Solving Problems in Couples and Family Therapy

Techniques and Tactics

Solving Problems in Couples and Family Therapy

Techniques and Tactics

Robert Sherman, ED.D.
Paul Oresky, M.S., A.C.M.F.C.
Yvonne Rountree, PH.D.

BRUNNER/MAZEL, *Publishers* • NEW YORK

Library of Congress Cataloging-in-Publication Data

Sherman, Robert
    Solving problems in couples and family therapy : techniques and
tactics / Robert Sherman, Paul Oresky, Yvonne Rountree.
        p.   cm.
    Includes bibliographical references and index.
    ISBN 0-87630-647-4
    1. Family psychotherapy.   2. Marital psychotherapy.   I. Oresky,
Paul.   II. Rountree, Yvonne.
    RC488.S47   1991
    616.89'156—dc20   91-25757
                                                                             CIP

Although the techniques, tactics, and tips described in the book have been
successfully used in the field, the authors cannot take responsibility for the
use of any one of them implemented by the reader not directly under the
control or supervision of the authors. The information is provided herein
for use by mental health professionals at their professional discretion.

Published by
BRUNNER/MAZEL, INC.
19 Union Square West
New York, New York 10003

MANUFACTURED IN THE UNITED STATES OF AMERICA

10 9 8 7 6 5 4 3

Contents

Preface

There are now many books and articles that address the theoretical framework and therapeutic processes of family and marital therapy. However, knowledge of theory alone does not guarantee smooth sailing across the oceans of clinical practice. At times, even the highly experienced therapist is unable to convert theoretical constructs into the fuel needed to move the therapeutic ship forward. The therapy drifts while the therapist struggles with the machinery.

The purpose of this book is to provide a body of tested and established techniques to help accomplish important therapeutic tasks encountered by clinicians practicing couples or family therapy. For example, how do you help a couple or a family to achieve greater intimacy, establish boundaries to reduce enmeshment, negotiate conflicting differences, overcome severe feelings of hurt toward one another, bring in a resistant family member, stop abusive behavior, increase feelings of optimism and empowerment, cope with grief, or cope with pathological behavior? These are some of the many common therapeutic tasks discussed in this book.

Since no one technique is likely to be the "magic bullet" for every task, we have brought together a wide variety of multidisciplinary techniques to solve each of the problems considered. The practitioner can adapt the techniques to his or her own theoretical approach, style, and specific situation encountered.

The techniques chosen reflect our own firm belief that therapy typically works best when it emphasizes the positive. Most of the techniques focus on strengths and foster the development of constructive beliefs, roles, resources, and skills. Through these, the system is reorganized into more effective patterns.

The book is designed for quick and easy reference to the specific area of help required by the clinician. Chapter 1 provides a general integrative model for behavior change. It lists specific strategies to change beliefs, roles, and skills; increase optimism and pride; promote social interest and social feeling; and improve patterns of communication.

Each succeeding chapter addresses one major problem area. Each chapter begins with a theoretical introduction to the problem and some of the key therapeutic issues involved. Then one to three major structured techniques, models, or strategies are presented. Included are theoretical rationale, description of the procedure to implement it, a case example, and alternative uses of the technique. This is followed by a description of a variety of additional tips, tactics, and less complex techniques. Finally, references and additional sources of information are listed at the end of each chapter.

All together, the book makes available more than 200 tested methods for solving the 14 common major therapeutic problems considered. Most of these are listed in the detailed Appendix of Techniques and Tactics at the end of the main text.

The authors are well aware that just as theory cannot function without appropriate techniques to operationalize it, techniques cannot stand alone without being used within a careful theoretical frame and selected as appropriate to clients and therapists in their particular context and circumstances. We believe that good theory is the most valuable tool in the possession of the therapist and that good techniques are evolved from good theory and the sensitivity of the therapist. We see no magic in the techniques and tactics described and do not subscribe to "technolatry," the worship of techniques. In this book we offer options and possibilities that have been helpful to others and that can be creatively adapted by the therapist to carry out the goals of therapy in a given set of circumstances.

This book is seen as a complement to the *Handbook of Structured Techniques in Marriage and Family Therapy* by Robert Sherman and Norman Fredman (1986) and the *Handbook of Measurements for Marriage and Family Therapy* by Norman Fredman and Robert Sherman (1987) both published by Brunner/Mazel. The first describes many tested complex techniques in each category—fantasy and metaphor, paradoxical, structural, behavioral, and so on. The second describes over 40 popular instruments and inventories for use in family therapy. For a discussion of how to invent and construct techniques, readers are invited to consult the first chapter of the *Handbook of Structured Techniques in Marriage and Family Therapy.*

For ease of reference in this book, unless directly quoted, therapists are usually referred to as "she" and "her" and clients as "he" and "him."

Solving Problems in Couples and Family Therapy

Techniques and Tactics

1

AN INTEGRATIVE
THERAPEUTIC MODEL
FOR CHANGE

I. INTRODUCTION: THE THERAPEUTIC CHALLENGE

Every marriage and family therapist is faced with several major tasks: (1) to join with the clients without being absorbed into the system; (2) to assess the patterns of dysfunctional behavior, strengths and resources; (3) to assist clients in changing their patterns of interaction and the individual motives and behaviors which contribute to those patterns; and (4) to terminate in a way that leaves the clients feeling more empowered and behaving with greater effectiveness in a better functioning and more satisfying system than when they arrived. Each marriage and family theory attends to those four tasks with varying degrees of emphasis.

The human system is not a machine. Individual members interacting create the system and the roles undertaken by them in it. They are propelled by their own motives and goals. An individual can change the system by refusing to play by the existing rules and roles. The system also acts upon its members, either forcing conformity or reinforcing existing reciprocal patterns of interacting guided by a hierarchy of system myths, beliefs, and values. Therefore, system and individual are constantly influencing each other. A number of books deal with the individual and the system such as Wachtel and Wachtel (1986), Sherman and Dinkmeyer (1987), Nichols (1989), and Sander (1989).

The therapist embarking on a case is faced with a variety of interesting challenges. The veteran therapist knows that every couple and every family have their own unique ways of being and situations to cope with. Even though they may be similar to many other couples or families, the differences require innovative differentiation of treatment plan and invention of suitable techniques for purposes of diagnosis and change. Even formula-type models with invariable prescriptions such as developed by Selvini Palazzoli and associates (1984) need to be adapted to each case. Further, the style, personality, age, gender, race, or ethnic background of the therapist may impact differently on each family (and, indeed, on each member).

The typical clients arrive feeling discouraged and frustrated with their inability to come to satisfactory solutions to their situations. They are frequently engaged in a power play to convince one another, or external institutions such as school or the court, that they are okay or right and the others are wrong. Often, the therapist tends to be seen either as a representative of the referring authority, the representative of the person in the family who initiated going to see the therapist, an interfering stranger, a potential ally to help overcome the others in the conflict, some kind of mediating judge, an interfering charlatan, or a rescuing expert who has all the answers. Such differences in perception of the family's problem and of the therapist's place, purpose, and person may lead to competing values and goals among the participants relative to the therapy and the techniques implemented by the therapist. Culture plays an important part in forming such perceptions. Observing the overt reactions of the family members provides an invaluable source of data for direct assessment of the family interaction processes and belief systems.

When one looks at such challenges as those, it is clear that the therapist needs a wide repertory of tactics and techniques to join with the family, assess their behavior, and assist them in bringing about desirable changes.

This chapter presents an outline of an integrative therapeutic model and focuses primarily on the process of change. The model focuses on four stages of work: (1) defining the problem, joining, and structuring the therapeutic system; (2) assessing how the couple or family functions and the meaning of the behavior patterns displayed; (3) reorienting and reorganizing the couple or family; and (4) evaluating and reinforcing the changes, planning next steps, and terminating. The sequence is suggestive and is more a function of emphasis than a rigid structure. We are, in fact, working to join, assess, and change the system at all times simultaneously. For a more detailed discussion of the model than is presented here and case examples, see Sherman and Dinkmeyer (1987).

II. DEFINING, JOINING, AND STRUCTURING

A. Define the Problem as Seen by the Clients

Each participant is asked to describe the situation. Rather than ally with any one perception, the therapist affirms that this is how each sees it. She then formulates a generalization to encompass all the positions stated, such as, "You would all like to see more cooperation in this family."

B. Have Clients State What Will Make It Better

Clients are asked to indicate what would make the situation better. Again, the therapist affirms each person's position and then tries to identify a generalization to incorporate what the family wants. "So, if each of you were more responsible for your own activities and more respectful of one another, you think that might help."

C. Join With the Clients

In joining with the family, the therapist validates them as individuals and as a family. She makes some connection with each member, validates the subjective position of each as he or she presents it, and assigns good intention to each. She also structures the interaction so that each member listens carefully to whoever is speaking. Validating the identified client, who often feels like a scapegoat, as well as validating all of the others who are frustrated trying to help the identified client, provides some measure of positive recognition and understanding. "So, George, it is very hard for you to keep these assignments in mind and it hurts when you think mother is criticizing you for it. And Mom, you watch George and work very hard, as good mothers do, to get him to see that he needs to be more mature and responsible so that he will grow up well."

D. Reframe in Positive Terms

The behavior complained about, particularly the symptomatic repeating pattern, can be reframed in positive terms. State it as a tentative hypothesis about what is going on. The object all through the therapy is to change minuses into pluses. Give a new positive meaning to the various roles being played out. For example, the seldom present father is striving to be a good husband and father by providing for his family, while Mom is trying to convince him that he is sacrificing too much, that he deserves more time and pleasure with his family, and that he needs to have more opportunity to be a father to his children.

E. Set and Clarify Tentative Goals

Setting and clarifying tentative goals are the first efforts at tackling a major cooperative task in the session. A good question is, "If the therapy is successful what will the family be like?" Suggestions are valued, but are examined in terms of their consequences for the system as a whole and for each member. This introduces the concept of paying attention to and being concerned for others, while beginning to implement negotiating skills. The therapist also observes the family's pattern of behavior as they interact in the goal-setting process. The next question is, "What does each of you need to do individually to make that happen?" This is to indicate that each person concentrates on changing his own behavior in order to change others and the system.

F. Prescribe an In-Session Task To Move Toward an Agreed-Upon, Less Stressful Subgoal

The task accomplishes several purposes: it permits the therapist to refine her assessment of the system; it assists her particularly to observe the power structure and the most likely source of resistance; and, if successful, it is very encouraging to the family to see that they can move in a positive way and that the therapy may be helpful. For example, "To create more harmony in this family, could you now plan for a fun family outing this coming weekend that everyone can enjoy?"

G. Structure the Therapeutic System

All through the session the therapist assumes the specific type of leadership role desired and introduces the rules of the game by her actions. These include who is permitted to speak when and to whom, how agreements are to be made and kept, how generational boundaries are to be observed, how long the sessions are, payment policies, and policies relative to record keeping and recording of sessions.

III. ASSESSING THE SYSTEM

A. *Select the Data To Be Gathered*

The amount of data that may be obtained is overwhelming and likely to be very confusing. Therefore, it is imperative to focus in on the kind of data likely to be most useful. The theory held by the therapist will determine the kind of data that is to be considered significant, particularly in terms of such variables as beliefs about human nature, how behavior is formed, how behavior is changed, and what constitutes functional or dysfunctional behavior. The theory will direct the search in relation to the past, the present or the anticipated future. It will suggest whether to emphasize patterns of organizational structure, communication, beliefs, thought processes, behavioral skills, or habits. It will point to unconscious processes, individual motivations, self-structures, object relations, structural configurations, interpersonal dynamics, multigenerational interactions, circular reinforcement, goal-directed lines of movement, or any of many others. There are a multitude of different theories.

Based on their own theory, the authors suggest that the assessment carefully track the behavior surrounding the defined problem and examine how it is organized around some central, ongoing theme that will constitute the systemic hypothesis. The theme is both cognitive and structural, with each impelling and reinforcing the other. The operative theoretical principle is that the subjective view or meaning given to a situation depends upon the point of view brought to the situation; the point of view in turn depends upon the place held by the person(s) in the situation (the world looks different to the teacher than to the student, to the wealthy than to the poor, to the firstborn than to the baby, to the parent than to the child); and the meaning of the place depends in part on the cultural and personal values, privileges, demands, and social roles assigned to the place, which then influence both the view and the point of view. The whole system is thus created by the continuing organized complementary interactions among the parts. The human system is organized for two purposes: to maintain itself and to accomplish some conscious or unconscious cognitive goals.

The authors attend to the following dynamics: (a) the distribution and use of power in the system and the power play inherent in the symptom; (b) the interplay around intimacy, closeness, distance, and territoriality; (c) the boundaries set to include and exclude, as well as their permeability; (d) the coalitions formed among the members in terms of alliances and collusions; (e) the myths and beliefs that govern the system; (f) the rules devised to enforce the myths and beliefs; (g) the roles established to operationally implement the beliefs; (h) the similarities that bind the members together and create cohesiveness; (i) the complementarities that allow for reciprocal role relationships; (j) the patterns of communication within which these dynamics are played out; and (k) the pathological patterns that can develop within the family system around any of the above issues. These factors are examined as they are organized developmentally in any system or specifically as they are organized around the symptom. They can further be observed thematically as part of the continuing life-style of the system multigenerationally or as they are enacted here and now in the sessions.

The therapeutic task is to discover the central organizing tendencies.

B. General Assessment Techniques

There are a multitude of tactics and techniques available. Each theory postulates several of its own favorite ones. Some of the more popular categories are: (1) questioning—specific, general, or circular; (2) tests, inventories, and questionnaires on a wide range of couple and family characteristics—formally evaluated commercially developed instruments or informal ones developed by the agency or practitioner; (3) close observation of behavior in session—non-verbal, seating arrangements, roles assumed, alliances in effect, the uses of power, metaphors verbalized and many more; (4) exercises to explore beliefs and patterns of interaction—tracking, examining a typical day, drawing the family floor plan to see how the family organizes around space, descriptions of early recollections to identify expectations and life-style themes, experiencing and expressing love to explore the reciprocal expectations and individual languages and needs of the members, discussing family photographs, making the success chart to discover achievement themes, playing the name game to better understand places in the family, and many more; (5) sculpting, the physical expression of the relationships—done by the identified client, done by each member, done by the therapist; (6) metaphorical methods such as autobiographies, composing stories or story endings, keeping diaries, making drawings, and analyzing dreams; (7) behavioral tasks prescribed in-session or to do at home or work in order to allow observation of both the willingness and ability to cooperate and function—solving a problem, making a plan, or playing together; and (8) constructing a genogram to chart the family constellation, relationships, nodal events, triangles, and developmental themes—done by the clients or taken in interview by the therapist.

C. Identify the Central Organizing Factors or Get to Essence

The therapist can use a number of techniques to help her sort through the maze of data and formulate her major systemic hypothesis. Some of them are:

1. *The symptom as a metaphor.* The symptom may not merely be a dispute or reflect only the behavior of the identified client. For example, if a child is running away, this may signal that there is a lack of respect for individual behavior and needs within the system. Asking each member what he does in order to get away from the family and what he needs to get away from may help to elaborate the central dynamics.

2. *The word, phrase or caption.* The therapist sits back and allows a word or phrase to form in her mind which identifies this system. For example, struggle for control, need for separation-individuation, need for mutual appreciation, an unnegotiated change in the marital contract, lack of a map to cope with this situation, and others. More challenging and more fun is to construct a newspaper headline or movie title to describe the family. Such a word, phrase, or headline can help focus the therapist's attention.

3. *What the therapist feels and wants to do.* The therapist is invited by the family into its system. By identifying what feelings are elicited in the therapist—anger, pity, frustration, enjoyment—and what the therapist feels stimulated to do—work harder, disengage, shake one or more members, reassure, come to the rescue—will provide important clues to the way the family functions.

4. *The animal or object game or sculpture.* The members are asked to identify each other and then themselves as some animal or object in relation to the problem presented. They can discuss their reciprocal identifications, sculpt them, and enact them in a fantasy role play (Papp, 1982). The therapist can observe the central organizing dynamics in these interactions.

5. *Tracking.* By tracking the exact sequence of interactions through the continuing posing of questions as to who does what and who does what next, the therapist can elicit the entire cycle of behavior that maintains the system and the symptom. Each behavior sequence elicits the next one in the pattern and each reinforces the other to maintain the repeating process. For example, mother feels abandoned and is angry with a distant husband. The child misbehaves. Mother complains to the father about the child. The father engages with her in disciplining the child. The father then leaves. Mother is lonely again and the child misbehaves to bring in the father.

6. *Identify priorities as organizing principles.* Values are organized in a hierachical structure, with the person and system giving the most attention

and resources to the most important ones. Bitter (1987) describes four major priorities of behavior derived from the works of Adler, Kfir, and Satir—superiority, pleasing, comfort, and control—or the four negative goals of misbehavior—to dominate, gain attention, get revenge, or manipulate by playing helpless. There are many other lists in the literature. Each encompasses a personality structure which emphasizes particular patterns of behavior. When these patterns are examined in terms of complementary relationships, the therapist can understand how they function as they do. The family can organize to keep a depressed mother mobilized, protect an alcoholic member, or maintain an identifying tradition such as faith, business, or myth.

7. *Identify reciprocal role relationships.* The family may organize around such roles as pursuer/distancer, rescuer/victim, or overadequate/underadequate. The symptom may be expressed in such role interactions. Similarly, if two firstborn individuals with younger siblings marry each other and each is habitually in the role of leader of his/her siblings, they may well fight over who will be the dominant partner in the marriage. A fight may also occur in a remarriage when two step-siblings previously occupied the same position.

8. *Look at the direction of the behavior and then to the opposite.* If behavior is purposive and moving toward goals, then the behavior can be assessed by examining its consequences. Any pattern that is often repeated as a symptom has useful consequences evidenced by each person's reactions. If a child wants attention and gets a lot of it from others through misbehavior, then his behavior works in getting him the desired attention. It may also serve to divert attention from a more risky situation such as parental fighting or to mobilize a depressed mother. The consequences inform us of the purpose.

IV. CHANGING THE SYSTEM:
SIX MAJOR VARIABLES OF CHANGE

The authors offer six major areas of variables through which to bring about change within the individual, couple, family, or institution as a system. Each interacts with and influences all the others to make up the whole.

1. *Beliefs.* The beliefs, myths, ideas, attitudes, rules, and object projections that underlie the problem behaviors and perceptions of the problem within the system give purpose to the behavior. Within this internal framework of logic, the behavior both makes sense and is useful. The beliefs include goals to be attained that are anticipated, consciously or unconsciously, to yield either satisfaction and growth through connec-

tion, cooperation, and assertion, or greater safety through aggression, manipulation, or avoidance. The behavior constitutes the line of movement toward those goals.

2. *Organization.* The places, roles, coalitions, and interaction patterns operationally express the beliefs and values within the family's organization of behavior and the pursuit of both individual and family goals.

3. *Skills.* These are the skills and knowledges that are available to implement existing beliefs or to identify and carry out new options for reform.

4. *Feeling of optimism and empowerment.* These feelings permit the members to be proactive, to take the risks of change, and to be open to change because they expect to succeed. They experience most failures as an event requiring additional learning and improvement rather than as a catastrophe. These feelings also include the family's sense of worth and the worth of belonging to it.

5. *Social interest and cooperation (Adler, 1979).* Social or community interest and social feeling involve a sense of being connected with others in a larger unity, concern both for the others and that larger unity, and therefore working together, rather than against one another, for the common good. This requires seeing past the self, or this family unit, paying attention to others, being sensitive and empathic toward them, and perceiving events in relation to a larger and caring perspective. Social interest generates a feeling of equality with others. Equality does not imply sameness. We all have different roles, talents, and inferiorities in relation to one another. But we are equally worthy and all are faced with the challenges of life. Equality requires mutual respect.

Social or community interest is not synonymous with social conformity. It is an agreement to participate as equals in varying roles in caring ways for both the individual and the common good. This quality in people and systems allows them to live together via social contract and agreement rather than by force or fear. It applies alike to family, school, employment, community relationships, and the relationship between man and his physical environment. Social interest is the opposite of alienation, which separates us from one another or represents splits within the self-system.

6. *Communication patterns.* These are the methods used to exchange or withhold information, beliefs and emotions; to express expectations and needs; to share intimacy; to include and exclude participants; to resolve differences; and to make decisions.

The reader can readily identify that different theories will emphasize different points while giving somewhat less attention to the rest. For example, Structural theory will load on #2 above; Analytic and Object Relations on

#1; Strategic on #1, #2, and #6; Cognitive Behavioral on #1, #3, and #6. Adlerian theory would focus on all of the above.

Following is an illustrative guide to the multitude of different kinds of techniques that could be employed to accomplish changes in each of the six areas defined above: beliefs, organizational patterns, skills, communication patterns, attitudes of optimism, and social interest. In fact, most complex techniques can be designed to address most, or even all, of them simultaneously. The kinds of techniques are listed, some with brief examples, to help illustrate the possibilities. However, there are many more complex or subtle techniques that fit into each category. Many will be discussed and described in the remainder of this book in terms of bringing about change in a particular therapeutic task, such as improving intimacy, joining, or boundary setting.

A. Changing Beliefs

1. *Interpret the dysfunctional belief* or myth to the clients to help them better understand what they are doing and the purposes they are pursuing. ("Is it possible that in this family men are supposed to take care of women, so that George does . . . in order to . . .?")

2. *Confront clients* with the consequences of their beliefs and behavior. ("Are you aware that if you must make all the rules and be right every time, then you make your partner wrong and stupid? Your partner then becomes angry with what is experienced as your put-down behavior each time there is a difference of opinion between you." Or, "What is the risk of accepting that you really are more grownup, competent, and powerful now than when you were a child frequently criticized by your father?")

3. *Dramatize the beliefs* to show their inappropriateness by exaggeration. ("This must be a depressed family of failures. If perfection is the only acceptable standard, who in the family can meet that standard?" Or, "When you achieve perfection, surely you will be at the right hand of God and above all mere mortals. Would you please put in a good word for me?")

4. *Match a strongly held belief with a strongly held opposite belief* to weaken the first one. ("When did you realize that to be a good father you have to spend some more good time with your children as well as working hard to be a good provider?")

5. *Introduce new beliefs* to expand the options of the system. ("I notice, Mrs. M., that even though you complain about your husband's domination, you are a very powerful person. Look at all the things you are doing—*list*

them—which he opposes, but has learned at least to put up with. Is it possible that you are both very strong individuals who need to learn how to negotiate your differences?")

6. *Encourage rebellion against an old belief* that is dysfunctional. ("How much longer do you think that you must be punished at age 41 for fondling the girl next door when you were both 13?")

7. *Insert crazy ideas* that are more crazy than the existing ones.

8. *Use Socratic questioning* to attack the logic underlying existing beliefs.

9. *Make up a story or fairy tale* or read one to the family that puts their situation in a more favorable context of beliefs.

10. *Use imagery and visualization* to help clients come into touch with all kinds of new material within themselves. Similarly, experiencing the family situation in role playing, sculpting, drawing, or through the results of projective tests or family inventories may provide new insights and challenge old beliefs and myths.

11. *Use traditional analysis and analytic techniques* to help clients gain insight into their behavior and the emotions attached to the insights—for example, free association, analysis of dreams, early recollections, interpretation of the resistance, etc.

Texts on cognitive and cognitive behavioral therapy will contain additional types of techniques to change belief systems (Bellack & Herson, 1985; Cerio, La Calle, & Murtha, 1986; Kanfer & Goldstein, 1986; Margolin & Jacobson, 1979).

B. Changing Position and Role

1. *Assign clients to new places and new roles.* ("Could you pretend for this week that you are the person that you wish you were and behave just that way and be a good actor?" Or, "At work you behave in an initiative and assertive way, so you know how to do that. Can you do that in the family this week?")

2. *Strengthen existing natural roles.* ("You are very protective of your younger brother in school and on the street. Could you be his kind older brother at home this week?") Or, encourage parents to take proper charge of their children in session; have parent and child negotiate an agreement in session so that the child feels he has a voice too; and define together the tasks and expectations that go with each place in the family.

3. *Positively relabel existing roles* to give them a more positive connotation and place in the system. ("Is it possible that, rather than being a rebel,

your daughter is fun-loving and trying to encourage this entire family to develop a much needed sense of fun?")

4. *Prescribe role reversals* to create more empathy and a better balance of power and resources in the family. ("Mrs. R., you've been working very hard to discipline and care for your children while your husband comes home and plays with them, leaving you the bad guy and he as the good guy. Could we try for a week that you, Mr. R., will take charge of the discipline and you, Mrs. R., will figure out all kinds of ways to enjoy being together with your children?")

5. *Block inappropriate roles or role behavior.* The therapist can interrupt the behavioral flow and introduce a new pattern in place of the blocked one. ("You are about to get into one of your typical fights. Instead, John, would you please make a proposal to solve this problem?" Or, "John, please speak for yourself. Mother is about to speak for you again.")

6. *Spread out a symptomatic role among all family members* to expose the family secret or remove the symptomatic member from the scapegoat position. For example, in the case of a runaway child, the therapist asks each family member what he or she does to run away in this family. Discussion then might reveal either that the family is too tight or that there is insufficient recognition of individual members and their needs so that each has to run away in some fashion.

7. *Establish, strengthen, or weaken boundaries.* ("Pamela, when Mother and Father fight, could you please leave the room so that they can work it out between them? Mom and Dad, do you want your daughter in the middle of your disagreement?" Or, "Do you suppose that some other families may be faced with a problem such as yours? Would it be helpful to know how others handle it?")

8. *Fashioning new alliances* to adjust the balance of power and improve patterns of communication. The therapist can join with one member to create a shift in the existing pattern, such as helping Mother to better manage her children in session. The therapist can assist the father to join with the mother in dealing with the children and meeting together to work out their joint policy for child rearing.

9. *Provide more structure in a chaotic organization.* The therapist can help the family define rules for functioning as a group, agree upon a distribution of tasks and responsibilities, assign roles, and introduce customs and traditions to be followed, such as celebrations of holidays and birthdays. Then, she follows up and reinforces these to be sure that the new structures are working.

10. *Reduce rigidity in an inflexible structure* to permit changes to occur.

The therapist can validate all of the members to decrease the need for defensiveness; create a climate of encouragement (see section D below); introduce some humor and fun in the sessions and as homework tasks; ask the members to try out some new behaviors in the form of brief "experiments"; and engage the family in creative tasks such as writing new endings to their current family story, making up a fable about their family, or drawing a picture of their ideal family. Reducing rigidity to permit change is so central to our work that a great deal of what we do in therapy under any heading is, in fact, dedicated to this purpose.

C. Change Knowledge and Skills

There are numerous direct and indirect methods for adding new information, reformulating existing information, introducing new skills, or sharpening desirable, existing ones.

DIRECT METHODS

1. *Give direct instruction.* The therapist may provide useful information to the family in a direct, straightforward way.

2. *Coach the clients* during a problem-solving activity, sculpting, or in performance of any task within session by correcting behavior or suggesting other possibilities. Clients have the opportunity immediately to practice the new skills under supervision of the therapist.

3. *Suggest new ideas, possible options, prescriptions, or tasks.* The family can make more informed choices if they are aware of additional possibilities. Performance of in-session or homework tasks will, hopefully, add new skills or sharpen underdeveloped ones.

4. *Refer clients to appropriate resources.* The therapist is not the sole resource for the family. They can be referred to other experts for information or advice, such as an attorney, physician, or older family member. Similarly, the therapist may refer the clients to specific readings, movies, or T.V. programs to obtain information and new perspectives, overtly demonstrated skills, or vicariously acquired skills.

5. *Request that the client(s) enroll in a particular training course or psychoeducational program* such as those for parent education, marriage enrichment, assertiveness training, men's or women's issues, or support groups like ALANON or Cancer Care.

INDIRECT METHODS

1. *Formulate questions based upon an entirely different premise than is currently accepted in the system.* ("Now that you are more grown up and mature than you used to be, you probably don't want to do that (*symptomatic behavior*) anymore.")

2. *Use "circular questioning"* as described by Tomm (1985) and the Milan group (Boscolo, Cecchin, Hoffman, & Penn, 1987) in which one person is questioned about the relationships among others. The responses are then utilized by the therapist to introduce new formulations.

3. *Present "interpretation" or "tentative hypotheses"* ("Is it possible that what is going on here is . . .?") to inject information and new ideas.

4. *Construct a simple "paradox" or a complex paradoxical prescription* to confront the family with the truth about how this system functions, hopefully leading to a recoil from the existing dysfunctional pattern of behavior based on an unpleasant recognition of what they are doing and the adoption of a more satisfying pattern of behavior.

5. *Utilize imagination and visualization* to put the client in touch with resources within the self, such as the Inner Adviser (Sherman & Fredman, 1986), and to practice skills through behavior rehearsal in imagination (Wolpe, 1969).

6. *Model skills through your own behavior,* particularly by being positive, respectful, encouraging, attentive, caring, and cooperative. Model clear communication so that all members know where they stand. Engage in negotiations with the clients to demonstrate skills in conflict resolution and handling differences.

7. *Introduce new pleasing customs and traditions or reinstate old familiar ones related to roots and ethnicity.* Such customs and traditions involve both myths and ritual behaviors to be performed. This provides the family with both culturally rooted and approved new ideas and new skills for dealing with the challenges of life.

D. Increase Feelings of Optimism and the Sense of Empowerment

1. *Affirm the family and each member.* Be attentive, respectful and caring. This, in itself, is very encouraging to the clients. When the therapist further expresses genuine understanding and empathy and provides affirmation and validation to the family, self-concepts and family pride are enhanced.

2. *Identify and recognize strengths.* Prescribe strength bombardment techniques such as the Family Appreciation Party (p. 29–31) to recognize

member contributions and importance or the Encouragement Meeting (p. 32–35) in which members emphasize each others strengths.

3. *Promote assertion and negotiation rather than aggression.* Stop the members from complaining to and about each other and help them instead to propose constructively in positive operational terms what they want and to be prepared to negotiate for it rather than command it.

4. *Identify and make choices and joint decisions.* Help the members to see that they are not trapped and that they have a range of choices. Whenever decisions are made, stress that this is their choice and their use of power. Ask them to list decisions they have recently made, including those within sessions.

5. *Set common workable goals.* Help the family to set a common goal that they can all agree on. Then break up large goals into smaller, more manageable ones that they can handle with more assurance.

6. *Identify and emphasize positive changes and movement.* Sometimes, clients attend mostly to negatives. They therefore fail to see the improvements occurring. It is helpful to point out the good things that are happening, to label them, and to summarize them periodically. This can be done either by therapist or clients, or by both.

7. *Reframe negative meanings and negatively charged events* in the family system into new positive formulations which bring new perspectives and include new possibilities.

8. *Recall incidents that worked successfully in the past.* ("Is there anytime when you handled this situation or that family member well? What did you do? Describe it exactly. Can you do the same thing now or next time this comes up?")

9. Positive changes in any of the other five areas for change described here are encouraging and empowering.

E. Develop Increased Social Interest and Social Feeling

1. *Focus attention on others.* Coach the clients to pay careful attention to one another's needs and feelings and to what is needed by the family as a unit rather than focusing narcissistically on themselves. Teach them to listen carefully and check out the other's intentions by asking if they understood what the other is trying to do.

2. *Help clients to assess the impact and consequences of their behavior* on themselves, others, and the family as a unit. This helps them both to take responsibility for what they do and to become more sensitive to the results of what they do. They become aware of how others experience them.

This can be accomplished at many levels by therapist and family thinking through together the possible consequences of plans, goals, and decisions being made; by feedback sessions in which consequences of acts being performed are described to the actor; and through role reversals to enable members to feel what it is like to be in the other's place.

3. *Present differences as assets rather than liabilities.* Differences and complementarities can be portrayed as the cutting edge of growth and as adding strength and excitement to the family system. Differences properly regarded can lead to new creative syntheses. The family is described as having a diversity of talents and interests which add both stimulation and more options for improving the family quality of life.

4. *Teach negotiating skills* (See pp. 258–261). Negotiation is very different from demanding. The therapist bases her teaching on the assumption that all involved have legitimate differences among them in power, needs, interests, and styles, which they have to respect in order to come to mutual agreements. She introduces a model involving proposals and counterproposals rather than assumptions and commands.

5. *Prescribe positive exchange types of tasks.* Each person is asked to identify things that he/she could do that would be pleasing to another and to surprise that person by doing such nice things in his/her behalf. The other person must discover the surprises, thus catching the first person being "nice" rather than "bad." Each is thus engaged in being positively interested in the other.

6. *Organize the family to engage in a couple conference and or family meeting* (See pp. 175–179). A couple conference gives each partner an equal alternating opportunity, such as 30 minutes each, to make him/herself known to the other without interruption while being fully attended to. The family meeting is run as a democratic meeting under the leadership of a different family member each session. Anyone in the family can introduce an agenda item and the family discusses its needs and plans.

7. *Create a mutual self-help group.* Constitute the family as a self-help group in which each member is dedicated to helping the others to develop and achieve what they need and want. When each is experienced as working for the other, defensiveness is reduced and there is a willingness to compromise for the common good so that everyone wins.

8. *Initiate cooperative games in session.* The family can be asked to use building blocks to build a sturdy house together, put on a play, or draw a mural depicting some aspect of family pride.

9. All the items mentioned under section "D" above, "Increase feelings of optimism and empowerment," will also serve to improve social interest.

F. Change Patterns of Communication

All the other five areas discussed above are intended to also change the patterns of communication since that is the essence of how a human system operates. Some of the specific tasks to attend to that have not been previously described are: creating a safe environment; sending out clear positive messages about what is wanted rather than not wanted; usually, giving rather than withholding information and sharing feelings; usually, being specific rather than vague; informing rather than expecting the other to know; eliminating double messages such as "yes, but" or kind words in a steely voice, and double-bind messages in particular; and correcting projections about what I think the other thinks of me.

Communication patterns can be changed through such diverse techniques as: direct instruction and coaching, describing patterns to the members, sculpting, the family floor plan, family photographs, checking out the intentions of the other, behavior rehearsal directly or in imagery, changing seating arrangements, blocking specific types of communication by cutting them off, unbalancing the system through alliances with one or more members, in-session or homework tasks, playing back videotapes of the session, having members keep a diary of their interactions, or shifting or redefining roles in the system.

Therapeutic change is not intended to be a capricious event, although sometimes it is. It emanates from a carefully designed plan evolved from assessment of the problem, persons, system, and context within a theoretical framework and from common sense. The theory will dictate which techniques are likely to be suitable. However, the therapist can also benefit by taking into account the internal private logic of the system; her own private logic about the meaning of what is going on; how the culture defines the meaning of the events being studied; and her own intuition and analogical thinking. The purpose is to come up with a profound understanding and a creative design for change.

V. TERMINATION, EVALUATION, AND FOLLOW-UP

Just as it is important to begin well, it is important to end well. This final stage of the work includes evaluating together the progress made, reinforcing the appropriate and effective new behavior patterns, determining next steps to be undertaken, and following up after three months, six months, or a year to see how things are progressing.

A. *Evaluation*

Evaluation involves an assessment of outcomes in relation to the presenting problems, contracts for change, and goals to be achieved. Briefly, to what degree quantitatively and qualitatively have the goals been met? The change model presented in this chapter implies both remediation of dysfunction and growth in the form of reoriented beliefs, new skills and knowledges, more favorable attitudes, and a more efficient pattern of organization as the general goals of the therapy. We would expect changes in individual behavior and in the systemic patterns of interactions.

1. *Some of the major criteria* that need to be evaluated are: satisfaction, effectiveness, appropriateness, and positive identity. (a) How *satisfied* are the clients with the therapeutic process, the work accomplished, and the way in which they are functioning now compared with before? (b) How *effectively* is the system functioning in relation to current and ever changing personal and systemic goals and needs? Are they practicing workable communication and negotiation skills? Do they have a practical plan to get where they want to go? Are they sufficiently open and flexible or, if needed, structured and organized? Are they more optimistic about their ability to deal with change and the challenges of life? (c) How *appropriately* are the clients interacting in relation to their situation as a family and within the community? Do they manifest respect and social interest for one another and for others? Are they cooperative? Are they organized within appropriate boundaries and coalitions? (d) Do they have a *positive sense of identity* and place in the community and feel better about who they are? These factors need to be measured to assess the outcomes.

2. *Measurements* can be obtained through many different methods and techniques.

(a) *Questioning for self-report.* The therapist frames questions to have the couple or family identify the presenting problems and the goals established to improve the situation, symptoms, or conflicts. Then they are asked to assess what progress and improvements were made and what work remains to be done. They are asked specific questions in relation to each of the above four criteria. The members can also be asked to answer similar questions about each other. The therapist may have to remind the clients about some of the issues that came up and some of the work pursued. It is helpful for both clients and therapist to participate in summarizing the therapeutic experience to better evaluate it.

(b) *Before and after administration of tests and inventories.* Available instruments are listed and described in Fredman and Sherman (1987) and

Touliatos, Perlmutter and Straus (1989) There are instruments on family or couple satisfaction, conflict, sexuality, jealousy, and many other areas.

(c) *Early and later prescription and enactment of major structured techniques.* The therapist can use before-and-after structured techniques such as sculptures, sociograms, floor plans, family photographs, autobiographical pieces, drawings, early recollections, dream interpretations, fantasies, sentence completions, role card sorts, written contracts, and games to observe changes in the patterns of interactions.

(d) *Careful observation and comparison of before-and-after in-session behavior.* The therapist observes the evolving use of metaphors in speech, seating arrangements, posture, tone of voice, dress, patterns of communication, ability to negotiate differences and resolve conflicts, changes in role taking or role behavior, presentations of optimistic or pessimistic moods, willingness to cooperate, openness to new ideas or options, willingness to try new behaviors or seek new information.

(e) *Behavioral reports from collaborative sources.* Does the child get better grades in school, have a better attendance record, fewer disciplinary reports? Did the husband apply for and get a job or a better job? Did the family members report a significant weight loss? Is the anorexic child maintaining a healthier weight and diet? Is the family eating dinner together? Are parents consulting on child rearing practices and coming to agreements? Is the wife on time for work? Is the "recovering" gambler or alcoholic bringing home his wages? Has the symptom disappeared?

B. Refinement, Reinforcement and Projection

1. *Refinement.* Based on the evaluation process, the therapist acts to reframe or sharpen the major changes which have occurred and to encourage whatever minor corrections will improve the clients' functioning. ("Do you think it might help further if you would soften your voice when asking your husband to do something?" "If Tuesday evening is an inconvenient time for your weekly family meeting, how about Sunday before lunch?") Misunderstandings, misinterpretations, and distortions that are revealed are clarified and corrected.

2. *Reinforcement.* The family or couple are validated as individuals and as a unit. Their strengths are once again enumerated and valued. Their accomplishments are noted and summarized and connected to their strengths. Newly acquired beliefs, myths, and attitudes are restated in the positive and their helpfulness to the system is affirmed. Newly acquired roles, places, or role behavior patterns are labeled and positively connoted.

However, if particular changes were brought about through paradoxical interventions, then the therapist continues to caution against change unless the change is firmly embedded. If it is firmly embedded, the therapist may choose to confess that maybe she was incorrect about those things or that they are no longer necessary. Newly acquired knowledges and skills are restated and reconfirmed in terms of their value to the members. Finally, statement of positive feelings about self, the other member(s), we as a unit, our mutual caringness, and we in the world are further encouraged.

3. *Planning for next steps.* Life is a continuity. We were, are, and will be. The present situation is part of a continuing line of movement. We are aware of a history, a present, and an anticipation of the future. According to social learning theory, we behave in the present in anticipation of the future. Therefore, as part of our "ending," it is useful to ascertain that the couple or family and each member have some appropriate short-term, intermediate, and long-term plans and some reasonable notion of how to carry them out. We also need to examine the possible consequences of those plans upon the system and its members. In effect, we return to Stage I of the therapy, helping them to define problems and goals and to proceed toward their attainment without the assistance of the therapist. The couple or family are now ready to leave.

C. Issues in Termination

1. *Termination before completion.* As therapists, we hope that termination will occur when the work is successfully completed. There are many forces that may mitigate against that. The clients may make a large geographic move; the therapist may move, retire, become ill, or change jobs; clients may encounter financial adversity; the case may be inappropriate for the worker or agency and require referral; there may be a personality clash or misfit of some kind between therapist and clients; the therapist may not be able or wish to accept the contract that one or more members of the group insist upon; and the inability to get vital members in for sessions. Probably, the most frequent source of premature termination is resistance to the changes proposed. The issue of resistance is discussed in chapter 4.

2. *Separation.* Typically, in systemic couple and family therapy we do not encourage or emphasize transferential relationships. Rather, we encourage the people involved to connect appropriately and interact with each other. Therefore, disengagement between clients and therapists tends to be a less emotional process than in psychoanalysis with individuals. But therapeutic alliances are formed and we intimately enter the lives of our clients.

To help in the disengagement process, we summarize with our clients their strengths, their ideas, their courage, their successes, and the changes they made. We reaffirm their mutual respect and mutual support. Sometimes, clients will come up with an entire new set of problems or a crisis to avoid termination. The therapist reassures them that they know how to handle these problems now and can do it on their own. She further indicates that she will be available in the future if needed and schedules a follow-up session (section E below). Occasionally, just as some couples pointing toward divorce will escalate the fight between them in order to make the separation possible, a couple or family will pick a fight with the therapist to make it easier for them to leave. They may even withhold payment on rare occasion, thus engaging the therapist in pursuit.

The therapist, too, may have difficulty letting go. She may need the money. She may feel like a member of the couple or family. She may want to do more than is necessary. She may feel needed or nurtured by these people. She may be in the midst of trying to work out some issues in her own life through her work with these clients.

Sometimes, clients and therapist may collude together to set up a new dual relationship socially or in business.

One way to make separation easier is to make it clear from the beginning that this is a business arrangement and the therapist is not a rescuer, parent, nor best friend, but a caring helper. This is equally true in schools, churches, and businesses in which the services may be free.

D. Follow-up

1. *Planning the meeting.* A follow-up meeting is planned for the future and scheduled. The couple or family's permission is requested for such a meeting. The content is described: "We'll be checking up on how you are doing and see what your current needs are, if any. Is the symptom still removed? Are you using the skills you developed in our meetings? Are you carrying out the next-step plans that you made? Are you satisfied with the service that you received? Are there any new issues or problems? How are you handling them?" Questions will be directed toward the specific issues and work that was done. It is made clear whether or not the clients will be expected to pay for this session. The meeting is planned in terms of the medium or media that will be used: office session, double session, telephone interview, mailed packet of questionnaires or tests, or home visit.

In general, the stage IV process is briefly repeated in the follow-up, including evaluation, refinement and reinforcement of the new functional behavior, and encouragement of the members.

2. *Using the results.* The results provide a check on the effectiveness of one's work, lead to forming hypotheses and generalizations about systemic behavior, and provide questions for formal research. Clients may be further validated and reinforced in their new behaviors. If needed, clients can be referred for particular assistance needed or invited back for another round of therapy. The follow-up indicates their continuing worth and importance as people who deserve to be cared about.

Every session involves some aspects of termination since every session hopefully will end well. Unless the effort is to raise anxiety to produce change, the therapist will summarize the session with the clients, validating and reinforcing progress made, planning next steps, or prescribing a homework task to be followed up by telephone, mail, or at the next session.

REFERENCES

Adler, A. (1979). *Superiority and social interest.* (3rd Rev Ed.). H. L. Ansbacher and R. R. Ansbacher, Eds. New York: Norton.

Bellack, A. S. and Hersen, M. Editors. (1985). *Behavioral assessment. A practical handbook.* (Third Edition). New York: Pergamon.

Bitter, J. R. (1987). Communication and meaning: Satir in Adlerian Context. In R. Sherman and D. Dinkmeyer, *Systems of family therapy: An Adlerian integration.* New York: Brunner/Mazel.

Boscolo, L., Cecchin, G., Hoffman, L., and Penn, P. (1987). *Milan systemic family therapy.* New York: Basic Books.

Cerio, J. E., La Calle, J. F., and Murtha, J. P. (1986). *Eliminating self-defeating behaviors system.* Muncie, IN: Accelerated Development.

Duhl, B. S. (1983). *From the inside out and other metaphors.* New York: Brunner/Mazel.

Fredman, N. and Sherman, R. (1987). *Handbook of measurements for marriage and family therapy.* New York: Brunner/Mazel.

Kanfer, F. H. and Goldstein, A. P. Editors. (1986). *Helping people change. A textbook of methods.* (3rd Ed.) New York: Pergamon.

Margolin, G. and Jacobson, N. S. (1979). *Marital therapy strategies based on social learning and behavior exchange principles.* New York: Brunner/Mazel.

Mills, J. C. and Crowley, R. J. (1986). *Therapeutic metaphors for children and the child within.* New York: Brunner/Mazel.

Nichols, M. (1989). *The self and the system. Expanding the limits of family therapy.* New York: Brunner/Mazel.

Papp, P. (1982). Staging reciprocal metaphors in a couples group. *Family Process.* 21: 453–467.

Sander, F. (1989). *Individual and family therapy.* New York: Jason Aronson.

Selvini Palazzoli, M. and others. (1984). *Paradox and counterparadox.* New York: Jason Aronson.

Sherman, R. and Dinkmeyer, D. (1987) *Systems of family therapy: An Adlerian integration.* New York: Brunner/Mazel.

Sherman, R. and Fredman, N. (1986). *Handbook of structured techniques in marriage and family therapy.* New York: Brunner/Mazel.

Tomm, K. (1985). Circular interviewing: A multi-faceted clinical tool. In D. Cambell and R. Draper (Eds.), *Applications of systems family therapy: The Milan method.* New York: Grune and Stratton.

Touliatos, J., Perlmutter, B. F., and Straus, M. A. Editors. (1989). *Handbook of family measurement techniques.* Newbury Park, CA: Sage.

Wachtel, P. L. and Wachtel, E. F. (1986). *Family dynamics in individual psychotherapy.* New York: Guilford.

Wolpe, J. (1969). *The practice of behavior therapy.* New York: Pergamon.

ADDITIONAL RESOURCES

Allen, D. M. (1988). *Unifying individual and family therapy.* San Francisco: Jossey-Bass.

Beavers, W. R. and Hampson, R. B. (1990). *Successful families. Assessment and intervention.* New York: Norton.

Brock, G. W. and Barnard, C. P. (1988). *Procedures in family therapy.* Boston: Allyn and Bacon.

Budman, S. H. and Gurman, A. S. (1988). *Theory and practice of brief therapy.* New York: Guilford.

Carlson, J. and Sperry, L. (1990). Psychoeducational strategies in marital therapy. In *Innovations in clinical practice. A source book.* Sarasota, FL: Professional Resource Exchange.

Carnevale, J. P. (1989). *Counseling gems. Thoughts for the practitioner.* Muncie, IN: Accelerated Development.

Combs, G. and Freedman, J. (1990). *Symbol, story and ceremony.* New York: Norton.

Compher, J. V. (1989). *Family centered practice. The interactional dance beyond the family system.* New York: Human Sciences Press.

Corsini, R. J. Editor. (1981). *Handbook of innovative psychotherapies.* New York: Wiley.

DeAngelis, T. (1989). Playfulness in therapy opens new dimensions. *APA Monitor,* July, p. 27.

deShazer, S. and Kral, R. (1986). *Indirect approaches in therapy.* Rockville, MD: Aspen.

Dossick, J. and Shea, E. (1990) *Creative therapy II. 52 more exercises for groups.* Sarasota, FL: Professional Resource Exchange.

Guerin, P. J., Foy, L. F., Burden, S. L., and Kautto, J. G. (1987). *The evaluation and treatment of marital conflict: A four-stage approach.* New York: Basic Books.

Huber, C. H. and Baruth, L. G. (1989). *Rational-Emotive family therapy. A systems perspective.* New York: Springer.

Imber-Black, E. (1988). *Families and larger systems.* New York: Guilford.

Jacobson, N. S. and Gurman, A. S. Editors. (1986). *Clinical handbook of marital therapy.* New York: Guilford.

Kaslow, F. W. Editor. (1990). *Voices in family psychology.* Vols. I and II. Newbury Park, CA: Sage.

Klein, R. S. (1990). *Object relations and the family process.* New York: Praeger.

L'Abate, L. and McHenry, S. (1983). *Handbook of marital interventions.* New York: Grune and Stratton.

Leupnitz, D. A. (1988). *The family interpreted. Feminist theory in clinical practice.* New York: Basic Books.

Levant, R. F. Editor. (1986). *Psychoeducational approaches to family therapy and counseling.* New York: Springer.

McMullin, R. E. (1986). *Handbook of cognitive therapy techniques.* New York: Norton.

Mosak, H. H. (1987). *Ha ha and aha. The role of humor in psychotherapy.* Muncie, IN: Accelerated Development.

Paradoxical interventions. (1986). Special issue. *Counseling Psychologist.* 14:2.

Piercy, F. P. and Sprenkle, D. H. (1986). *Family therapy sourcebook.* New York: Guilford.

Powers, R. and Griffith, J. (1987). *Understanding life-style: The psychoclarity process.* Chicago: American Institute of Adlerian Studies.

Prata, G. (1990). *A systemic harpoon into family games. Preventive interventions in therapy.* New York: Brunner/Mazel.

Reynolds, D. K. (1989). *Flowing bridges, quiet waters. Japanese psychotherapies, Morita and Naikan.* Albany, NY: State University of New York Press.

Robertiello, R. C. and Schoenewolf, G. (1987). *101 common therapeutic blunders: Countertransference and counterresistance in psychotherapy.* New York: Jason Aronson.

Schaeffer, C. E. Editor. (1988). *Innovative interventions in child and adolescent therapy.* New York: Wiley.

Schulman, B. H. and Mosak, H. H. (1988). *Manual for life style assessment.* Muncie, IN: Accelerated Development.

Sheikh, A. A. and Sheikh, K. S. Editors. (1989). *Eastern and western approaches to healing.* New York: Wilcy.

Schoenewolf, G. (1990). *101 therapeutic successes: Overcoming transference and resistance in psychotherapy.* New York: Jason Aronson.

Special Interest: Social interest. (1991). *Individual Psychology Journal of Adlerian Theory, Research and Practice.* 47:1.

Sperry, L. and Carlson, J. (1991). *Marital therapy: The integrating theory and techniques.* Denver, CO: Love Publishing.

Varieties of brief therapy. (1989) Special issue. *Individual Psychology. The Journal of Adlerian Theory, Research and Practice.* 45: 1&2.

White, M. and Epston, D. (1990). *Narrative means to therapeutic ends.* New York: Norton.

Whitaker, C. A. and Bumberry, W. M. (1988). *Dancing with the family.* New York: Brunner/Mazel.

Yapko, M. D. (1990). *Trancework. An introduction to the practice of clinical hypnosis.* New York: Brunner/Mazel.

Zeig, J. K. and Gilligan, S. G. Editors. (1990). *Brief therapy. Myths, methods, and metaphors.* New York: Brunner/Mazel.

2

THE ART OF ENCOURAGEMENT

I. INTRODUCTION

Positive feelings of optimism, empowerment, and pride are nourishing forces that enable persons and families to face the challenges of life and relationship with courage and openness.

The emphasis in therapy is to change or "fix" what is wrong. Therefore, the focus of attention is typically on problems and weaknesses rather than on the strengths to be found in the system and in its members and their inherent worth. By doing so we are at risk of reinforcing negative feelings, a sense of powerlessness, and increased rigidity and resistance. Recognition of strengths, inherent worth, and emphasis on positive expectations tend to make people feel more positive and able.

Adlerian Psychology deals in depth with the issues of optimism and pessimism and the consequences of each on behavior. Adler (1980, Chapter 3) believed that the optimistic person is flexible, proactive, and willing to take risks, while viewing life as a challenge with problems to overcome rather than people to overcome. The person is self-confident and believes he is able to achieve. He has the power and influence to do so. Some failures and mistakes are inevitable and are opportunities for learning. He is interested in other people and their well-being. He has the capacity for both intimate connections and independent activity. Such a person has the courage to be imperfect and, therefore, to continue on the proactive path of improving himself (Dreikurs, 1973).

On the other hand, the pessimistic person feels threatened and unsure of himself. He is discouraged by the challenges of life and does not view himself as capable of meeting them successfully. Therefore, he develops a safeguarding life-style which is extremist and rigid. He protects and avoids rather than risks. Although he may complain a great deal, change is frightening and avoided as being beyond his power (Adler, 1980, Chapter 3).

During development, hostility, inconsistency, neglect, and overpampering are most likely to lead to the emergence of pessimism. Negative expectations emerging from erroneous beliefs also foster the attitude of pessimism. If I think that everything I do always turns out badly, then I will be very reluctant to undertake new activities (Powers & Griffith, 1987). Believing oneself to be in roles in which one is inferior, undervalued, victimized, exploited, or ignored can be very discouraging. The actual or perceived lack of information or specific skills can also induce a pessimistic outlook.

One could arrive at somewhat similar generalizations from the principles of behavioral learning, cognitive, imaging, and hypnotherapy theories.

The American Heritage Dictionary (1970) defines *optimism* as "a tendency or disposition to expect the best possible outcome, or to dwell upon the most hopeful aspect of a situation."

To *encourage* is "to inspire to continue on a chosen course; impart courage or confidence to; embolden, hearten."

Empower means "to enable."

Pride is "1. A sense of one's own proper dignity or value; self-respect. 2. Pleasure or satisfaction taken in one's work, achievements, or possessions."

The purpose of this chapter is to identify techniques through which the therapist can build on the strengths of the clients and client system, improve individual and systemic self-concept and morale, and encourage the clients toward more effective behavior based on a more optimistic outlook on life.

The process of encouragement is the overall term that we will use in this chapter to describe how to enable people to feel more optimistic and acquire the courage to behave more effectively.

Encouragement is a much broader concept than praise or reinforcement. It involves accepting the clients as persons of intrinsic worth; paying attention to them; listening to them carefully and demonstrating that they are being understood; validating that, given their beliefs and situation, what they are doing makes sense; assigning good intention to each; letting each person know that he/she counts (the opposite of discounting by putting down, attacking, complaining, or ignoring); fostering mutual respect; providing positive feedback; using humor to provide perspective; reframing negatives to positives by searching for the constructive elements in situations; identifying strengths; and focusing on efforts, contributions, and positive movement (Dinkmeyer & Losoncy, 1980; Sherman & Dinkmeyer, 1987).

Such actions by the therapist impact on the person's sense of worth, belonging, and capability. Someone really believes in him and backs it up in social interaction! The same is true for the family as a system. When each member is treated by the others as one who counts, is worthy, and contributes something of value to the family unit, a positive climate is created. It is now much easier to generate cooperation among the members, modify distorted beliefs, and reshape roles and boundaries.

The family, too, possesses a concept of itself as a unit. There is a sense of pride or of frustration and discouragement about "us." The therapist can help the family develop feelings of legitimate pride in itself and optimism by focusing on many of the above listed actions in the encouragement process. More specifically, the family can examine its multigenerational constructive accomplishments, loyalties, values, customs, traditions, mutual protectiveness, mutual helpfulness, diversity of interests, and strengths. The family can explore what useful things each member has learned from others and what useful things each contributes to the whole. Further, they can specify each member's special talents, value, and positive differences.

The therapist accepts, values, and validates the family and its efforts to cope with the problems of living. She helps the family to identify the wisdom and skills already present and to build upon them to find new solutions. Any positive movement is stressed as the work proceeds. Negative movement is interpreted as having some useful purpose that needs to be explored.

The therapist structures the sessions so that family members practice the same encouraging behavior toward one another as she models with them. The primary effort is to accentuate the positive and convert negatives into positives while building respect, trust, and cooperation.

Some of the issues that arise in therapy are how to: stop family members from discounting or putting each other down; overcome the egocentrism that emerges when people are frustrated and discouraged; introduce a wide range of options to replace the extremist either/or, good/bad, right/wrong modes of thought; reduce the defensive rigidity of a system with discouraged and pessimistic members; convert power plays into a more cooperative pattern; and obtain firm commitments to action. Getting started is itself very encouraging. Much of the conflict in families is related to resistance to perceived disrespectful demands or lack of caring. When people feel respected and cared about, the meaning of events and behavior is changed.

The techniques which follow in this chapter are designed to encourage and empower the clients and enhance their feelings of optimism and pride.

II. STRUCTURED TECHNIQUES

A. *The Appreciation Party*

1. RATIONALE

The Appreciation Party is a technique adapted by Sherman (1987) from a custom common in organizations to honor members who have made important contributions. Often, an award ceremony, breakfast, or dinner is given and prizes are awarded. The purposes are to recognize the efforts of the members who performed well, to stimulate others to greater achievement, and to create bonds and pride among the members for their individual and collective accomplishments.

The same idea and purposes can be applied to work with couples and families. The family is encouraged to adopt the award ceremony as a family custom and to honor each of its members for his/her contributions. Individual feelings of pride, belongingness, and significance are enhanced within the group. To organize and execute such programs, the group members learn to cooperate and share. Thereby, both group cohesiveness and individuation are promoted simultaneously. Attention is focused on the positive, which, hopefully, increases feelings of optimism and empowerment of both the individual and family system.

This technique is somewhat similar to the Encouragement Meeting (see pp. 32–35), but much more extensive and dramatic.

2. PROCEDURE

The therapist asks each person to identify his/her special interests, needs, talents, successes, and contributions to the family. The therapist may need to help with suggestions. "Have you ever helped out another family member? Do you like music? What kind? Are you good at any sport? Did you ever do a good job of something? Were you ever praised for anything? What's your job in this family—do you start things, try to make peace, have new ideas, teach people how to fight, take charge of cleanliness or finances or fun, and so on? "After each presents, ask the group to add other things that are special about the person and other contributions he/she makes. The therapist affirms these positives and points out that there are many strengths and accomplishments here.

"Clearly, each of you has some strengths and talents and does some valuable things for the family. Sure, you may also do some things that others complain about. But you would like the others to recognize the good person that you are and the good things you do, too. For example, take *(start with the name of either the most overadequate or underadequate member)*. Look what this person tries to do and how hard he/she works at it? Wouldn't it be nice for the group to show its appreciation to him/her? Hold an Appreciation Party (lunch, dinner, day) with *(name)* as your guest of honor, with speeches, small presents, and pledges of support for him/her just like they do in all the charities, churches, and businesses to honor their important members. You may want to plan games, costumes, or an outing. Make it a festive occasion for everyone to enjoy. The rest of the family will plan it for *(negotiate the date)*."

The therapist may wish to have the family plan the party in session in order to teach skills in working together and negotiating differences. She may also assist in helping the group invent an award that will produce some shift in roles among the members in order to change the pattern of organization in the family. A firm commitment is obtained from each person to do his/her part.

"Who will be the next person honored? When will that be?" It is important to indicate that each member will be honored. The therapist enjoins the group that the feedback and pledges of support given the honoree must be sincere. The first event should be within two or three weeks. Subsequent events might occur monthly.

Birthdays can be celebrated as appreciation parties.

A variation of the technique is to have a similar party in which every family member is an honoree at the same party. The members form multiple subcommittees to plan the awards and pledges of support. The honoree is not a member of the subcommittee planning his/her awards. The entire group plans for the general festivities.

3. CASE EXAMPLE

The "T" family consists of Mother and Father in their 40s, both working, and two sons aged 14 and eight. There is much conflict over household chores and family responsibilities. Mother is very demanding, is critical of the others, and usually fills most of the gaps while feeling very alone and victimized. The males are resentful of her criticism and nagging and withhold in their performance. Father sometimes joins Mother in criticizing the children, which also engenders, among other reasons, serious resentments toward him. There is a discouraging, negative climate in the home.

The Appreciation Party was introduced to the family following an identification and affirmation of strengths, talents, and accomplishments. With the focus on the positive, it was accepted that Mother was certainly working very hard for the family and deserved some recognition. It was understood that each other member would also be honored.

Mother went off for a brief visit to her family of origin in a distant city. The males planned the party and the awards and greatly enjoyed doing it. They also cleaned up the house in their own fashion. Unfortunately, the therapist did not warn Mother that the event also would be done in their fashion. Her first comment on arrival was to bemoan that the house was not cleaned right. This threw a temporary damper on the affair, but as the event unfolded a good time was had by all. Mom felt that her efforts were indeed noticed and she felt less alone. The men enjoyed working on a fun thing together. In league with the therapist, one of Mother's presents was that the men pledged some support by undertaking some of the household responsibilities that she had been doing. In return, she was instructed to accept this present graciously and realize that they would not be done exactly her way. She was to take a well-deserved vacation and allow the men to undertake the responsibilities. This had to be reinforced at each session, but it helped to disengage the power play in the family and reduce feelings of resentment, while focusing more on the positives.

Subsequent parties were held at monthly intervals for the others. The members each felt better about their respective places in the family and themselves as persons. In each case, with the therapist coaching, the presents received were directed in part toward shifting roles in the system. Mother was placed in charge of fun, Father of finances, the 14-year-old of distribution of family chores, and the eight-year-old of family history.

4. USES

The Appreciation Party is useful in helping to disengage power plays, create a positive climate, and shift roles or introduce new roles within the system. It creates warm lifetime memories which bond the family members together. It provides an opportunity for fun and appreciation rather than neglect and hostile attacks. It encourages the family as a system to feel worthy and it encourages individuals to feel significant, potent, and needed.

B. The Encouragement Meeting

1. RATIONALE

The Encouragement Meeting was designed by Dinkmeyer and Carlson (1984b) to strengthen individuals and relationships. It is based on the traditional model of the Adlerian Family Meeting described in Manaster and Corsini (1982) and Sherman and Fredman (1986). Providing positive feedback around the circle is an old group work technique. These meetings are held to regularly identify positive characteristics, behaviors, and contributions of each member of the system. The system could be a family, couple, class group, work group, etc.

Each member is affirmed as a worthy person by the positive attention received from the others and by stress placed on the positive in him/herself. Similarly, the technique can be used for the group to toot its own horn about its accomplishments and character. As a result, feelings of belonging, recognition, and personal and group pride may be enhanced. A climate may be created which facilitates the next steps of developing more effective conflict resolution skills, the willingness to change relational elements in the system, and the confidence to tackle the challenges posed by life both within and outside of the system. The technique also teaches skills for positive communication, mutual respect, cooperation, and democratic leadership.

2. PROCEDURE

The therapist suggests the Encouragement Meeting as a desirable activity to be added to the current life of the group in the context of their prior behavior and discussions. It is presented as something that could add good feelings and strengthen the group. The therapist conducts the first meeting in session in order to instruct the group in the process. A family will typically need 15–30 minutes for each meeting, usually held at least once a week.

The rules are that the meeting is to occur at the same time and place and without any interruptions permitted. Each person is given a chance to speak positively about every other member and to talk about his/her own positive moves or feelings. Negative feelings and gripes are not permitted to be aired at these sessions, which are not designed to solve problems. The members face each other and maintain eye contact as they speak. The chairperson role is rotated each session so that all who are old enough to chair are given the opportunity to do so.

The therapist chairs the first meeting in session in order to train the couple or family. She says: "Please think silently for a moment about yourself. Are there some things about you—some traits, strengths, something that you did, felt, or thought—that you are pleased about? Is there something that you tried even if you didn't fully succeed?" She then selects a member who would be most likely to share and suggests that the person tell the group what he/she was just thinking about. She congratulates the person on what was shared and thanks him/her for describing those special feelings and news. Everyone follows in turn, telling good things about the self while looking directly at the members and is congratulated.

Next, the therapist invites the group to stop for a few moments and silently consider the members present. "Can you think of some positive things about each person here; some trait, special strength, or talent, something the person did or tried to do that you appreciate?" She then asks one member to begin to share with each other person in turn the good things that he/she noticed. "Say only what you honestly believe." Insincerity is likely to be picked up by the listeners and this will destroy any sense of trust and good feeling in the meeting. When the speaker is finished with each person, the one addressed is asked to respond. "Please summarize the ideas, beliefs, values, or events you heard and acknowledge that you understood them. Just accept that this is what the speaker is thinking about you. Don't correct, defend, or depreciate the speaker." Each person gets a turn as speaker and to respond briefly to each speaker about what was heard about him/herself. No interruptions of the speaker are permitted.

The therapist then requests that the group silently reflect upon the group as a group and identify the good talents, resources, and accomplishments of the group. These are shared and discussed. The therapist congratulates them on their accomplishments and strengths.

A variation is for the members to go around the circle identifying some quality or action of each other one that they wish they could acquire for themselves or do themselves. To set up goals for behavior change, they might then be asked what they would be willing to give up about themselves in order to acquire the selected qualities or behaviors of the other members. After discussion, a commitment to the change is obtained and the group is asked to cooperate to facilitate the change. Thus, relationship patterns are shifted and the group reorganizes.

3. CASE EXAMPLE

The H. family consisted of Mother and Father, each in the 40s, and two sons, Jonathan, 20, and Paul, 15. The parents reported that Paul was the identified client who had physically violent temper tantrums and was doing poorly in school, academically and socially. Assessment further revealed that there was much conflict between the parents over finances, fun, and child-rearing. Mother was obsessive about cleanliness. Everyone blamed everyone else for all kinds of disappointments and difficulties and the vicious put-down was the typical mode of family communication.

The therapeutic strategy was first to acknowledge each person in the group and the importance of the personal needs and expectations each professed. These were reframed into positive statements. Each family member was then asked to acknowledge the needs of others as at least somewhat legitimate. Second, the therapist prescribed a family truce. (See pp. 255–257) The members were not to put each other down, be violent or nasty, or buy the bait laid down by any other member. Third, the therapist pursued what was "right" with this family. The roles of members were positively reframed: Mother was trying very hard to push the family forward toward greater achievement and more efficient organization; Father was the nice guy trying to keep the peace; Paul was striving for independence and modeling for Father how to be more assertive in the family; and Jonathan tried to support Mom, who was very discouraged, alternately falling apart and trying to whip the family in line.

At this point the Encouragement Meeting was introduced and practiced in session. Each person received a lot of strokes from the family. For example, Father was seen as a strong fighter in a tough vocational world and neighborhood, a good athlete, an excellent salesman and businessman, and very loving, among other things. Paul was seen as very passionate, helpful to neighbors, loving of animals, and ambitious and persistent about his hobbies. Jonathan was told that he is very bright, very knowledgeable about music and electronic equipment, a fine salesman, and a caring person. Mom learned that she was much loved in spite of the fighting, had a great sense of humor and fun, was considered by her "men" to be very attractive, was a good cook and housekeeper, and was very passionate and caring.

There were many efforts by the members to insert "Yes, but" messages: "You are a good housekeeper, but you are too finicky." The therapist stopped the "but" part of the message immediately, pointing out how strong the habit of putting people down is in the family. She then restated that this meeting concentrates only on honest positives.

The family also identified many things "right about themselves" as a family. They would protect each other against the outside world. They enjoyed preparing and eating good food. They were strong and healthy. They were intelligent.

Occasionally, the therapist moved in to help by identifying some positive quality that she noticed so that the family could be triggered to identify some more of its strengths.

The depth of discouragement in the family is probably directly correlated with how short a list of positives they make.

The members gradually relaxed and began to enjoy the strokes they were giving and receiving. They saw that all was not bad and maybe there was some hope for them. The meeting was then prescribed as a family ritual to be carried out twice weekly at home for a month.

With a more relaxed, positive atmosphere, it was possible to disengage Paul and Jonathan from the couple conflict, to make them more responsible for themselves, to get Mom much more off their backs, and to help Father become more assertive as Mom became softer.

4. USES

The Encouragement Meeting can be used to help disengage power plays, as illustrated in the above case. It helps people feel good about themselves and one another. It focuses attention on discovering the strengths and positives rather than the negatives. These can then be utilized as the basis for therapeutic interventions using strengths to overcome weaknesses or dysfunctions. People learn to relate together in a positive, cooperative way, employing the skills of a democratic meeting. Such skills can then be transferred through coaching to a wide range of other kinds of communication from the family meeting and couple conference (See pp. 175–179) to the impromptu interaction.

This is also a good technique to introduce when one encounters heavy resistance and bad feelings in the session. It provides for a complete change of pace and reversal of content. One reason for resistance is a misalignment of goals among the participants. Recasting to the positive the behavior patterns and roles in terms of systemic complementarities, as described in the case above, paves the way for acknowledging the disparity and cooperatively finding some accommodation among goals.

C. The Name Game

1. RATIONALE

The Name Game is a familiar technique with many variations widely used in group counseling and in encounter groups. Participants are asked such questions as how they wish to be called, for whom they are named, what have been their nicknames, and what is their ideal name. The purpose is to assist each person to get a better understanding of his/her identity, self concept, and ideal self. Group members also become better known to one another.

Sherman adapted this technique for use with couples and families in his practice. The purposes are the same as above, plus a means for helping people place themselves constructively within their multigenerational family systems. They may then discover that in the context of a past, present, and future they can appreciate what feels good to them and make changes for a more amenable future. It helps each person to both assert his/her individuality and connect with the family. The family and its members discover a sense of continuity, typically seeing that they are part of a larger whole.

People have beliefs about names. A Sheldon is the kind of person who . . . Babe is a name for a child, not an adult . . . being George Adams 3rd carries a distinguished past or great burdens from the past . . . being named after great Aunt Suzie means that I should . . . I really see myself as a Joshua. This technique uses names to discover identities, meanings, and places in the system, and to enable some shifts in the patterns of interaction.

2. PROCEDURE

The therapist introduces the procedure by inquiring, "What's in a name? Perhaps we can find out a little more about how this family fits together by exploring the meanings of your names." The therapist then throws out the following questions to the group, discussing each one in turn in terms of individual identity and place in the family.

"What is your formal given name? Are you pleased with it? Does the name have a literal translation? What does it mean to you?"

"Are you named after someone or something? What are the stories about that person or thing? Are there a succession of people in your family history who carry that name? Is there an ultimate ancestor? What are the stories about that ancestor? What does it mean to you to be named after that person or thing? How does it influence you? Does it imply that anything particular is expected of you? How are you like your namesake and how are you different?"

"Do you or have you had any nicknames? What nickname did your parents give you? How do you feel about it? Are there any stories about it? Have you had any other nicknames? How did you get them? How did they get changed? How do you feel about them? What did the nicknames tell about what kind of person you are and how you behave?"

"Did you invent any fantasy names growing up? What did they represent for you?"

"Ideally, by what name would you like to be known now? How would that suit you and represent you better than your present name?"

Allow the partner or family to jump in at any time to share reminiscences, stories, or opinions. If parents are present, ask them what they had in mind when they gave the names they gave.

When all have spoken, inquire of the family:

"How do the names describe who you are and what is expected of you in this family and what you expect of yourself? How does it influence your behavior and relationships?"

"Do you see yourselves as part of a continuing chain?"

"What power do you have to take the best from your past and fashion the best possible future?"

The therapist throughout the discussion works to affirm and validate each person in the family and to identify as many positives as possible. Those seeming negatives that could be usefully reframed to the positive are reframed. The intention is to use the exercise also as a means of building individual and family pride.

3. CASE EXAMPLE

The identified client, Ben, age 24, an only child, complained of depression, isolation, and worthlessness. His parents were invited to join the therapy. At first, they pushed him away with their admonishments when he shared his complaints. The therapist validated Ben's mood as what he was experiencing and his desire to overcome the negative mood he was in. Ben claimed he didn't really fit or belong in this world. The therapist did a multigenerational genogram (see the Genogram technique on pp. 56–60 and McGoldrick & Gersen, 1985) on a large sheet of paper tacked on the wall. Based on the discussion and the visual representation of his extended family on the wall, he could see that he was part of something larger than himself. He could feel some sense of belonging, but still thought of himself as worthless. The therapist used a variety of cognitive and simple paradoxical tactics during the discussions (for example, "For someone who thinks he is so worthless, you certainly spend an awful lot of time thinking about yourself") and helped the parents to truly listen to the son and the son to appreciate that his parents really did care about him.

At this point, the Name Game was introduced. The purpose was to help Ben define his identity within the connections of a family group and to enhance his sense of belonging and significance. His given name is Benjamin after his mother's father whom she loved dearly and who was very warm and loving of Ben until his death when Ben was 11. It was discovered that Grandfather's death was very much an unresolved issue in this family, especially for Ben and his mother. Ben was the family nickname as it had been Grandfather's nickname. Talking about Grandfather gave Ben warm feelings and he was proud to be named after him. But he worried if Father resented his connection to Grandfather. He was angry that his father was a more distant and less affectionate person. Conversely, he was angry with his mother, whom he described as too intrusive.

Presenting and discussing the other questions described in the Procedures section revealed, among other data, that a Ben is supposed to be a gentle and sensitive person much loved by others. Mother had to be protective to carry on the tradition of the person she was named after and Father honored what he perceived as his macho nickname, Jake. Jake is cool and takes what he wants. He was somewhat disappointed with his more gentle and sensitive son and indeed would have preferred to have given him a more manly name. "Maybe he would have been less of a mother's boy."

The therapist used this information to work on the positives. Ben was descended from a long line of Benjamins and carried a distinguished name in history. He was very much loved by all the members of his extended family. He indeed agreed with his father that he wanted to be more independent and assertive, as well as warm, sensitive, and gentle. He was asked to obtain permission from his father to develop both sides of himself to be a broader, more effective human being. Father stated that he respected his son's sensitivity and would like to learn some of that kind of behavior for himself. Therefore, a plan was developed so that they could teach each other. Mother realized she had to differentiate between protection and affection and, with her husband's help, turn her son loose. The information gleaned in the Name Game about the spouses was then used to make some changes in the spouse relationship.

Ben felt very much impacted by this experience. He became more worthy in his own eyes, felt that he had something to contribute, and felt encouraged that he could become more independent, assertive, and respected by his father. Father recognized that being sensitive and less distant was not unmanly.

4. USES

The Name Game can be used to help the couple or family better understand themselves individually and as a unit. It can help to identify myths, mistaken beliefs, hurts, unresolved issues, expectations, and patterns of interaction. It can be used to build self-esteem; family pride; and a sense of belonging, empowerment, and optimism. By bringing people together, it can reduce tensions and power plays.

III. TIPS AND TACTICS FOR ENCOURAGEMENT

A. Affirm Rather Than Discount

A discouraging cycle is perpetuated when family members compete in attacking or criticizing one another. Often the criticism is well intentioned to get the other person to change and be "good," "right," or "successful." Other times it is to defend against perceived hostility. It may also be modeled by one member to help another one become more aggressive and assertive. For example, a boy may act out against his mother to show his passive father that he should not put up with his wife's apparent domineering behavior. It can be a way of compensating for feelings of inferiority by making oneself superior to others. It can also be a habit acquired in one's family of origin as the way to connect, deal with problems, and try to get what you want.

Discounting further occurs when: decisions are made without consultation; one tries to do more than is appreciated for another; important information is withheld or simply not shared; a person's communications or feelings are ignored; and attention is not paid in general.

The therapist can intervene with blocking techniques to stop the behavior or join with affirming and validating methods to encourage the couple or family.

B. Blocking Tactics

1. *Describe back and assess intentionality.* The therapist observes the pattern of hostile behavior and describes it back to the participants to make them aware of their process. She then inquires as to their intentions through questions such as the following: "What did you hope the outcome of your communication would be? Do you want to hurt, get something, or settle something? What effect did the communication actually have as you per-

ceived it? Does this pattern usually work for you? If it seldom works, what stops you from changing it? Is it possible that it does serve some purpose other than what you say you intend? What might that be? Do you know any other ways of accomplishing your intentions?"

The idea for this tactic is derived from the communication model used by Gottman (1976) in his teaching film that every communication has an intention, a delivered message, and an effect, impact, or consequence. Having the participants become aware of and examine the sequence may prepare them to stop it. The therapist can then work toward substituting a more effective pattern by focusing on the positive intentions.

2. *Dramatize roles.* Assign a dramatic role label to each person. In the case of a critical wife and resistant husband, you might suggest that the wife comes across as a critical mother and the husband like a rebellious son. "Is that who you really are? Given the taboos of our society, it must be very hard for a mother and son to make love together." Similar interventions might be: "Where did you learn to become the inspector general or judge of this family and who else agreed to it?" "When did you decide to accept the job of being the lightning rod who collects all the negative criticism for everyone else in this family?" The dramatization may have a paradoxical effect in highlighting each one's responsibility in the pattern.

3. *Praise expertise in put-downs.* The therapist describes the hostile pattern just enacted and exclaims, with complete sincerity: "Boy, you people are really good at these put-downs! I feel so inadequate next to you. You hurl nuclear bombs at each other and you absorb the blows with such effectiveness and don't get destroyed. You are really strong and certainly are worthy opponents. Clearly you are both so strong that neither one can win. Every fight ends in a draw, with nothing resolved." After this sinks in the therapist might use some of the following questions and comments: "Where and how did you learn to do this? Do you each need more practice to further hone your skills to convince yourselves how powerful you really are? Obviously, neither of you would be pleased if the other were not a strong person. Mutual strength leads to a stalemate. So what do you do now?"

4. *Take umbrage on behalf of a friend.* The therapist allies herself with the system as a whole and with the individuals in it by declaring that as worthy human beings they deserve not to be abused and that any kind of abuse is intolerable and must be stopped immediately. If she wishes to risk it, she can declare even more strongly that she likes the members of this group and finds it intolerable that anyone would hurt the people she likes. If she prefers a milder approach, she can ask if the people in this group

deserve to be treated well. If so, how can abuse be tolerated, especially among people who at many levels care for each other?

C. Affirming Tactics

1. *Model and coach attention and acceptance.* The therapist models her attention to the family and each member and accepts each one as worthy. She does this through eye contact, leaning slightly forward in her chair, and positive nodding of the head. She can restate briefly what was said and acknowledge the statement or reflect the feelings in a process of active listening (Rogers, 1951). She can interpret the meaning of the behavior in the form of a tentative hypothesis to both indicate understanding and provide an opportunity for the group to examine the behavior (Dinkmeyer, Dinkmeyer, & Sperry, 1987). She can stress her own interest in the importance of the other person and state the rule that each person must be attended to and heard in this group. She may ask others to acknowledge what was heard and what it might mean.

In these ways group members learn to be attentive and to acknowledge one another rather than to criticize or ignore.

2. *Shift labels.* This technique is a form of reframing. However, the objective is to teach the family how to put alternative, positive meanings on the actions of their fellows rather than negative ones. Negative labels create negative expectations, hostility, and anxiety. McMullin (1986) uses this as a cognitive therapy countering technique to change negative or irrational beliefs when working with individuals. With families, the therapist has the members make a list of the negative meanings or labels which they assign to one another's behavior. They then practice identifying alternative meanings for the same behavior until they see the many possible interpretations. They are encouraged to assign good intention to their fellows and focus on the more positive explanations. This, in turn, encourages and reinforces more positive intentions. They must practice using the new labels every day.

Some examples of relabeling provided by McMullin (1986) are: A person who changes one's mind a lot can be seen as wishy washy or, alternatively, as flexible; one who sticks to projects can be compulsive or determined; one who believes what others say is either gullible or trusting.

The same process can be used to have the members positively relabel their problems or symptoms.

3. *Inform.* Sometimes people feel very discouraged because they lack necessary information or skill. The counselor may put information into the system through a number of different techniques.

a. Simply tell the clients what they need to know.

b. Elicit the knowledge through a series of leading questions.

c. Prescribe appropriate bibliotherapy materials or practical readings.

d. Make tentative hypotheses or interpretations. (Is it possible that what is going on here is . . . ; what your feeling is . . . ; what your thinking is . . .?)

e. Project information within the premise or content of a question. ("Do you think you could more often get what you want and trigger fewer fights with others if you could speak of what you need rather than what is wrong with the other one?" "When did you realize that you are more grown up now and have better ways of getting what you want than by having temper tantrums?")

f. Coach the clients in performing some new, agreed-upon behavior and practice it in session and in the setting in which the lack of that skill is a problem. This can be done while the clients are enacting their relationship in session as they work on an issue or play with children (Minuchin, 1974; Minuchin & Fishman, 1981), through role-playing a situation, or through behavior rehearsal in which the clients fantasize the situation in their own imagination (Flanagan, 1990; Sherman & Fredman, 1986, Chapter 2).

g. Refer the clients to an appropriate expert or course.

h. Have the clients observe an appropriate model of the behavior in action or the therapist may serve as the model.

i. Refer the clients to an appropriate psycho-education group to learn about a particular problem area such as parent education, schizophrenia, retardation, or alcoholism, and how better to cope with it.

4. *Normalize.* Clients often engage in self-recrimination and blaming and see their situation as extraordinary and, therefore, super serious. They look at their perceived circumstances with extremist eyes so that their position appears incredibly bad, if not hopeless. The intention of normalizing actions by the counselor is to move the experience from the extreme to a more manageable position. The counselor can cite statistics or indicate that in the experience of her practice this is a fairly common phenomenon. She might share that in the same circumstances she might be inclined to do the same things. She can ask if this is a catastrophe or a life-threatening situation. Clients who totalize (all or nothing, good or bad, always or never) are asked to be specific about when and how the situation occurs and when it doesn't. The therapist then points out that this happens only *sometimes* and not *always* or *never*. The counselor further examines the consequences of the problem so as to track and assess the actual damage.

REFERENCES

Adler, A. (1980). *What life should mean to you*. London: George Allen and Unwin.

Dinkmeyer, D. and Carlson, J. (1984A). *Time for a better marriage*. Circle Pines, MN: American Guidance Service.

Dinkmeyer, D. and Carlson, J. (1984B). *Training in marriage enrichment. TIME*. Circle Pines, MN: American Guidance Service.

Dinkmeyer, D., Dinkmeyer, D. Jr., and Sperry, L. (1987). 2nd Ed. *Adlerian counseling and psychotherapy*. Columbus, OH: Merrill.

Dinkmeyer, D. and Losoncy, L. (1980). *The encouragement book. Becoming a positive person*. Englewood Cliffs, NJ: Prentice-Hall.

Dreikurs, R. (1973). *Psychodynamics, psychotherapy and counseling*. Chicago: Alfred Adler Institute.

Flanagan, C. M. (1990). *People and change. An introduction to counseling and stress management*. Hillsdale, NJ: Lawrence Erlbaum.

Gottman, J. (1976). *Behavioral interviewing with couples*. (16mm. color film). Champaign, IL: Research Press.

Manaster, G. J. and Corsini, R. J. (1982). *Individual psychology*. Itasca, IL: Peacock.

McGoldrick, M. and Gersen, R. (1985). *Genograms in family assessment*. New York: Norton.

McMullin, R. E. (1986). *Handbook of cognitive therapy techniques*. New York: Norton.

Minuchin, S. (1974). *Families and family therapy*. Cambridge, MA: Harvard University Press.

Minuchin, S. and Fishman, R. (1981). *Family therapy techniques*. Cambridge, MA: Harvard University Press.

Morris, W. Editor (1970). *The American heritage dictionary of the English language*. Boston: Houghton-Mifflin.

Powers, R. L. and Griffith, J. (1987). *Understanding life cycle: The Psycho-Clarity process*. Chicago: American Institute of Adlerian Studies.

Rogers, C. (1951). *Client-centered therapy*. Boston: Houghton-Mifflin.

Sherman, R. (1987). Psychoeducational techniques for improving relationships. Workshop. Eighth Annual Conference in Marriage and Family Counseling, Queens College, City University of New York, November 13th.

Sherman, R. and Dinkmeyer, D. (1987). *Systems of family therapy: An Adlerian integration*. New York: Brunner/Mazel.

Sherman, R. and Fredman, N. (1986). *Handbook of structured techniques in marriage and family therapy.* New York: Brunner/Mazel.

ADDITIONAL RESOURCES

Alpert, L. (1982). *Linda Alpert's advice for coping with kids.* New York: Dutton.

Dreikurs, R. (1946). *The challenge of marriage.* New York: Hawthorne.

Dreikurs, R. and Soltz, V. (Reissued 1987). *Children the challenge.* New York: Dutton.

Efran, J. S. and Lukens, M. D. (1990). *Language, structure, and change.* New York: Norton.

Freeman, A. and De Wolf, R. (1990). *Woulda, coulda, shoulda. Overcoming regrets, mistakes, and missed opportunities.* New York: Morrow.

Harper, J. M. and Hoopes, M. H. (1990). *Uncovering shame. An approach integrating individuals and their systems.* New York: Norton.

Imber-Black, E., Roberts, J., and Whiting, R. Editors. (1988). *Rituals in families and family therapy.* New York: Norton.

Kvols-Riedler, B. and Kvols-Riedler, K. (1979). *Redirecting children's misbehavior. A guide for cooperation between children and adults.* Boulder, CO: RDIC Publications.

Lankton, C. H. and Lankton, S. R. (1989). *Tales of enchantment. Goal-oriented metaphors for adults and children in therapy.* New York: Brunner/Mazel.

Lichstein, K. L. (1988). *Clinical relaxation strategies.* New York: Wiley.

Mosak, H. H. (1987). *Ha ha and aha. The role of humor in psychotherapy.* Muncie, IN: Accelerated Development.

Schaeffer, C. E. Editor. (1988). *Innovative interventions in child and adolescent therapy.* New York: Wiley. (Some examples of encouraging techniques in this book are: phototherapy, videotherapy, animal therapy, and making life books.)

Wallas, L. (1988). *Stories for the third ear.* New York: Norton.

Wallas, L. (1991). *Stories that heal. Reparenting adult children of dysfunctional families using hypnotic stories in psychotherapy.* New York: Norton.

3

JOINING

A man is a bundle of relations, a knot of roots, whose flower and fruitage is the world.

(Emerson, Essays: History.)

I. INTRODUCTION

A. Discussion

The process of forming relationships begins with joining. As social animals, people are joiners. We live purposeful lives in the company of other people: family, friends, coworkers, acquaintances, and strangers. We belong to churches, synagogues, mosques, and temples, political parties, civic organizations, unions, parent-teacher organizations, environmental groups, health and photography clubs. Within these groups, relationships are shaped, ostensibly by a person's desire and ability to establish rapport.

How one "hits it off" or initially connects opens the door to the beginning of an association. First impressions do not simply determine whether an association will be formed. Expectations and limitations are also estimated by both parties. These may change as the parties get to know each other better and some bonding takes place—a stranger becomes an acquaintance, a coworker may be added to one's circle of friends.

In the process of adapting to new relationships, some amount of blending, an understanding and acceptance of the ideas and behaviors of others, takes place. There is a give and take, negotiation and compromise; accommodations are made. A group of children may decide to ride their bicycles at Dana's suggestion because they have already played at activities suggested by the other children. Both sets of grandparents can't have their grandchild for her first sleepover at "their" house.

In therapy, joining is also a process. It begins with the initial contact over the telephone, in person, or through a third party. As the process proceeds, the therapist's ability to join with her clients will determine the quality of the therapeutic relationship and serve as an indicator of the possibilities for positive change. Without the acceptance of the therapist by the family, change cannot take place.

Although joining is often seen as a primary concern only during the beginning phase of therapy, it is important to remember that it also needs to be attended to during the entire course of the therapy. The therapist continually builds upon the relationships established with family members. Weaving effective joining strategies and techniques into the therapeutic process enhances the family's acceptance of the therapist. This acceptance will serve to reduce the potential for resistance (see Chapter 4) throughout the various stages of the therapy. Generally, a client's level of resistance is indicative of the therapist's success in joining with that individual.

1. JOINING TAKES PLACE ON TWO LEVELS

The therapist needs to join with each family member on two levels—the personal and the professional. She must be accepted as a human being capable of developing an empathic understanding of the family system and of the individual members living within that system. The family members need to feel comfortable in the therapeutic environment. All need to feel respected by the therapist for who they are. They need to feel included and understood.

The therapist is also recognized as a professional, possessing the skills necessary to guide the family out of their difficulties. The family needs to perceive the therapist as a person who can help them to move in the direction of relief. As the family experiences positive results from the therapeutic process, resistance to future work and suggestions generally decreases. Success tends to breed success.

2. CHALLENGING CIRCUMSTANCES

Despite our knowledge of human behavior and various life-styles, clients will occasionally bring to therapy difficulties related to a markedly different life experience than that known to the therapist. Some examples are: a woman who indicates to a male therapist that she is experiencing difficulties with her family during her PMS; the parents of a foreign-born husband who refuse to accompany their son and his American wife for therapy with an American therapist; a homosexual or lesbian couple who come to a heterosexual therapist for therapy; or a court order that brings a lower class family with teenage gang members to a therapist from a middle class family orientation.

The particular circumstances of clients can present significant challenges for the therapist. To meet such challenges, the therapist must convert strangers into cooperative clients. Use of the specific techniques and tactics included in this chapter can facilitate the process.

B. Definition

The Latin, "jungers," means join or yoke (Barnhart & Barnhart, 1985). Joining, the therapeutic construct, is the connective link or the intermedium through which systemic changes are more easily brought about. However, it also imposes restrictions upon the therapist, as the yoke does on the oxen. The therapist needs to remember to work within the limitations of the existing gestalt brought to the therapy by the clients.

Joining is an active process. Select aspects of personality, background and experience, social skills, and learned techniques, as well as theoretical approaches, are called upon to facilitate the success of a particular brand of therapy. Some therapists may seek to "capture," while others "establish rapport." Perhaps, as a therapist, I choose to "join," you may choose to "blend," and two other therapists might "connect" and "bond," respectively. For the purposes of this book, the generic term "joining" will be used to represent the variety of theoretical constructs identified in the different theoretical orientations as having the purpose of gaining the trust and acceptance of the clients.

II. STRUCTURED TECHNIQUES

Change is inevitable. It is the pain, frustration, anxiety, lack of confidence, fear, or perception of an inability to continue which moves family members to seek help. The initiation of the search outside the family system is significant. The therapist, through joining, coheres with the family in their pursuit of functional patterns for interaction.

The techniques included in this chapter were selected from a variety of therapeutic approaches. They were chosen to provide the practitioner with specific joining interventions which could be useful at the various stages of therapy while moving the venture forward.

A. *Questioning to Form Connections*

1. RATIONALE

Questioning is a fundamental aspect of communication in our culture. We use questions to accomplish a wide variety of tasks. Through the use of questions, we make inquiries to acquire information. ("What time is it?" "How does it work?" "What do you think about this?") We use questions to limit conversation or to open it up. ("Would you like to go to the beach today?" "What would you like to do today?") We can put others down. ("Haven't you figured it out, yet?") We can attempt to put words in another's mouth. ("You are interested in solving this problem, aren't you?") We can also project our own thoughts, feelings, and motives. ("Are you still allowing your mother to tell you what to do?") The kinds of questions asked in the therapeutic situation, in large measure, forge the therapist/client relationship and determine the extent to which joining is possible.

Establishing rapport need not be a belabored process replete with fancy techniques. The family coming for therapy is usually interested in explaining their problems to a concerned and understanding professional. The therapist is interested in obtaining information from the family about their unique system of relating to one another and the difficulties they are experiencing. The interests of both can be met through the effective use of questions. Acceptance of the therapist is facilitated and strategies can be formulated by the demonstration of receptivity and acceptance of the information a family presents through the use of questions designed to acquire needed information.

2. PROCEDURE

The questioning style of the therapist cues the client as to what the therapeutic process will be like: painful, enjoyable, capable of being manipulated, client or therapist focused, and so on. In order for the therapist to most effectively open the family system up to accept her as helper, it is important that the questions asked be necessary for understanding the problem presented by the family.

Awareness of the different types of questions and their impact is important for effective utilization in establishing ties to the family. Ivey and Gluckstern (1974) and Grunwald and McAbee (1985) identify two categories: closed and open, which are illustrated in the following examples.

3. CASE EXAMPLES

a. *Closed questioning.* Closed questions are worded so as to result in a brief, to-the-point, factual response. Yes or no answers are indicative of the asking of a closed question. Choosing a pattern of closed questioning is generally used to establish control or focus in session. This can be effective with chaotic families or in families with small children. For example:

Therapist: Do you go out without the kids?
Husband: Yes, we go to the movies on occasion.
Wife: Sometimes we see friends.
Child 1: Yeah, they go out, sometimes, Not much without us.
Child 2: They go out and leave us home, sometimes.
Therapist: Do you enjoy yourselves?
Wife: Yes. I miss them, but it's nice to be with H.
Child 1: I don't like it.
Child 2: I don't like it neither.
Therapist: How do you feel, H?
Husband: It's okay. We enjoy ourselves.
Therapist: Do you prefer to take the children along when you socialize?
Wife: Well, I would. I like having them around, knowing where they are, what they're up to. You know. Do you have kids?

"Is" or "Are" questions tend to confine responses to brief descriptions around a yes or no answer. "Why" and "Do" questions can be demeaning and accusative in nature, as well as restrictive. Although "Why do you do that?" may be appropriate at some point in the therapeutic process, it is not the kind of question that promotes bonding with a family member. The asking of the question, with the expectation of obtaining a response, is dependent upon the bonding that has already taken place.

b. *Open questioning.* The use of open questions allows the family members to communicate and explore their thoughts, feelings, and behaviors. The limited structure allows for greater movement and growth, with support from the therapist. Within this framework the sessions remain focused on the family's problems. For example:

Therapist: What do people in this family do with other family members, but not with the whole family?

Husband: The wife and I go to the movies together every once in a while. I take the boys to Little League practice, usually. She helps them with their homework. The boys do a lot of things together, don't you guys?

Child 1: Yup. We go to school together. We go to the movies together. We play together. We practice hitting and catching together. We watch television together, but sometimes we like different programs. So, I watch in our room and my brother goes into the living room to watch his program.

Child 2: Yeah, but sometimes I want to watch in our room and he won't let me. He pushes me out of the room.

Therapist: He does?

Child 2: Yeah, but we don't hate each other.

Wife: Their fighting drives me crazy. And my husband never breaks them up. He says that's how boys are. As long as they don't break anything or really hurt each other, it's okay. Do you have any kids? But to get back to what you asked, we, my husband and I, try to get out at least twice a month without the kids. We go to friends or to the movies. I also take the kids to the library and to their music lesson. What else do we do together? Oh, we go bicycle riding. Sometimes just he and I; sometimes I go with the kids; sometimes he takes them alone.

Therapist: Could you tell me if you enjoy yourselves?

Wife: Yes. I miss them, but it's nice to be alone with him. It's also nice to be with the kids sometimes. I get a chance to be a little silly and do things I wouldn't do if he was there, like trying to imitate our older one by standing on my head.

Child 1: Yeah. Mom can be really funny. You should see the faces she makes sometimes when my brother plays the piano.

Child 2: And when you play, too, sometimes. And I miss Mom and Dad when they go out sometimes and Mrs. S is our babysitter. She is mean.

Therapist: How do you feel (to husband)?

Husband: It's okay. We enjoy ourselves. I don't miss them. W and I need time to be together.

Therapist: How would it be to take the children along with you when you socialize?

Wife: I would like that. I like having them around, knowing where they are, what they're up to. Do you have kids?

The use of an open questioning pattern encourages family members to include a wide variety of responses. Being able to talk to the therapist in this manner signals the family that the therapist is interested in all they have to say.

"What" and "How" questions encourage quantity and more descriptive input from the family. "Could" questions acknowledge family members' right not to offer the information and accepts the possibility that some things may not be forthcoming at this time.

c. *Continuation questioning*. This is another form of questioning that encourages clients to provide additional information. It facilitates establishing rapport through the demonstration of interest in what the client is offering. Examples include: "He does?" "Oh?" "Yes?"

It is helpful to review audio and video tapes of sessions with an ear and eye on the kinds of responses obtained from questioning patterns utilized in session. Observing one's present style of questioning and client responses can reveal a good deal of information regarding their effectiveness in establishing rapport. Questioning, when carefully utilized, can be a powerful joining technique.

4. USES

Awareness of questioning styles, coupled with the ability to utilize them selectively, provides therapists with a useful diagnostic tool. The pattern of questioning most effective with a family in session is indicative of their needs and their perceived "normal" state. Families in which the closed type of questioning is more effective may require boundary strengthening or role delineation and structural emphasis. Clients for whom open questioning patterns are successful may also respond better to fantasy and imagery techniques with a more cognitive/perceptual emphasis.

B. Tracking

1. RATIONALE

Minuchin and Fishman (1981) identify tracking as a structured technique which allows the therapist to join with the family from a medial therapeutic position. The therapist actively interacts with family members from a position of neutrality, primarily as a listener in search of information. She helps the family tell its tale. The content presented, however, is juxtaposed with the process observed. Process clues picked out during the telling are followed up by a therapist coming from the position of curiosity. For example:

"When your mother criticizes your father, do you think she is a bad person?" Tracking allows the therapist to move from content to process and to link process with content, providing a well-rounded, full story for the family and therapist.

The tracking opens new vistas through which the family can safely view their interactions. The therapist gains acceptance and credibility by acknowledging each person's behavior, by describing the interactive pattern of the system, and by communicating her understanding of the process. Her encouragement and acceptance of the family and their story strongly enhance the joining of the family with the therapist.

2. PROCEDURE

To track, the therapist adopts a position of impartial involvement with the family. A presenting problem is chosen to explore the operation of their system. The family's story is elicited by the therapist's following up what is offered by a family member with comments or questions indicating the therapist's interest and desire to know more about the particular event or concern being expressed. The careful wording of comments and questions will allow the therapist to guide the course and flow of the interactions to reveal information about family history, boundaries, roles, values, symbols, and myths.

The therapist needs to determine how much control she wishes to exert with the tracking intervention. If the object is to observe the systemic inter-actions firsthand, therapist questions or comments should be made to the family unit. This would encourage the members to interact as is customary within the system.

If the goal is to investigate the system in a more controlled atmosphere, the therapist would address questions and comments to individual family members. This approach would tend to alter the communication network in many families. It is also possible to use both methods within a session.

Through the use of clarifying questions, repeating and paraphrasing what is said, and interjecting positive remarks, the therapist can move to develop a rapport with one family member at a time or with the entire family. Simple comments such as, "I see" and "Yes" or "Uh huh" are used as encouragers signaling family members that the therapist is listening and they should con-tinue. The therapist's demonstrated interest in guiding family members to relate what is happening facilitates her acceptance by the family members.

Some questions might include the following: Who? Where? How? Could you give an example? a description? a demonstration? Is there a specific time of day? sequence of events? Has anything been omitted? Do you agree? What are your feelings about this? What do you mean by that? What has been tried to change the behavior? Was it at all successful? Why, do you think?

It is necessary for family members to refrain from sidetracking the discussion by switching to a related topic. The therapist needs to guard against such maneuvers by asking for clarification as to what the information offered has to do with the topic under discussion or by requesting a return to the subject at hand. This can be accompanied with a promise to return to the related area at another time.

Minuchin and Fishman (1981) caution the therapist to pay attention to her own behavior in tracking a family's process. This will provide useful information about the family and operate to prevent entrapment-by-content. The therapist might assess whether the topic chosen for tracking is significant to the interest of the family, the therapist, or both. Her reactions to a family member may be indicative of other family members' covert perceptions. Does one family member seem to invite rescuing while another comes across as being above the others? Do you need to force yourself to exclude or ignore a family member? Awareness of these feelings allows the therapist to better organize her interventions. Selectively giving in to those feelings can help to facilitate the joining process. Overdoing it, however, sucks the therapist into the family whorl.

3. CASE EXAMPLE

The Philips family came to therapy because of difficulties in dealing with their son, Robbie, 12. Over the phone, the possibility of separation was mentioned. At the beginning of the session, name calling dominated the family member interactions. Robbie was the IP.

Mother: We just don't know what to do with that son of ours. He's so stupid. The things he does. We just don't know any more.
Therapist (To father): Do you think your son is stupid?
Father: No, not really stupid. He just doesn't use his head sometimes.
Therapist: What do you mean by not using his head?
Father: He forgets to do things or isn't careful.
Mother: He had three bicycles stolen because he forgets to lock them up. No, two. The third was run over by a truck or a car because Robbie didn't wheel it over to the sidewalk after he had fallen off the thing. He left it in the middle of the road while he came in to wash off his

bruises. His father always tries to defend his son, no matter what he does or I say.

Father: I do not. One time he painted the ceiling of his room without putting down any dropcloths to cover anything. In school he's always doing the wrong homework. He gets 80s on his tests but zeroes for homework, so he winds up with 65s or 70s on his report cards. He's not stupid. One time he helped a kid do a project and wound up being late with his own project.

Therapist: Do you have an explanation for any of the things?

Robbie: In school I'm trying to improve my memory, so I'm not writing down my homework assignments.

Therapist: Has your memory improved?

Robbie: I think so, a little.

Therapist: When your mother was very upset with what you had done, has she called you stupid?

Robbie: Yes.

Therapist: When your mother calls you stupid, what do you do?

Robbie: I tell her that I'm not stupid.

Therapist: And how do you tell her?

Robbie: Sometimes I cry and scream at her. Sometimes I keep saying "I am not" or "Am not" every time she says it.

Therapist: What happens then?

Robbie: She sends me to my room or hits me and then sends me to my room. She usually yells and cries too. When my father comes home, she yells at him about me. "What are you going to do," she yells.

Therapist: And what does your father do?

Robbie: He usually comes upstairs and talks to me. Sometimes he yells at me.

Therapist: (*To parents*) Is that pretty much how it is?

Mother: Yes, but my husband doesn't do anything about it. He just thinks that Robbie will grow up and this will all disappear.

Therapist: What do you think?

Mother: I don't know. Maybe it will. I guess I think that he will grow up to be a bumbling idiot. Not an idiot, but not very smart, clumsy.

Therapist: Unsuccessful?

Mother: Yes, unsuccessful.

Therapist: (*To father*) Do you agree?

Father: I don't think so. He'll outgrow all this, I think, and he will do just fine.

Therapist: What do you say to Robbie when you go up to talk to him?

Father: Sometimes I'm very angry and I also yell, especially about school. But, usually we talk about whatever it was that he did and how he could avoid it happening again. Sometimes we talk about why his mother gets so upset and he understands.

Therapist: Have you told your wife what you do with Robbie when you go up to talk with him?

Father: She's never asked. I just tell her what we decided, like Robbie promises to take better care of his bicycle or to ask me before he paints again.

Mother: I get so upset, I guess, I just don't want to know. And it's never the same thing twice. It's always something else the next time. The bicycle this week, the week before it was the painting, the week before that it was the report card, and the week before that it was something else. I forget. I can't keep track.

Therapist: Who asks you to keep track?

Mother: No one. I just do, not too well, I guess.

Therapist: Uh-huh. You know, Robbie, you are a very lucky boy. You have two parents who are very concerned about you and your future. They're so concerned that sometimes they get angry at each other and themselves because they cannot help you to live up to their expectations of you. Perhaps you can help them not get so angry, if your parents would want your help. . . .

4. USES

The tracking technique is useful at any stage in the therapeutic process. The family members are assured and reassured by the therapist through the elicitation of information. The therapist joins the family in examining their system. Myths and symbols, values, roles and history can be accessed and attended to by use of the tracking technique. It can also be used to set the stage for eliciting changes, or to obtain feedback concerning movement made earlier in the therapy. Tracking is particularly useful when one is dealing with chaotic families and families in which differences are rarely resolved.

Caution needs to be exercised in application, however. In families in which the identified person (IP) or any other family member is sensitive, possible resistance to therapy could develop as a result of that member becoming the focus of attention. Positive, caring attention is best when one is utilizing the tracking technique.

C. Joining Effectively Through the Use of the Genogram

1. RATIONALE

Family of origin data have proved to be helpful in understanding the origins of interactional patterns operating within present family systems. The instrument widely used by family therapists as a framework within which cross-generational information can be efficiently organized is the genogram. All important facts, including names, ages, dates, relationships, gender, geographical location, occupations, and other significant data can be depicted graphically for easy retrieval.

The genogram is a diagrammatic representation of the extended family of both spouses, as described in detail by McGoldrick and Gerson (1985). Squares are used to represent males; circles represent females. Family members of the same generation are placed on the same horizontal plane and extended family members, such as grandparents and children, are placed on horizontal planes above and below the spouses, respectively. Relationships are delineated through the use of horizontal and vertical lines. Horizontal lines depict intergenerational relationships, such as marriage and cohabitation. The vertical lines connect generations: parents with children. There are a variety of additional symbols to indicate separation, divorce, friendship, death, twins, abortion, strong ties between family members, and negative interactional patterns among family members.

Many therapists regard the genogram as an effective device for gathering and organizing family history data to facilitate a diagnosis. Beck (1987) points out that little attention tends to be given to the use of this instrument as a means of enhancing the joining process by moving the therapy, along. This disregard for process dynamics in genogram construction may have developed from Bowen's approach to family therapy, which seeks to minimize the emotional dynamics at work in dysfunctional family systems.

Frequently, family trees are quickly roughed out in a session or two, with additional content material to be filled in as the therapy progresses. Overlooked in this mechanistic approach to genogram construction are many opportunities to establish a better rapport with family members by attending to client affect.

2. PROCEDURE

In the course of putting together an intergenerational family picture, the therapist responds to the process material as well as to the content material being presented. The therapist selects opportunities to convey interest, caring, and empathy for family members. She can accomplish this by attending to the feelings and thoughts of all family members during the brief descriptions of family-of-origin relationships tendered by each spouse.

A question about the appearance of a sour expression on a family member's face communicates sensitivity on the part of the therapist to present feelings as well as to the past. Probing the nonverbal clues revealed by family members can facilitate the joining process by underscoring the therapist's intent to comprehend the scope of their relationships within the extended family. The drawback that results from joining with a family through the affect material while noting the content being presented is that the genogram will take longer to complete.

3. CASE EXAMPLE

Thomas, a 32-year-old divorced, noncustodial parent, had been involved in several unsuccessful relationships with women since his divorce. At the time he came to therapy, he was remarried. His wife, Jean, agreed to accompany him in the hopes of saving their marriage. After talking with the couple, the therapist suggested that some background information about their families of origin might be helpful in working out their difficulties. Both consented, although they felt that the past did not reflect their individual growth and their present situation. A genogram was begun the following session.

The names, ages, present location, occupations of Thomas' parents, and a few additional facts were glibly offered when requested. When asked about his relationship with his parents, he became more thoughtful and serious. He sat up in his seat, put his hands together into a praying position covering his nose, and paused a while before answering that they had had their ups and downs. Instead of moving on to collecting information about grandparents or siblings, the therapist picked up on the change in posture and mood and decided to pursue the causes for the changes observed.

Therapist: Let's talk about your relationship with your parents a little, okay?
Thomas: Sure.
Therapist: Is that okay with you, Jean?
Jean: Yeah, sure.
Therapist: So, how do you and your parents get along?
Thomas: Pretty well, I guess.
Therapist: Pretty well?

Thomas: Yeh. I think they're still disappointed that my first marriage didn't work out after we had a child. I don't know. They've been disappointed in me for a long time. We see each other occasionally. They've met Jean.

Therapist: You said they were disappointed in you for a long time. How long is a long time?

Thomas: Everything was all right until about the 10th grade. (*Smiling, leaning forward in chair.*)

Therapist: You're smiling.

Thomas: Yeah. It's amusing now, looking back.

Therapist: You have thought about this before?

Thomas: Yeah.

Therapist: What happened in 10th grade?

Thomas: My mother didn't like the kids I was hanging around with and we started getting into arguments. It was as if all of a sudden I couldn't do anything right. My marks weren't good, so I raised my grades. Then my friends weren't the type of people someone with my grades should be associating with. I didn't know what she wanted from me. Everything was fine until around then. (*Serious expression, leaning back in the chair with hands in his pants pockets and legs stretched out in front of him.*)

Therapist: You're not smiling.

Thomas: It was serious then. We argued a lot.

Therapist: And now?

Thomas: Things are okay. We manage.

Therapist: You were very strong-willed. You didn't give in.

Thomas: No, I didn't.

Therapist: Were any other important things happening in your family at that time?

Thomas: No, I don't think so. I really can't remember any.

Therapist: Could you find out?

Thomas: I think so. I'll ask.

Therapist: Good. And how did you get along with your father at this time?

Thomas: He was great. He would defend me and argue with my mother. But it seemed that she always won. Even though there were times when I know my father convinced her that what I wanted wasn't unusual or bad, it seems that I always wound up doing what she wanted. (*Initially much brighter, smiling, then fading a little.*)

Therapist: And how did you feel about that?

Thomas: Really frustrated . . . frustrated.

Therapist: How did you always wind up doing what your mother wanted you to do?

Thomas: . . . .I don't know. I just did. I just wound up doing what she thought best. (*Jean cleared her throat and leaned forward looking at Thomas.*)

Therapist: How do you feel about Tom's parents, Jean?

Jean: We only went out with them twice, but they seem to be nice people. About what Tom was saying about his parents, it's true. When Tom introduced us, his father wanted to go to a fish restaurant for dinner. His mother wanted to go to one of these new pasta places. Tom had been wanting to try shark for quite a while, but chose the pasta place. So we went for pasta. The second time we went to the movies. His father suggested one movie at one theater and his mother wanted to see a movie at another theater. I said that I would like to see the movie that his father wanted to see. Tom agreed. So we went to see Superman II. When we arrived there was a small line. Tom said that he changed his mind and suggested that we go to the other theater to see how long the line was there. When we got there, the line was pretty long. But Tom didn't want to go back to the other theater, because the line would be longer there by the time we drove back. I don't even remember the movie we saw.

Therapist: Is that the way things went, Tom?

Thomas: Yes. I don't know why. Things just work out for my mother.

In the course of gathering information, the therapist chose to use the affect instead of letting it be forgotten or artificially brought up in a later session. In so doing, interest and concern are communicated to the family. In addition, a more comprehensive understanding of each member's perceptions of family-of-origin roles and relationships can be obtained. Jean was also included in the preliminary exploration to acknowledge the importance of her perceptions, establishing a better rapport with her.

Later in the session, the therapist was able to link Thomas' frustration over doing what his mother suggested to frustrations he was experiencing in his relationship with Jean. Difficulties with his brothers were also addressed in the process of drawing up the genogram. In the same manner, Jean's patterns of interaction with her parents, brother, and sister were explored.

4. USES

For joining purposes, working together on a genogram is a way of entering the family. The scope of the system being studied is enlarged, which
can defuse tension between the couple or between a parent and child. The
problem is spread out and can be normalized within a larger context by a
focus on different family styles. Observing other family members while
working on one member's genogram can provide insight into the feelings
of others about the "side" of the family being studied.

The effective construction of a genogram has the potential for affecting
the therapy in a variety of additional ways. It can provide an organized introduction to the therapy as the therapist gathers important data useful in diagnosis. Clients may be moved to consider themselves from a different
perspective. Treatment goals may be clarified for both the client and the
therapist. It can also be used to draw a client into the therapeutic process.
All of this is helpful to promoting the joining process.

D. The Dynamic Duo: Matching and Pacing

1. RATIONALE

Our relationships with others are based largely upon shared interests.
When strangers meet at a party, the conversation moves to identify a common ground. Relationship to the host or hostess, complimentary remarks
of one kind or another, and thoughts about the weather are universally
employed as get-acquainted techniques. Sharing similar weather concerns
could lead to talk about the effect it has had on business or leisure activities. Strangers may discover that they work around the corner from each
other, belong to the same health club, enjoy shopping at flea markets on
weekends.

The longer they converse, the more attuned they become to each other's
manner of communication. If one party communicates in an upbeat, ani-
mated style, others may take on a similar upbeat cadence and mannerism.
Through shared interests and behaviors, the acceptance of others occurs.
Having things "in common" smoothes the way for establishing an aquain-
tanceship, a relationship, or a friendship.

In therapy, the need is to establish rapport, to join with clients. Families
come to therapy steeped in their spoken and unspoken family "language."
Effective therapy requires that we connect with our clients in a manner that
is acceptable to them. The neuro-linguistic techniques of matching and pac-

ing, as described by Cameron-Bandler (1978) and Lankton (1980), allow the therapist to interact with a family in a language which they understand. The therapist meets each family member at the door to his universe and they become kindred spirits in their quest for change.

2. PROCEDURE

The goal is to establish a positive therapeutic relationship on a conscious and, more importantly, on an unconscious level. The more fluent a therapist can become in using the family members' language(s), the more acceptable the therapy can be. This involves matching and pacing as many of a client's behaviors as the therapist is capable of. In effect, the therapist becomes each client's mirror.

The process commences with the therapist choosing and casually expressing one particular behavior she has observed to be naturally exhibited by a family member. It is best if the chosen behavior is representational of the member's character or style. A therapist might begin by matching the physical behaviors of a client, such as the rate of breathing, the angle of a client's head, the positioning of legs, hand gestures, posture, voice volume, or eye movements.

Begin with something easy and integrate one match at a time. Moving too quickly may be interpreted by a client as mimicry or parody. It is generally better to be able to match one behavior for each of four family members prior to mastering three or four matches for one member.

As the therapist becomes more comfortable with the matching of a person's behavior, such as head positions, the matching of another member's behavior, such as hand gestures, might be nonchalantly introduced. This is called direct matching.

Matching some clients' behaviors directly may be either impossible or not to the therapist's liking: sitting in yoga position on a chair, fingernail biting, asthmatic breathing. These kinds of behaviors can be matched indirectly. Instead of crossing her legs, the therapist might cross arms; the placement of the finger of the nail being bitten might be next to the corner of the mouth instead of inside the mouth; and moving one foot up and down could be used to pace an asthmatic. Substitutions of this nature are called indirect matching through the use of "cross-over" channels. In using indirect matching, one must remember to be consistent.

Pacing also usually requires a few sessions to attain a match with a client. To pace a family member, the therapist begins her matching behavior at the same time client behavior is being expressed.

3. CASE EXAMPLES

a. *Direct matching:* In the following dialogue, the therapist matches the client's predicates.

Client: My husband doesn't *understand* me.
Therapist: What is it that he needs to *understand* about you?
Client: He doesn't *understand* my *needs and wants.*
Therapist: Have you helped him to *understand* what those *needs and wants* are?
Client: I'm not a *teacher.* He should *know.*
Therapist: How can he *know* if you don't *teach* him?
Client: I've tried plenty of times. He should *know* after seven years of marriage. We've argued enough about it.
Therapist: *Teach* him now, here. What does he need to *know* you need from him? Don't argue about it. Explain what he needs to know you want from him.

b. *Indirect matching:* A blended family with two children, 12-year-old Arlene and eight-year-old Adrian, come to therapy for help in dealing with issues common to such families. At about the time Ms. M. began to seriously consider remarrying, Adrian became a consummate nail biter and Arlene began gum chewing and snapping in a big way. Both these behaviors became a source of annoyance and disagreement over how to deal with the children.

During the first session, both of the activities were quite in evidence. By the second session, the therapist had indirectly matched Adrian's nail biting with rubbing the side of her nose and Arlene's masticulating and snapping with rapid up and down movements of the therapist's right leg. Mr. M. tended to pair arm flailing with voice raising when excited or worked up. This display was matched with eye blinking. Ms. M. responded to all that was going on by averting her eyes and slowly lowering her head, which was mirrored by the therapist's slowly raising her head and looking up and away.

During the third session, both children began to attend to the therapist's mirroring behavior. About halfway through the session, Adrian laughed out loud as a smile appeared on Arlene's face. Mr. and Ms. M. responded by intensifying their displays as the therapist continued working her right leg up and down, rubbing her nose, and blinking her eyes, as she slowly lifted her head and gazed at the point where the wall opposite her met the ceiling.

Mr. M.: What are you doing?

Arlene: She's imitating us.

Therapist: (stops matching.) Motionless silence looking at the therapist, then each other.

Mr. M.: Is that how we look?

Therapist: What are your impressions of what you saw?

Adrian: You looked a little crazy.

Arlene: Yeah . . . but you kind of looked like . . . I don't know. I think you were imitating us,..but you really didn't.

Therapist: Ms. M.?

Ms. M.: I can't say. I . . . wasn't really watching you.

Mr. M.: I was watching. What you were doing really bothered me.

Therapist: I saw that. My intent was not to bother you.

Adrian: You were funny.

Therapist: I wasn't trying to make fun of you either.

Ms. M.: You were trying to tell us something about our behavior. Maybe some of the things we do are annoying even though we don't want them to be. . . .

Intermittently, in the subsequent sessions, the therapist continued to match and pace each family member, directly or indirectly. The family was able to talk about what they did to each other and how they communicated their feelings, including those which they would not verbalize. The therapist's matching and pacing communicated, in their language, to the family that their difficulties were understood by the therapist. The family seemed to feel more and more comfortable bringing up and dealing with issues which heretofore had ended up unresolved with an argument.

4. USES

Demonstrating clients' behaviors can have a significant impact on the joining process. Acceptance of the therapist is in part based upon the ability of the therapist to communicate to the family an understanding of their problem(s) and to each member an understanding of his/her perspective regarding the family problem(s). Matching and pacing accomplish this in a dynamic way.

This combination technique can be implemented at any point in the therapeutic process. It is advised, however, that the therapist ease into the imitating, especially if initiated after several sessions with the family. Matching and pacing also work well in conjunction with role-playing, psychodrama, and family choreography techniques.

III. TIPS AND TACTICS

1. Work Through Existing Structure

First and foremost, therapists must be agents of change. To facilitate this function, however, we may find it helpful if we also accept the role of care-taker, or maintenance person. It is important to protect and promote those aspects of our clients' gestalt which will help the exploration and aid the family members in making changes.

When we use structures already in place, changes in dysfunctional patterns can occur within an organizational framework known to the family (Minuchin, 1974). The members work on the familiar architecture to make the changes needed to improve their living arrangements.

If Father is the family rulemaker and Oldest Daughter is the family spokesperson, then, at least initially, the therapist could accept family information volunteered by the oldest daughter and navigate family rule changes through the father. In this manner, the family structure is acknowledged and maintained until the family moves into a position from which it can make a functional change in that structure.

2. Reframe

Families bring to therapy their unique perspective of themselves as a unit and as individual members within their family. Reframing, sometimes referred to as relabeling, can be used to alter a family's referential framework for a given behavior from a negative to a positive. The therapist validates the occurrence of the interaction, but changes its value judgement by juxtaposing a family member's negatively labeled pattern of interaction with one that is positive. In this way, an overly critical father may be relabeled the conscience of the family.

Minuchin and Fishman (1981) point out that in order to join through reframing, the therapist first has to observe the clients' reality. An understanding of the myths and symbols used to influence the dynamics of the family interactions is helpful prior to attempting to reframe. There, the therapeutic reality has to be circumscribed. Which interactional components are to be addressed? A client's being critical can have several goals: to call attention to oneself; to communicate the belief that the complainer is better qualified than someone else; to communicate concern and interest; to teach new behavior, and so on. Reframing the behavior to reflect a positive intention directs the system to another vantage point from which to work.

Many decisions and apparent solutions to families' problems are rooted in their perceptions. As an angry complainer, Mom pushes the family away in her undertakings to bring them together. As a concerned mother and wife, she stands a better chance to succeed at bringing the family together for meals. When one changes the negative frame in which a family member is viewed to one that facilitates the recognition of positive attributes, the perception of that person's behavior and that of others could change significantly. This, in turn, affects patterns of interaction.

Sherman and Fredman (1986) point out that moving from a negative to a positive position makes all members feel better about themselves. Through reframing, the therapist communicates an affirmation of the family members. The negative behaviors overshadowing the ascribed, positive intentions can then be addressed in a new, encouraging light. As the family is guided in the direction of positive self-regard, the therapist will tend to become associated with the positive image and thus facilitate joining.

3. *Joining Families Whose Backgrounds Differ From That of the Therapist*

A. DISCUSSION

A frequent concern of therapists is a lack of confidence in their ability to join effectively with families or family members exhibiting marked experiential differences from those of the therapist. Effectively joining with members of the opposite sex, with families from markedly different cultural or socioeconomic backgrounds, with families with physically sick or handicapped members, and with family members who are markedly different in age present challenges to the family therapist.

How can a male therapist understand premenstrual syndrome? Can a Black therapist, who grew up surrounded by poverty, establish a rapport with an upper middle class White Protestant family? How effectively can a therapist without children of her own blend with a family in which there are three children? The lack of trust in one's ability usually stems from the therapist's perception of the observable differences between the prospective clients' and the therapist's life experiences.

Admittedly, a referral to someone more experienced, to a therapist who specializes in a particular area, or to a therapist who is not as busy and has more time to devote to the case may be appropriate. In cases involving sexual dysfunction, eating disorders, and alcoholism, it is possible to work in conjunction with a specialist who sees the client separately to deal with that aspect of their relationship. However, the following tactics offer the therapist opportunities to get underneath the surface differences and begin to work with the dysfunctional interactions with which the practitioner is more familiar: taking a one-down position and the family floor plan.

B. TAKE A ONE-DOWN POSITION

The one-down position is an information-gathering technique which opens the family's door to the therapist by allowing the family to explain who they are, what they do, or how they feel. The therapist tells the family: "I am interested in helping you. I may not understand you. I want to understand you so that we can work together to help you. Please explain so that I will be able to understand and work with you."

The fact that the therapist does not know what it is like to be a family member or a particular family member does not in any way change her ability to understand the dynamics at work in the family system. However, if therapist and family are working through triangling, the formation of coalitions, overcompensation coupled with resentment when criticized, parentified children, or other dysfunctional patterns of interaction, it is necessary that the clients accept the therapist as one who understands their unique situation. By taking the one-down position, the therapist demonstrates respect for the client and gains therapeutically valuable information.

A bored, handicapped wife and mother in session with her husband and two children balked at the therapist's suggestion by saying: "Do you know what it's like being in a wheelchair all day, day after day, month after month? No, you don't. So how can you think you know what I could do?"

The therapist responded by taking a one-down position. Following the client's explanation, the therapist thanked her and continued by saying, "You're right. I can't really know. I recognize that you have a difficult time. Please tell us what kinds of things you can do. If you can do all that you just described to me, could you please help me by explaining why what I had suggested before cannot be done?"

By taking the one-down position, the therapist communicated her interest in the client's condition, a willingness to listen, learn, and use the knowledge acquired in a therapeutic manner. The client did follow the therapist's suggestion.

C. FIND OUT ABOUT THE PHYSICAL LIVING CONDITIONS OF THE NUCLEAR FAMILY OR OF THE FAMILY OF ORIGIN

The therapist requests the family members to draw a floor plan of their living quarters. As they draw, specific questions are asked about what it is like to live in that environment.

Three variations of the family floor plan are commonly used. The parents may be asked to outline the floor plan of the homes in which they grew up. If they had lived in more than one home, then the one which they remember best would do. The children are instructed to observe. In another version, the children are directed to draw their present living quarters while their parents look on. To include all family members, parents and children can be directed to sketch the layout of their present home. It is important that the same home layout be drawn by all family members in situations where a family has lived in a few residences.

As the family members are drawing, the following directions and questions are slowly interjected (Coopersmith [now Imber-Black], 1980):

1. As you draw each room, be aware of the mood you ascribe to it.
2. Remember the odors, the sounds, the colors, and people in the house.
3. Is there a room in which people usually gather?
4. Where do members of your extended family go when they come for a visit?
5. Are there rooms you could not go into?
6. Have you a special place in the house?
7. Think about issues of privacy or the lack of it, closeness and distance. How were they experienced in the house?
8. What is the place of this house in the community? Does it fit or not?
9. Allow yourself to remember a typical event which occurred in this house.
10. Allow yourself to hear the words that were commonly spoken by family members.

Internalized family rules and attitudes are frequently uncovered, which can then be compared and contrasted with the perceptions of other family members. The use of space is a strong indicator of underlying inclusion and exclusion, boundaries, power, tension, and comfort. The amount of space allocated to different persons and their respective pursuits indicates the value placed upon those activities, such as eating, working, socializing, fighting, playing. Family goals and myths are also frequently uncovered.

The therapist is guided through rooms concealing areas of agreement and conflict within the family's living space. The identification of heretofore unknown information about family members demonstrates the ability of the therapy to impact on their lives. Whatever new information surfaces provides, at the very least, background information useful in facilitating exploration. With exploration comes the hope that change is possible. With hope comes a measure of the trust and acceptance that are essential for effective joining to take place.

In effect, the therapist joins by being admitted to the clients' homes as perceived by them. The therapist can then join further by utilizing the physical and emotional uses of space within the family domicile in formulating changes in the system.

4. Use Psychological Testing

Testing is widely accepted by the general population as a reliable source of evaluation. It is used in schools, the professions, and government to qualify for promotion, the receipt of a degree, licensing, and civil service jobs. Informal assessment is also an accepted component in our daily lives. One child daring another to climb a tree tests the other child's courage, ability, and willingness to accept challenges. Photographers show their portfolios to prospective clients as a matter of course.

The inclusion of psychological testing in the family therapist's catalogue of tactics could do much to facilitate joining with some clients. As Fredman and Sherman (1987) point out, many clients tend to view testing as moving in the direction of solving their difficulties.

Informal instruments such as Harris' (1963) Draw-A-Person (D-A-P) or Hammer's (1980) Draw A House-Tree-Person could be casually integrated into the therapy by the therapist without breaking the pace or tone of the session. Formal assessments would require the services of a competent psychologist, preferably one familiar with the family therapist's therapeutic orientation. Ziffer (1985) offers detailed discussion regarding the use of psychological testing by family therapists.

In the interpretation of the results of a testing process, it is important to maintain a family systemic perspective. Might a high score on a dependence variable indicate positive or functional behavior within a given family context?

Fredman and Sherman (1987) identify some subtests of instruments which seem appropriate for understanding family interactions. These include cards 2 and 3 of the Thematic Apperception Test, the five items in the Picture Arrangement Subtest of the Wechsler Adult Intelligence Scale concerning male-female interaction, and the Rorschach.

There are many instruments which deal specifically with marital adjustment, intimacy, satisfaction, and other areas of family interaction. Such questionnaires, inventories, scales, and surveys quickly provide therapeutic direction by suggesting pertinent areas for exploration. They tend to add a sense of "objectivity," sometimes described as a "professional touch," which is reassuring to many clients. The use of tests may also be experienced as empowering since clients have control over the responses and there are no right or wrong answers.

REFERENCES

Barnhart, C. L. and Barnhart, R. K. (1985) *The world book dictionary* (Vol. 1, A-K), Chicago, IL: Doubleday.

Beck, R. L. (1987) The genogram as process. *The American Journal of Family Therapy, 15*(4), 343–354.

Cameron-Bandler, L. (1978) *They lived happily ever after.* Cupertino, CA.: Meta Publications.

Coopersmith, E. [Now Imber-Black.](1980) The family floor plan: A tool for training—Assessment and intervention in family therapy. *Journal of Marriage and Family Therapy, 6,* 141–145.

Fredman, N. and Sherman, R. (1987) *Handbook of measurements for marriage & family therapy.* New York: Brunner/Mazel.

Grunwald, B. B. and McAbee, H. V. (1985) *Guiding the family.* Muncie, IN: Accelerated Development.

Hammer, E. (1980) *The clinical application of projective drawings.* Springfield, IL: Charles C. Thomas.

Harris, D. (1963) *Children's drawings as measures of intellectual maturity.* New York: Harcourt, Brace, and World.

Ivey, A. E. and Gluckstern, N. B. (1974) *Basic attending skills.* North Amherst, MA: Microtraining Associates.

Lankton, S. (1980) *Practical magic: A translation of basic neurolinguistic programming into clinical psychotherapy.* Cupertino, CA: Meta Publications.

Lazarus, A. A. (1981) *The practice of multimodal therapy.* New York: McGraw-Hill Book Company.

McGoldrick, M. and Gerson, R. (1985) *Genograms in family assessment.* New York: W. W. Norton.

Minuchin, S. (1974) *Families and family therapy.* Cambridge, MA: Harvard University Press.

Minuchin, A. and Fishman, H. C. (1981) *Family therapy techniques.* Cambridge, MA: Harvard University Press.

Sherman, R. and Fredman, N. (1986) *Handbook of structured techniques in marriage and family therapy.* New York: Brunner/Mazel.

Ziffer, R. L. (1985) The utilization of psychological testing in the context of family therapy. In R. L. Ziffer (Ed.), *Adjunctive techniques in family therapy.* Orlando, FL: Grune & Stratton.

Additional Resources

de Shazer, S. (1985), *Keys to solutions in brief therapy.* New York: W. W. Norton & Company.

Kottler, J. A. (1991). *The compleat therapist.* San Francisco, CA: Jossey Bass.

Myers, M. F. (1989). *Men and divorce.* New York: Guilford Publications.

Sue, D. W. & Sue, D. (1990). *Counseling the culturally different: Theory and practice* (2nd ed.). Somerset NJ: John Wiley & Sons.

4

TAKING ON
THE OPPOSITION

Resistance

"We must view with profound respect the infinite capacity of the human mind to resist the introduction of useful knowledge."

(Thomas Raynesford Lounsbury, 1913, p. 44)

I. INTRODUCTION

A. *Discussion*

1. PURPOSES OF RESISTANCE

Resistance to change is a universal phenomenon. It is not therapy specific. In the affairs of humankind, it has been and continues to be a powerful force. On the one hand, resistance to outside influence is responsible for the maintenance of unique cultural, political, family, and individual characteristics which account for diversity in today's world. On the other hand, it offers a potential threat to one's well-being when resistance demands rigid adherence to uniqueness.

A sizeable investment of client time and energy goes into establishing and maintaining a status quo. Individual patterns of interaction tend to be rooted in the family-of-origin patterns established during childhood. Interaction with others enables perceptions of identity to be worked out and rede-

71

fined during the school years and young adulthood. Adult choices and relationships usually complement one's established perception of self. In the process of making choices and forming relationships throughout one's life, however, self-perception continues to change. In families with children, such choices also presage which paths will lead to the fulfillment of parental expectations for their offspring.

Families generally come to therapy seeking relief from the pain which the established interactive patterns could not correct and a return to the way things used to be. A change in life-style is not often a goal. Even highly motivated families may experience difficulties dealing with changes in patterns which have become aspects of perceived collective and individual identities. However, the request for help is a first step in the direction of change.

2. IS THERAPEUTIC RESISTANCE REAL?

Dealing with client resistance to therapeutic intervention has been, for the most part, buried in the various theoretical approaches to therapy. In theory, if the therapist follows the guidelines of a model, resistance should not become problematic. It is assumed that the therapist will be able to handle any derailment by assessing where she strayed and then getting back on track. Some approaches do not mention resistance at all. In practice, however, situations in which client resistance influences the therapy may develop even among experienced therapists.

De Shazer (1984a,b) objects to the inclusion of the concept of resistance within the systemic boundaries of family therapy. He postulates that the old therapeutic gremlin ought certainly to be put out to pasture at this stage in the development of family therapy. Should the therapist become aware of an unfolding oppositional attitude on the part of a client, the therapist needs to move toward changing the direction of the therapy to one of cooperation. Adopting a cooperating client-therapist mindset is more likely to foster, nourish, and open up the closed, homeostatic patterns of dysfunctional families than attempting to anticipate resistance. Why look for obstacles to change? Certainly, if it has a place at all, resistance lives within the realm of the "family-as-a-system."

Yet, a rose by any other name still has thorns. Papp (1976) views therapy as the process of overcoming resistance. In the psychoanalytic community, resistance is manifested in the form of denial. Behaviorally, it is frequently referred to as noncompliance. Intergenerational approaches to family therapy root out family of origin issues to work around client resistance. Structural therapists presuppose resistance and join and accommodate in the hopes of avoiding it. Most strategic therapists adopt strategies which are predicated upon its existence to bend it to therapeutic advantage.

The nomenclature employed regarding clients' resistance to therapy and oppositional attitudes and behaviors seems to obfuscate a universally recognized concept within the field. It appears that each approach deals with different parts of the same beast. On a pragmatic level, the fragmentation of the construct poses difficulties in accessing useful techniques and tactics outside one's adopted therapeutic approach. To the extent that a therapeutic approach functions from within a closed or limited system, the range of interventions available to the therapist to effect change in clients' oppositional attitudes and behaviors is restricted. As a result, some models may be more effective than others in working with different family dysfunctional patterns.

It may now be time for the therapeutic community to come together to define and address the various aspects of resistance as well as the tactics and techniques proven successful in dealing with it. Once these are addressed, perhaps we can then move toward integrated modes of therapy incorporating de Shazer's (1984a) "cooperating mindset" and Papp's "overcoming" to improve the effectiveness of family therapy in producing desired changes.

Although resistance is regarded as a negative client position, the value of resistant behavior also needs to be considered. Sherman (1986) points out that oppositional attitudes and behaviors function as checks and balances within the family system. Resistance aids the therapist in identifying issues of conflict necessitating the use of negotiating skills and the ability to compromise.

The fact that resistance is manifest in session is indicative of client individuation, ability to perceive effects of interventions, and an ability to mobilize and act. The level or intensity of opposition is indicative of a family's or family member's need for stability or the degree of risk willing to be undertaken to accomplish a goal.

Lusterman (1979) conceptualizes a family's therapeutic field as a motile one in which the therapist occupies a central position. Resistance within this field is subject to increases and decreases in intensity and shifts from member to member. Maintaining focus while dealing with clients' oppositional activities requires self-confidence and an awareness of one's present standing within the group. Being aware of the levels of resistance being encountered and of the members who are involved in resisting can be useful in determining the relative position of the therapy and therapist at any given moment.

That there is movement toward an integrative approach to resistance is evidenced by Anderson and Stewart's *Mastering Resistance: A Practical Guide to Family Therapy* (1983) and Otani's (1989) article "Client Resistance in Counseling: Its Theoretical Rationale and Taxonomic Classification." However, a good deal more integrative material would be welcome.

3. IDENTIFYING CLIENT RESISTANCE

It is important to remember that the occasional occurrence of a behavior described in this chapter does not necessarily constitute a resistant pattern of behavior. The activity needs to occur in a variety of situations over a period of time. Resistance may also be issue specific, occurring repeatedly only when a particular problem is brought up for discussion.

Prior to labeling a family or individual member(s) as resistant, it may be helpful to attempt to identify anything that might be done differently to enhance cooperation and facilitate change. The effect of a larger system's procedures may produce resistant client behavior. It might also be worthwhile to inquire about the family members' involvement with additional helpers, such as individual members' therapists, the school, other agencies, and support groups like Gamblers Anonymous. Different points of view from a variety of helpers can impede progress, which may be interpreted as client resistance (Imber-Black, 1989).

B. Definitions

Derived from the verb "to resist," "resistance" has its origin in the Latin "resistere" and "resisto." "Resistere" is translated to mean "to take a stand" (Webster's Seventh . . . , 1965); "resisto" can be translated to mean "setback" (Funk & Wagnall's, 1963). Resistance, the noun, is defined as "1. the act or power of . . . opposing. . . . 2. the opposition offered by one thing, force, etc. to another" (Random House, 1987). To pursue avenues for change, it is important for the therapist to be able to recognize and deal with client resistance. Therapeutic progress becomes vulnerable to setback when a client takes an oppositional position.

Despite clients' agreement that change is needed, departures from the dysfunctional homeostasis are often met with resistive maneuvers. When family members' self-perceptions and roles are brought into question, their relative positions become unstable. Attempts to make changes in established patterns of interaction can become threatening as systemic modifications are experimented with in their daily lives. While achieving family goals in therapy is predicated upon change, the primary goal of most clients is symptom removal and a return to the way things were.

As a point of departure, we will define resistance as a class of client actions or ". . . behaviors in the therapeutic system which interact to prevent . . . [that] system from achieving the family's goals for therapy" (Anderson & Stewart, 1983). Client resistance often represents a difference of opinion between therapist and client (Sherman, 1986).

Anderson and Stewart (1983) identify two additional categories of resistance: the therapist and the larger system which surrounds the therapy. The therapist's level of confidence in herself and in the effectiveness of a family therapy approach are possible sources of resistance for the client. A few of the obstacles to therapy functioning outside the client-therapist relationship include availability of time, the accompanying paperwork, office space, referral procedures, and lack of recognition by insurance companies. Further investigation with regard to these other forms of resistance, however, is beyond the intended scope of this chapter.

DEALING WITH RESISTANCE—THREE APPROACHES

Client resistance can be handled directly and indirectly. The therapist can choose to confront the family or member with the oppositional nature of the manifested behavior(s) and attempt to move in the direction of exploration of the resistance in relation to the accomplishment of family goals. In assuming this therapeutic stance, the therapist places the responsibility for lack of movement in the client's lap.

An alternative means of dealing with resistance is to assume inherent client resistance and to structure the therapy accordingly. Interventions would be designed to reduce the possibility of resistant behaviors. Should the therapy become bogged down or meet with opposition, the fault lies with the therapist.

A third means of handling resistance is through negotiated agreements. The parties are aided by the therapist in the art of giving and taking to arrive at some middle ground acceptable to all. Manifested resistance in one family member is dealt with by the other member(s) through making concessions, trading, or strengthening demands in other areas being negotiated. The therapist's role is to keep the negotiations going until a settlement is reached.

II. A STRATEGY AND STRUCTURED TECHNIQUES

A. *Contracting-for-Results Strategy*

1. RATIONALE

Brief, "goal-oriented," contractual therapy can go a long way to facilitate focusing on family problems while minimizing the possibility of resistance. It is useful primarily in working with difficulties that are clearly observed, measured, and defined. The process of goal setting is also helpful and is transferable to life outside therapy. Inappropriate issues would be those which are nonnegotiable and those which require longer periods of time to work through.

The need for brevity forces family members and therapist to focus deliberate attention on an issue for a period of eight to 10 weeks. The end is always in sight, which may tend to foster greater commitment and willingness to participate. In addition, the family members and therapist do not have an opportunity to become disinterested, frustrated, or bored with the process.

The goals frame the therapy. Fox (1987) identifies three kinds: 1. "Final goals"—what is to be achieved; 2. "Facilitative goals"—what needs to be done to make the achievement possible; and 3. "Functional goals"—what each member will do to help reach the final goals. The family's goals, once established, are best written as the contract between family members and therapist.

The purpose of the contract is to serve as a guide for the family and the therapist. It must be amendable. The therapist's role also needs to be clearly delineated in the contract.

"Goals serve the important function of structuring the treatment in a positive direction" (Fox, 1987, p. 495). Knowing where the group wishes to wind up enables them to concentrate upon getting there. Obstacles they may encounter en route can be foreseen and negotiated before they are encountered. Given the family's resources, the more specific, explicit, realistic, and measurable the jointly agreed upon goals are, the less confusion there will be and the more likely the family will be successful.

Each group of steps outlined below will be followed by a description of Family R's progress in italics (Fox, 1987). The five goals identified and agreed upon by the family were accomplished using this strategy. For illustrative purposes, only Mr. R's relationship with his son, J, is included.

2. PROCEDURE AND CASE EXAMPLE

The procedure comprises eight tasks to be negotiated by the family members and the therapist. First, a clear picture of the family's present functioning needs to be established: baseline data. That description becomes part of the written contract. Next, a discussion regarding specific expectations identifies the general goal and subgoals, which are then prioritized and written into the contract.

Mr. R's lack of quality time spent with his son J was the main concern of the family. Punishment and criticism for not doing homework and for misbehavior constituted Mr. R's interactive pattern with J. Mr. R pushed his son to play in the Little League but didn't go to any of the games to watch J play.

Once the goals are identified, it is necessary to determine what will constitute change for each goal. The kind and quantity of behaviors which would signal that a goal has been accomplished need to be agreed upon by all. This is followed by therapist and family members outlining their respective roles and responsibilities. From this information, a plan is devised which includes alternatives for possible predictable obstacles.

Mr. R and J agreed that they would like to enjoy a better relationship and spend more positive time together. They decided that for one month J would be solely responsible for his homework and Mr. R would be responsible for taking J to one practice and one baseball game a week. In addition they agreed to begin building the treehouse which had been on hold for a long time.

The relationship between father and son was determined to be the most pressing family difficulty. To rectify the situation, it was agreed that father and son would spend at least four hours a week together. Mr. R would be responsible for keeping track of how much time was spent argument-free, as well as of the number of times he was tempted to criticize his son, but did not. J was responsible for keeping track of the number of homework assignments he completed each week.

Father and son decided to spend six hours per week together engaged in activities, keep the records suggested, and honestly log what had occurred each week. The therapist would be responsible for reading their logs, making suggestions when needed, and coming up with a plan for rewarding father and son. A gradual decrease in the negative behaviors was suggested, as well as the inclusion of positive activities, with progress to be scrutinized weekly, but more comprehensively from the second month on.

It is important to reiterate that the family was, at the same time, involved in working through related dysfunctional patterns that had contributed to the distancing between father and son. These included improving J's school attendance and homework, decreasing Mrs. R's involvement with J and his sister, S, and improving Mr. and Mrs. R's relationship.

The next step deals with the logistics and managing of the plan. The number and length of sessions, the amount of time needed to be allocated between sessions, and the sequence of implementation need to be clearly stated. The means by which the changes will be assessed need to be stipulated.

It was agreed that the six hours was acceptable and that the family would devote weekly sessions of one and a half hours to this problem for one month. At the end of the month, J would be completing his homework without his father's help, Mr. R would be attending one practice and one ball game per week without criticizing, and the treehouse would be half finished.

3. USES

The strategy could be employed as the primary orientation of the therapist with a resistant family. Whatever issues the family was able to clearly delineate could be dealt with all at once as subgoals under a more general heading. Depending upon the nature and intensity of the resistance, the identified goals could be addressed serially, one or two at a time in eight to 10 week blocks of time, and not necessarily immediately following each other. The strategy could also be useful as a change of pace intermezzo to deal with developing resistance patterns.

B. *Establishing a Positive Response Set*

1. RATIONALE

Clients' daily patterns of interaction include resistant strategies and behaviors. The therapist may engineer the therapeutic environment, making it conducive to exploration and change. This can be accomplished by establishment of a positive response set between the family members and the therapist at the beginning of the therapy. The goal is to develop an initial state of acceptance and agreement in such a manner as to make the commencement of therapy a welcome activity for each family member as well as for the therapist.

2. PROCEDURE

The therapist begins by reaffirming her confidence in herself and her abilities. She needs to feel relaxed and secure to be capable of identifying positive attributes with which she can identify in her clients. Upon initially meeting the family members, she needs to find something she can appreciate or admire about each individual. Recognizing something within herself that can serve as her bridge to the family system is highly beneficial (Silverstein, 1986).

A smile, an attitude, a voice inflection, their punctuality, and taste in clothing are observable characteristics, useful in promoting a basis from which the therapist's positive regard for the client can begin to grow. The seemingly insignificant observation can be the cornerstone for the building of a therapist-client relationship.

3. USES AND CASE EXAMPLE

A technique which makes the client impatient to begin the therapy can be utilized when suggestions and agreed-upon avenues of exploration meet with static and failure to follow through. The therapist may need to reestablish a positive mindset with the family or the resistant member(s). At the same time the importance of continuing with the therapy is conveyed. During medial and terminal stages, statements of the therapist's knowledge of the client and his surroundings may provide a therapeutic mental jog-in-place until the obstacle moves, is removed, or a way around it can be found. A confirmation of observable or known information about the family or individual family members can be amiably communicated in a conversational tone by the therapist to the client(s). This may be highly effective in circumventing resistance.

When this approach is used in an initial session, it is generally easier to begin with the person with whom the therapist has had contact in setting up the session. Once established, a positive mindset between client and therapist functions to reduce a tendency to resist. Added to this is the client's desire to move into more interesting or substantive issues. Therapy becomes the preferred alternative, chosen by the family member. Commencement is cued by the manifestation of client boredom or impatience. The amount of time necessary to predispose the client to choose to begin therapy tends to be related to the amount of resistance harbored by each individual (Dolan, 1985). For example:

Therapist: Your name is Charlene.

Charlene: (*Nods*)

Therapist: It's raining pretty hard outside and you arrived on time.

Charlene: Yeah, I guess so. (*Looking at her watch*)

Therapist: Your umbrella is soaked. (*Looking down at her umbrella on the floor*)

Charlene: Yes, it is.

Therapist: Your pants are soaked, too, at the bottom.

Charlene: Uh-uh, they are. (*Looking down, but not at her pants*)

Therapist: This is our first meeting although we've spoken on the phone.

Charlene: Yes, that's right. (*Glancing up at the therapist*)

Therapist: It took two conversations to set up this meeting.

Charlene: That's right. (*Looking at the therapist*)

Therapist: You said that you have experienced some difficulties in your family.

Charlene: Yes, I did. (*Maintains eye contact*)

Therapist: And it's now five o'clock in the evening on Thursday and you, your family, and I am here. . . .

Charlene: Yeah, we all managed to make it. (*Glancing down*)

Therapist: And you're sitting to my right in a chair just like mine and the time is passing. . . .

Charlene: (*Begins to slouch in her chair and appears impatient, looking at the therapist with a "let's get on with it" look*) Yes, that's right.

Therapist: Do you think you could describe the way you would like your life to be when we're finishing up with the therapy together. . . .

Charlene: I think so. Yeah. I'd like to be able to. . . . (*Looking around, but maintaining eye contact with the therapist*)

Therapist: (*Allows Charlene to fully explain*) Thank you, Charlene. And you are Edward.

The therapist continues to make easily verifiable observations about each family member, the weather, the room and the time to each member. In medial or terminal stages of therapy, the clients' goals, accomplishments, and expressed feelings could also be mentioned. Every statement is worded to elicit a positive response from the family member being addressed.

After working with each family member, the therapist could continue in the same vein to plan for future sessions. For example:

Therapist: Today you have conveyed information about how each of you would like things to be for you in your family when we finish working

together. Now we need to discuss when we could meet and work together on a regular basis to accomplish your goals.
    -or, in the medial stage:

Therapist: We have taken stock of your accomplishments this session. Now we need to consider what you have set out to do.

In the subsequent session(s) the therapist may continue to follow a similar procedure. She can begin by restating each family member's position at the close of the previous session. If corrections are made by a member, the therapist would restate the corrected position to reestablish the positive mindset with the client. It might also be helpful to close each session by stating each family member's position.

C. Call-Me-When-You're-Ready Technique

1. RATIONALE

One aspect of the therapeutic process which tends to be underutilized is the use of time between sessions. Standard operating procedure tends to be to schedule families once a week for a fixed period of time, regardless of what has occurred during that interval. It conveys the belief that commitment through regular attendance will lead to movement and change. For many families, regularly scheduled sessions forces them to deal with their difficulties and moves them toward accomplishing their goals.

For families in which there is greater resistance, however, weekly meetings may fan the resistant embers. Compelling consideration of what was said in session or completing assignments between session may be too much for all of the family to handle within a seven-day time frame. As the next session approaches, anxiety, frustration, and feelings of failure for not having done what had been agreed upon during the previous session may impact negatively upon the process.

This may become evident in the nonverbal cues such as lack of eye contact, inattentive body posture, and facial expressions in session. Participation may gradually decrease if some progress is not forthcoming. Tangential issues and complaints begin to fill the time without any resolve to concentrate upon alternatives. Client statements to the effect that movement or change is not forthcoming may be followed shortly by suggesting termination.

With a ready-or-not-let's-get-going schedule, the therapist may be encouraging resistant clientele to remain resistant. For some families, a change may need to occur before therapy can continue. No change; no therapy. Bergman (1985) calls this technique "reverse treatment."

In session, Family A demonstrates ableness and knowledge of the give and take necessary to work out their difficulties. Once outside the therapeutic walls, however, there is little carryover. They revert to the dysfunctional patterns which bring them back week after week angry, frustrated, and less hopeful.

Family B enjoys sharing their difficulties with the therapist, leaving little time to attempt to work toward resolving the problems. Every week the problems change or tangential issues take on the importance of the original. Frequently, one or two members complain about not having enough time in their busy schedules to do anything about their difficulties other than come to sessions once a week.

2. PROCEDURE

The Call-Me-When-You're-Ready technique requires a strong relationship between the therapist and the clients. The family must feel an overriding need to see the therapist despite the manifested resistance to the therapy. This type of client attends sessions regularly, attempting to use the therapist as a stabilizer and not as an agent of change.

This technique simply requires the therapist to insist upon completion of agreed-upon assignments prior to scheduling the next session. When a task is completed, a family member notifies the therapist and the scheduling of the next session is negotiated. As long as an accepted task remains incomplete, the therapist maintains the position that the next step cannot be reached; call me when you are ready to take the next step.

3. CASE EXAMPLE

Family A's goal was to equitably distribute household chores. In session, the family was able to function well enough to resolve a few minor concerns. At home, the discipline would break down the day following the session. The family was unable to complete a Family Council Meeting (Sherman & Fredman, 1986), despite everyone's acknowledgment of the importance for the individuals in the family to have a chance to be heard.

The therapist decided that this particular task could be handled by the family without her. Following a brief discussion, she announced to the family her confidence in their abilities and said that they were to call her to schedule their next session when they had successfully completed one Family Council Meeting. She reviewed the process and their roles, and instructed them to call her when they had succeeded. Three weeks later, a telephone call resulted in the scheduling of the next session.

What if Family A did not respond in three months' time? six months? a year? In Family A, the responsibility for the resistance (and change) was placed by the therapist on the shoulders of the clients. The family was considered not ready for undergoing the rigors of the change process until the assignment was completed. Should the family have needed six months or a year to complete the task, the underlying theory includes the assumption that it would not have been the fault of the therapist. With highly resistant families, it is possible that a therapeutic process constructed so that only the completion of a task would result in the assignment of another would facilitate the process of change.

4. USES

If the therapist believes that the responsibility is shared with the family members, or owned entirely by the therapist, then some modifications in the above technique may be in order. The task assigned might be a very simple one. It is more effective when designed to move the family toward their agreed-upon goals, however, and not merely as a demonstration to prove to the family members that they can work together successfully (unless that is a therapeutic goal, as with Family A). Another variation might be to call once, twice, or intermittently to let the family know that you have not forgotten them and that the therapy has not been terminated.

D. Bestowing Chivalries or Honorable Intentions

1. RATIONALE

Clients' fear of being blamed for past or present behavior frequently leads to resistance in therapy. Any critical or negative remark about family members can open up a Pandora's box of resistance maneuvers: denials, arguments, suspicion of covert alliances, refusals to participate, missed sessions, and possible premature termination, among others. Dealing with these resistance ploys sidelines the forward thrust of the therapeutic process for a while. Ignoring or denying the existence of these dysfunctional patterns impedes progress as well. Bestowing chivalries or "noble ascriptions" (Stanton, Todd, & Associates, 1982) provides a means to avoid getting one's shoes dirty when crossing a muddy road; it is a form of reframing from the negative to the positive. The chivalry the therapist bestows identifies a positive motive for the negative behavior.

2. PROCEDURE AND CASE EXAMPLE

The therapist, prior to bestowing a chivalry, must assume that the behaviors of family members are purposeful and positive when put into the proper perspective. If that is so, there must be a "good" reason individual family members act the way they do. The "bad" person is shown to have good intentions (Stanton, Todd & Associates, 1982).

The therapist might suggest that the wife who locks her husband out of the house when he arrives home drunk is acting not out of anger, but out of concern. He might do something to himself or another member of the family for which he would never be able to forgive himself. It might be pointed out to the family that their truant child's absence from school might not stem from peer pressure, but because several family members known to the child were school dropouts and managed to attain what appears to the child to be a comfortable life-style. The child may be emulating a pattern which already exists within the family.

In the first example, the therapist clothes the contrary conduct with a garland of good. In the second case, the family's jewel is placed in a more appropriate setting. Most frequently, such chivalries are welcomed by family members as truer representations of the facets of their behaviors or situations than they could have provided themselves. The therapist opens the closed system to new perspectives on the troublesome issues to begin construction on a bridge to more functional relationships.

III. TIPS AND TACTICS

Otani (1989) organizes 22 common types of client resistance into four definitive categories: "Response quantity resistance," "Response content resistance," "Response style resistance," and "Logistic management resistance." We will address at least one type of resistant behavior in each of these categories. The sources of the tactics cited below to deal with the specific types of resistance described by Otani are the authors of this volume unless otherwise indicated at the end of the description of each.

A. *Logistic Management: Poor Appointment Keeping*

The success of therapy is dependent upon the collaboration of the family members and significant others with the therapist to achieve the family's goals. To achieve this, the therapist needs to communicate the importance of regular attendance in the therapeutic process. The following tactics can be helpful in promoting regular attendance:

1. *Explain advantages.* Explain to the contact person the advantages of working with all family members and significant others. This will usually reduce anxiety somewhat and may be useful information for the contact person to have when he is discussing initiating therapy with other family members.

2. *Speak with resistant members.* Request or offer to speak with hesitant family members. This may be all that is necessary to empower the contact person to broach the subject of family therapy to family members perceived to be resistant.

3. *Stress first-session attendance.* Suggest to such clients that they attend at least the first session when a commitment to attend regularly is not forthcoming.

4. *Call absent member.* If a family member decides not to attend, the therapist might call during session and speak with the absent member in the following way: "I'm ____ and your ____ is here in therapy. I'm hearing ____ side of the story. I'd like to hear yours. Can you join us next week? [*If the response is negative* . . .] You mean you'll leave changing the relationship up to ____? Well, I'll try to protect your interests, but I can't promise you all that much. As your ____ changes, you may find yourself being depressed without knowing why" (Brock & Barnard, 1988).

5. *Use positive reinforcement.* Encourage positive reinforcement following sessions, such as going out to eat, having a special dessert out, or doing something special together over the weekend.

6. *Select a member to remind the family.* Have the family choose a member who is to be responsible for writing the date of the next session on a family calendar and reminding family members mid-week about their appointment.

7. *Audio or video tape sessions.* Sometimes family members find ways to prevent other member(s) from attending sessions. Make audio or video tapes of sessions so that clients can have access to what transpired.

8. *Refuse to meet.* Refuse to conduct sessions when members are unable to attend, coupled with an offer to reschedule at a time convenient to all.

9. *Include attendance issue.* Integrate the issue of attendance into the therapy, addressing it as a problem the family needs to resolve.

10. *Intervene with a paradoxical attendance contract.* For families who recognize their need for therapy but who chronically miss appointments, a paradoxical attendance contract can prove to be useful. (Dolan, 1985). An agreement is drawn up explaining, in writing, that therapeutic benefits tend to be more effective when the client wishes to accept treatment. Recognition of one's needs is a part of the therapeutic process. The client's recent past indicates the need for an interval of __ days between scheduled sessions. From this the therapist must assume that the client requires __ days between sessions. Therefore, each time an appointment is missed, it will be necessary to wait _____ days for the next session.

The agreement is dated and signed by all participants, including the therapist. The date of the next appointment is also written into the contract.

To continue to be oppositional, the client would need to increase the frequency of attendance. Compliance with the terms of the agreement would result in a strengthening of the therapeutic joining between client and therapist; the therapist is meeting the client's needs.

B. Response Style: Externalization

Recurring denials of responsibility for one's actions and blaming other family members for provoking a particular manner of dysfunctional behavior characterize one type of response style: externalization. The individual absolves himself from the problems within the system. These tactics facilitate clients' acceptance of responsibility of their contribution toward the maintenance of the dysfunctional patterns.

1. *Use "I" statements.* Encourage or insist upon the use of "I" statements in session.

2. *Encourage family members to talk about themselves* (Brock & Barnard, 1988): how they view themselves and the family, how they contribute to family problems, how another family member's behavior can become problematic for them, and how each reacts to the others' behaviors.

3. *Repeat the same question.* Pose one question to the family member, for example: Why blame him? or Why did you leave? Ask it repeatedly throughout the session whenever the client attempts closure or changing the topic. Following the reply, continue by acknowledging the response and adding ". . . but why blame him?" or "Okay, but what has that to do with why you left?" Following the next response, continue in the same vein, conclud-

ing with ". . . how is what you've said connected with why you're blaming him?" Whatever the blaming family member answers, the question remains the same. At the end of the session the therapist might assign the family the task of coming up with answers to the question posed (Anderson & Stewart, 1983).

4. *Communicate that change requires action.* Ask the question, "What would happen if we could prove who is to blame?" followed by "How would that knowledge make things better?" The aim is to communicate that the knowledge alone does not result in change. Something must be done to accomplish change (Anderson & Stewart, 1983).

5. *Question function of behavior.* Tell the family or hand them a letter stating: "I like the way you protect each other (the family). You are somebody as long as you oppose someone else. What would happen if you had no one to oppose? Could you still be yourself? It would really be hard" (L'Abate, Ganahl & Hansen, 1986).

6. *Identify intent* (Bagarozzi & Giddings, 1983). In many dysfunctional families, problems arise from incorrect assumptions or interpretations about the intentions of other members' behaviors. Negative reactions can often be traced to one's negative perception of another's conduct. It is important to intervene to clarify each party's motives. For example: A father is asked to discuss his inaccessibility to his daughter. Following this, the daughter is asked to relate her perceptions of the same behavior. The therapist accepts or reinforces neutral or positive intent. Should negative purpose be forthcoming, the therapist needs to guide the family into exploring the reasons for this. For example: The father avoids his daughter because he is preparing her and himself for the day when she will leave his home to go away to college or marry and never return. By limiting his contact with her now, he feels that both of them will be better able to handle her leaving later. From here, the therapist can reframe the father's intentions in a positive light and explore the father-daughter relationship further with the family in light of this new information.

7. *Pose something different* (Weiss, 1981). For example: Family relationships exist for mutual support. I wonder how each of you have supported each other. How do you attempt to make yourselves attractive to each other? Or, You know that it's possible for you to make your relationships look bad. Do you do this to each other? Do you sometimes make your relationship with other family members appear to be worse than it really is? What is it that you do? Is it fun; do you derive enjoyment from this? Do you think that the other person feels the same way about what you are doing as you do? How might you try to avoid doing such things?

C. Response Content: Emotional Display

An excessively emotional reaction pattern tends to affect the kind of information presented to the therapist. Eruptions of laughter or crying may be a family member's attempt to avoid further exploration of issues raised in session. The following tactics can be useful in dealing with this type of resistance.

1. *Refrain from reacting.* Remain calm and aloof; offer a crier a box of tissues; sit back and relax while a ranter raves. When the display is over, resume the discussion interrupted by the behavior.

2. *Set limits.* Insist that all family members agree to refrain from violence and destruction of property in session and at home while in therapy.

3. *Utilize time outs.* Employ time outs when discussions begin to become overladen with emotion. A five or ten minute break could be suggested. When all are calm, the discussion is resumed. By modeling this tactic in session, it can be suggested that the family members integrate it into their interactional patterns at home.

4. *Help identify reasons.* Help individuals identify the reasons particular issues lead to emotional outbursts by exploring family of origin material.

5. *Use biofeedback.* Use biofeedback to identify internal cues precipitating such displays. Once identified, ways to nip it in the bud can be explored.

6. *Relabel as intent.* Relabel the negative emotionalism as an expression of intent. "You tend to cry when you want to avoid dealing with an issue."

7. *Predict the next occurrence.* Predict the next outburst and discuss ways to avoid it.

8. *Play suitable music.* Play music suitable to the emotional display. If the client is crying, sad music to cry to; if the family member is shouting and carrying on, perhaps the 1812 Overture would be appropriate. This tactic can deflate the intensity of the emotional involvement and lead to exploration of the causes for the outburst (Bergman, 1985).

D. Response Content: Intellectualization

To avoid dealing with emotional issues, some clients employ technical terminology and abstractions during therapy sessions. Sessions can become bogged down in technical or philosophical discourse. The following tactics can be helpful in limiting, avoiding, or using this form of client resistance:

1. *Explore one issue at a time.* Explain to the family that one issue will be explored at a time. When one issue is resolved, then another can be undertaken. This will narrow the range of possible discussion.

2. *Use reenactments.* Have the family reenact the events instead of discussing them.

3. *Utilize sculpting and family choreography* (Duhl, Kantor, & Duhl, 1973; Moreno, 1946).

Anderson and Stewart (1983) suggest the following:

4. *Encourage others to talk.* Encourage other family members to talk about the intellectualizer's mode of communication: What do you think about this monologue (or dialogue)? Does this happen often at home? How do you feel when responded to in this manner? This could be the family's style of communication. It could also be that members employ it when specific issues are broached.

5. *Back up your position.* Utilize facts, studies, and prominent persons in the field under discussion to support a position. Interventions may be more acceptable when supported in this manner.

6. *Include feelings as a category of fact.* Encourage the family to set up a balance sheet to compare advantages and disadvantages, including emotional outcomes.

E. *Response Quantity: Silent and Minimal Conversationalist(s)*

Some clients attempt to control therapy by the amount of information they present in session. The following tactics are helpful in dealing with these types of resistance.

1. *Invite the silent member to contribute.* "Everyone else has had an opportunity to present their feelings, concerns, and thoughts about this issue. What are your thoughts on the matter?" In some families it may be the practice that one does not contribute unless asked to do so.

2. *Speak for the silent member(s).* The therapist sits next to or stands behind the person for whom she is speaking. She might then want to follow up by asking the non-talkative member(s) if she was accurate or if he had any additions or corrections to make (Brock & Barnard, 1988).

3. *Ask easy questions.* Ask questions which are easy to answer: How does this family celebrate birthdays, Thanksgiving, etc.?

4. *Ask the minimal talker about other specific family members.* "How do your brother and mother get along?" "What happens when your sister refuses to finish her dinner?" "When your husband is shouting at your son, what is your daughter doing? What is she feeling?" "If your wife answered this question as honestly as she could, what do you think she would say?" "How were things between your mother and sister six months ago?" "How do you remember your mother/sister being different then?" "If things do

not change, what do you suppose your sister/father might be most afraid of one year from now?" (Brock & Barnard, 1988).

F. Response Quantity: Verbosity

Some family member(s) regularly monopolize the sessions by talking for long periods of time.

1. *Limit time.* Set time limits on the amount of time each family member has to present a point of view. Place the talkative member(s) in charge of keeping track of the time.

2. *Identify limits.* Openly discuss the issue with the family to identify limits which would be acceptable to the family (Anderson & Stewart, 1983).

3. *Unburdening Members.* Suggest that the client is being used by the other family members. Through his actions, he accepts the unnecessary burden of being the family spokesperson.

4. *Role play.* Switch roles to encourage other family members to speak more frequently and the talkative member to practice controlling his verbosity, as well as experiencing what it is like to be on the receiving end of his actions.

5. *Stick to the issues.* The question to keep in the back of one's mind is: How does this relate to the problem at hand? Tangential topics or concerns introduced must be labeled as such and the conversation returned to the central difficulty being discussed.

6. *Signalling the IP.* Encourage family members to invent, identify, and employ verbal and nonverbal cues to signal the talkative member that enough has been said or that someone else would like to speak.

7. *Making equal verbal contributions.* Suggest that the family practice making equal verbal contributions by reading a book aloud together. The book, frequency of the reading sessions, the amount to be read by each member, and the amount to be read at each session would be negotiated by all family members.

8. *Incorporate nonverbal techniques* into the therapeutic strategy, such as family drawing, sculpting, and others.

REFERENCES

Anderson, C. A. and Stewart, S. (1983). *Mastering resistance: A practical guide to family therapy.* New York: Guilford Press.

Bagarozzi, D. and Giddings, C. (1983). The role of cognitive constraints and attributional processes in family therapy: Integrating intrapersonal, interpersonal, and systems dynamics. Wolberg, L. R. and Aronson, M. L. (Eds.), *Group and family therapy.* New York: Brunner/Mazel.

Bergman, J. S. (1985). *Fishing for barracuda: Pragmatics of brief systemic therapy.* New York: W. W. Norton.

Black, E. I. (1989, Fall). Queens College of the City University of New York Annual Marriage and Family Therapy Conference.

Brock, G. W. and Barnard, C. P. (1988). *Procedures in family therapy.* Needham Heights, MA: Allyn & Bacon.

de Shazer, S. (1984a). The death of resistance. *Family Process, 23,* 11–17.

de Shazer, S. (1984b). Post mortem: Mark Twain did die in 1910. *Family Process, 23,* 20–21.

Dolan, Y. M. (1985). *A path with a heart: Eriksonian utilization with resistant and chronic clients.* New York: Brunner/Mazel.

Duhl, F. S., Kantor, D. and Duhl, B. S. (1973). Learning space and action in family therapy: A primer of sculpting. In D. Block (Ed.), *Techniques of family psychotherapy: A primer.* New York: Grune & Stratton.

Fox, R. (1987). Short term, goal oriented therapy. *Social Casework: The Journal of Contemporary Social Work, 68,* 494–499.

Imber-Black, E. (1989, Fall). Queens College of the City University of New York Annual Marriage and Family Therapy Conference.

Keeney, B. P. (1986). *The therapeutic voice of Olga Silverstein.* New York: Guilford Press.

Kirschner, D. A. and Kirschner, S. (1986). *Comprehensive family therapy: An integration of systemic and family psychodynamic treatment models.* New York: Brunner/Mazel.

L'Abate, L. (1986). Beyond paradox: Issues of control. *Individual Psychology: The Journal of Adlerian Theory, Research, and Practice, 42,* 12–20.

L'Abate, L., Ganahl, G. and Hansen, J. C. (1986). *Methods of family therapy.* Englewood Cliffs, NJ: Prentice-Hall.

Lounsbury, T. Raynesford (1913). In F. Cummins Lockwood, *The freshman and his college.* Boston, MA: D.C. Heath & Co.

Lusterman, D. D. (1979). Creative uses of resistance. Presented at Queens College of the City University of New York Marriage and Family Therapy Course.

Moreno, J. L. (1946). *Psychodrama.* New York: Beacon.

Otani, A. (1989). Client resistance in counseling: Its theoretic rationale and taxonomic classification. *Journal of Counseling and Development, 67,* 458–461.

Papp, P. (1976). Family choreography. In P. J. Guerin (Ed.), *Family therapy: Theory and practice.* New York: Gardner Press.

Pugh, R. L., McColgan, E. B., and Pruitt, D. B. (1986). The role of the therapist in family therapy impasses. *The American Journal of Family Therapy, 14*, 304–311.

Sherman, R. (1986). The creative uses of resistance. North Shore Child Guidance Conference on Family.

Sherman, R. and Fredman, N. (1986). *Handbook of structured techniques in marriage and family therapy.* New York: Brunner/Mazel.

Silverstein, O. (1986). *The therapeutic voice of Olga Silverstein.* New York: Guilford Press.

Stanton, M. D. and Todd, T. C. (1981). Getting resistant families in treatment. *Family Process, 20*, 261–293.

Stanton, M. D., Todd, T. C. and Associates. (1982). *The family therapy of drug abuse and addiction.* New York: Guilford Press.

Stewart, S. and Anderson, C. M. (1984). Resistance revisited: Tales of my death have been greatly exaggerated (Mark Twain). *Family Process, 23*, 17–20.

Weiss, R. L. (1981). Resistance in behavioral marriage therapy. In A. S. Gurman (Ed.), *Questions & answers in the practice of family therapy.* New York: Brunner/Mazel.

Additional Resources

Erickson, S. K. & McKnight Erickson, M. S. (1988). *Family mediation casebook: Theory and process.* New York: Brunner/Mazel.

Friedman, E. H. (1991). *Friedman's fables.* New York: Guilford Publications.

Meth, R. L. & Pasick, R. S. with Gordon, B., Allen, J. A., Feldman, L. B. & Gordon, S. (1990). *Men in therapy: The challenge of change.* New York: Guilford Publications.

Talmon, M. (1990). Single session therapy: *Maximizing the effects of the first (and often only) therapeutic encounter.* San Francisco, CA: Jossey Bass.

Wallas, L. (1985). *Stories for the third ear.* New York: W. W. Norton & Company.

Watzlawick, P., Weakland, J. H. & Fisch, R. (1974). *Change: Principles of problem formation and problem resolution.* New York: W. W. Norton & Company.

5

BOUNDARIES
The Great Divide

I. INTRODUCTION

A. *Definition of Boundaries*

The concept of family boundaries is essential not only in defining who a family is but also in understanding how that family system functions. A boundary has been defined as "something that indicates or fixes a limit . . . or separating line" (Webster, 1967). Boundaries are invisible delineators which shape the pattern of family interactions both within the family and between the family and those outside its unit.

Boundaries vary from family to family along a continuum described by Minuchin (1974) as ranging from "enmeshed," where boundaries are diffuse or blurred, to "disengaged," where boundaries are rigid and basically impermeable. Members of families with diffuse boundaries exhibit overinvolvement with one another. The relationships are intense and frequently characterized by members speaking for each other, believing they share the same thoughts and feelings. Members of families with rigid boundaries remain detached and underinvolved. They seem unresponsive to or even unaware of each other's needs. Clear boundaries between family members are those that fall within the middle range between these two extremes, allowing not only for individuality and independence but also for a sense of belonging and interdependence.

B. Characteristics of Boundaries

Boundaries help determine family participation—who does what and under what circumstances. The family system is an organization of separate units or subsystems. The main subsystems have been defined as individual, spousal, parental, and sibling (Minuchin, 1974; Minuchin & Fishman, 1981). These subsystems interact and are dependent upon each other in various ways as a function of a particular situation and in response to the nature of that family's boundaries. For example, when the spousal subsystem is experiencing difficulties, in an optimally functioning family the boundaries are clear and the marital subsystem works on its problems without pulling in or triangulating a member of the family's child subsystem. Clear boundaries discourage dysfunctional alliances between one spouse and a child or prevent undue interference by in-laws or others.

In addition, each family member belongs to more than one subsystem simultaneously. For example, the mother is not just a member of a parental unit, but is also a part of a spousal, a female, and possibly a sibling subsystem. Relationship patterns, roles, and power in a family shift in accordance with membership in the several subsystems. Since families are living systems, they constantly change in response to their environment and their situational needs. While a well functioning family must have a clearly defined parental subsystem, ideally consisting of a mother and father, nevertheless a sibling can be temporarily placed—when boundaries are clear and well defined—in a parental role in the absence of parents without risking either family dysfunction or confusion (Goldenberg & Goldenberg, 1980). Boundaries must also be flexible and permeable so that families can be receptive to ideas, people, and things outside the family, but not so open that they become disorganized and chaotic, being flooded by constant and indiscriminate input.

C. Boundary Problems

1. BOUNDARY AMBIGUITY

Boss and Greenberg (1984) posit that an important source of familial stress results from "family boundary ambiguity" defined as a lack of clarity regarding who is in or out of the family system. This confusion regarding boundaries and, by implication, roles is usually a result of the loss of a family member. This loss might be psychological and can occur when a member is chronically ill, either physically or emotionally. It can also be through the physical absence of a divorced, deceased, or missing spouse. In fact, Boss (1980) first investigated boundary ambiguity as it related to "father-absent" prisoner-of-war and missing-in-action families.

A family struggling with ambiguous boundaries has difficulties effectively restructuring itself. Therefore, it is the lack of clarity surrounding the loss (whether the loss is ambiguous because of too few details surrounding the event or the loss is clear but denied) that is more important than the actual loss itself (Boss & Greenberg, 1984). Those families who are able to redefine their boundaries regardless of the circumstances of their loss are better able to redefine family roles and responsibilities and function effectively.

2. FAMILIES IN TRANSITION

Wood and Talmon (1983) are concerned with the tendency to look at family boundaries with a view toward pathology rather than toward health. They instead emphasize that transitional or life-cycle phases such as marriage, birth, launching, and death are a time for boundary reorganization facilitated by the "rite-of-passage" ceremonies that usually mark the occasions.

The restructuring of boundaries necessitates a change in both proximity and hierarchy within the family (Wood & Talmon, 1983). Proximity relates to the interpersonal boundaries in the family and includes issues such as the amount and quality of the time members spend together, how they share their physical space, their feelings, information, and decisions. A recently widowed mother might have to spend less time with her children because she has returned to work, but she might be emotionally closer to them as she relies on them in the absence of her husband. Hierarchy refers to generational boundaries, including areas such as nurturance, control, alliances and coalitions, and peers. These, too, are affected by family transitions and boundary reorganization.

Carter and McGoldrick (1988) believe that family stress is greatest during life-cycle transitions and that to effect a successful boundary reorganization the "entire emotional system" of the family must be explored. They believe this emotional system is comprised of at least three or four generations and extends across nuclear families as well. This is especially so when one considers the issue of boundaries in remarital situations, an area which has generated much interest in the past several years.

There is an ever-increasing divorce and remarriage rate in this country. Carter and McGoldrick (1988) cite statistics that indicate nearly half of those who marry for the first time will end those marriages and that over one half of those currently in their 30s will divorce not once but twice. With so many families facing multiple problems stemming from their reorganization, it is imperative that the boundary aspects of blended, step, or reconstituted families be seriously addressed.

3. STEPFAMILIES

The remarital family is another system in which confusion of role and definitions of who is in the family may often be found. For example, are noncustodial children in or out of the family? Lewis (1985) has looked at issues around stepfamilies and notes that the boundaries of such families must be more permeable than they are for original or "first married" families because of issues such as shared financial support of the children, dual custody or visitation rights, and multiple loyalties across households. To foster more control, stepfamilies often attempt to artificially close boundaries around their households. This is seldom the solution to the difficulties of shared control as it may promote guilt and confusion in the children and self-defeating competitiveness among the adults.

In one case, the parents of a seven-year-old girl had divorced a few years earlier. The girl and her mother lived in a different state from the father. He had subsequently remarried. The father had joint custody of the girl, which involved her spending summers with him and his relatively new wife. Although the girl and her stepmother worked through their relationship quite well, the girl's mother's presence was always felt. She constantly sent messages about how she wanted her daughter cared for, made frequent financial requests, and disrupted day-to-day plans in the stepmother's household. The stepmother initially attempted to close the boundaries around her household. That did not work. On realizing that was an ineffective way of dealing with the girl's mother, she was able to disarm much of the girl's mother's competitiveness by inviting her input into issues surrounding her daughter.

According to Lewis (1985), primary boundary problems occur within the stepfamily system as well as between households. The aforementioned case involving the seven-year-old girl is an example of the latter. The within-family boundary problem might be characterized by a hierarchical imbalance in which children, as a result of parents' guilt, uncertainties, difficulties in joining, and desire to "make up" for the children's discomfort, are allowed too much power either within the stepfamily or between the involved households. Marital boundaries must be reinforced if the hierarchical conflicts are to be successfully resolved.

4. CHRONIC ILLNESS

Chronic illness affects and is often affected by family boundaries in many significant ways (Masterson, 1985; Penn, 1983; Minuchin & Fishman, 1981). In exploring factors which contribute to poorly managed diseases, clinicians frequently find dysfunctional relationships within the family. In the case of families where there is an emotionally or psychosomatically ill child or adolescent, for example, there are several configurations of impaired family boundaries that might exist.

In some families, enmeshment occurs between one parent and the ill child. This situation either serves to distance the relationship between husband and wife or stabilizes an already conflictual marriage. The child may sense that intense conflict subsides only when he is acutely ill. He may thus exhibit difficulty with compliance either in taking medication or in some other area of medical followup. Overinvolvement by the parents can also foster overdependence by the child and contribute to failure on his part to attain age-appropriate milestones.

Another example of dysfunctional cross-generational boundaries occurs when a grandparent aligns with a chronically ill child against the child's parents. Still another variation may occur when the grandparent sides with one parent against the other around issues such as medical management of the child, thus diffusing the boundary around the marital subsystem. Even the sibling subsystem boundaries can be adversely affected by chronic illness in a family. In a case where parents are overinvolved with the ill child, the other children may feel there is too little response to their needs and may show their resentment through anger directed at their ill sibling.

D. Cultural Implications

One last but important point is the need to be ever mindful of cultural issues and how they affect the family's boundaries. The degree to which families either stretch their boundaries to embrace all past and future generations or, at the other end of the spectrum, carefully constrict their definition of family to encompass a small nucleus (Carter & McGoldrick, 1988) depends very much upon their ethnic and cultural background.

Landau (1982) notes that for families in cultural transition "The threat of the new culture, fear that the family's youth will be lost to it, and the family's unacceptability in its new environment may lead the system to close its boundaries to the outside world" (p. 556). Whether an adolescent is expected to join his parents, siblings, aunts, uncles, cousins, and grandparents for dinner each Sunday is not really crucial. Much more critical is whether his family boundaries are permeable enough to permit him to interact with his peers, become more autonomous, and generally master the tasks of adolescence.

The therapist must evaluate the question of boundaries not only on the basis of her own culturally defined yardstick but also on the ability of the particular family to function, grow, and appropriately negotiate life-cycle and developmental stages. There exist many ways in which families define themselves and it behooves clinicians to familiarize themselves with those customs and not take for granted what it means to a person to be part of a family in a particular culture or ethnic group.

II. STRUCTURED TECHNIQUES

A. Ghostbusting: The Empty Chair Technique

1. RATIONALE

As we have noted, confusion about who is or is not an integral part of a family system can stem from a number of causes. One such reason is what Boss and Greenberg (1984) term "ambiguous loss." Every family will at some time experience loss or separation. This is not necessarily a problem. However, some families fail to adequately cope with loss. They might experience either a physically absent member lost through death, divorce, or desertion as psychologically present or a physically present but ineffectual or chronically ill member as psychologically absent. These two conditions lead to ambiguity which can impede a reorganization of the family system along lines that would better meet the family's needs.

This concept of boundary ambiguity also relates to the problems surrounding stepfamilies, especially in those situations in which unreasonable attempts are made to effect cut-offs between children and their noncustodial parents or in which unresolved issues exist between divorced parents who must continue to relate to each other because of their children. A former spouse's "ghost" can be powerful.

2. PROCEDURE

The first step in addressing the topic of ambiguous boundaries or a ghostly presence in a family is to carefully assess the degree of ambiguity, the length of time it has existed, the extent to which it might have been initially helpful, and the degree to which it is now maladaptive. The second step is to help the family recognize its ghost or unrealistic expectations—for example, that the absent father will return and resume control; or that it is not possible for custodial and noncustodial parents to share in the life and upbringing of their children; or that their children will care about them less if allowed to care for someone else. The next step is to neutralize the power of the ghost by empowering the current executive subsystem—be it the divorced spouse or the new stepparent—through building self-assurance and a sense of competence.

One technique that can facilitate ghostbusting is a variation of the "empty chair" (Sherman & Fredman, 1986). This technique is usually attributed to Perls (Perls, Hefferline, & Goodman, 1951), who founded Gestalt therapy. He used this technique to help one get in touch with parts of oneself that were not being owned and integrated, but rather were being projected onto others. This procedure allows a family member to have an ongoing dialogue with another family member who is either absent or silently observing.

The actual procedure in the example of a divorcee would require that she address a facing empty chair as if her ex-spouse were sitting in it. The clinician would instruct her to role-play both herself and her ex-spouse, addressing and changing chairs depending upon what role she was assuming at the moment. In this way, with the help of the therapist who is either interpreting the interactions or confronting the patient on an ongoing basis, she is able to not only express her disappointment, frustration, anger, etc., but also experience the reality that her ex-spouse is no longer available as she might want him to be. In the process, she would be helped to realize that she is capable of doing many of the things she had been hoping her ex-spouse would return to do for her. The focus is redirected from her ex-spouse onto herself and her internal conflicts that had hampered her ability to feel empowered.

3. CASE EXAMPLE

Mrs. M. was a 37-year-old widow; her husband had died two years earlier. She had two children, a 17-year-old daughter and a 20-year-old son. She was referred for therapy by the employee assistance program at her place of employment because of prolonged and severe mourning. She had vegetative signs of depression and a high absentee rate at work. Her presenting problem, stated very tearfully, was that she could not get over her husband's death. Further discussion revealed that her husband had been her childhood sweetheart. She described him as having been everything to her—husband, friend, parent. Indeed, he had actually done everything for her, including grocery shopping, cooking, taking responsibility for paying the bills, and in general negotiating for them in the world outside their family. Although she had worked outside the home for many years, she had no close friends. Her family of origin was distant both geographically and emotionally. Her nuclear family had essentially been her world.

In using the empty-chair technique over a period of several weeks, she was encouraged to talk to her deceased husband. At first, she could only discuss how much she missed him and her expectation that he would voice the same sentiments, but encourage her to keep going. Gradually, she was able to confront him, via the chair, with the fact that she felt helpless and incapable of doing things on her own. Eventually, she was able to express her anger toward him for encouraging her to be totally dependent on him.

Throughout the period that this technique was being used, the therapist focused on Mrs. M.'s behavior that belied her contention that she was helpless and incapable of caring for herself and her children. For example, she was paying the household bills in a timely fashion, which also attested to her ability to organize and budget the family monies; she had guided her son into college; she arranged for minor repairs in the home; she did the grocery shopping; and, while no gourmet cook, she was appropriately taking care of the family's nutritional needs.

As the mourning issue abated, focus was directed toward her conflict with her family of origin and very early unmet dependency needs.

4. USES

The empty chair is a very simple technique that can be used to address various kinds of issues. Sherman and Fredman (1986) believe it to be especially useful when one is working with those who use projection, as it helps them own those parts of themselves that they inappropriately attribute to others. As in the case example discussed above, this technique can also shift the focus of treatment from external sources to internal conflicts. It is also very helpful as a means of integrating new roles and new interpersonal behaviors.

B. Interaction Diary

1. RATIONALE

In discussions of boundaries, mention is frequently made of enmeshed and diffuse boundaries and of structural and other techniques to clarify such boundaries. Just as disruptive to family functioning is the isolated or cut-off family member. He has essentially the same internal boundary conflicts as his overinvolved counterpart, but deals with those conflicts in an opposite way—by distancing himself from those with whom he is so involved emotionally. It is as though distancing is his only way to ward off feeling engulfed.

2. PROCEDURE

One technique to help the person who is cut off to loosen his internal boundaries is the compilation of an Interaction Diary. Each day he makes at least one brief notation related to his feelings about an interaction with a significant other. The interaction can be either one that has recently taken place, in the case of someone still involved to some extent with his family, or one that took place in the past. He should be encouraged to include notations about each family member and not just those with whom he feels he has had particularly difficult relationships. These diary entries are then brought into the therapy sessions on a regular basis, and the therapist helps the patient carefully explore all aspects of his relationships. Such notations not only force the patient to examine the boundaries and ties between himself, his family, and friends, but in the context of family discussions, where such are possible, provide avenues for more engagement between himself and other family members. Notations about friends might help him reflect on how his attitudes toward his family influence how he responds to his friends as well.

3. CASE EXAMPLE

Mrs. W. was a 40-year-old, twice divorced mother of three children who ranged in age from 8 to 22. She entered therapy because she was experiencing difficulties in her third marriage. Mr. W. had been in individual therapy for some months prior but refused to join Mrs. W. in couple therapy, insisting she needed individual therapy first. She agreed.

Mrs. W. described her husband as being emotionally distant from her. He had his own friends and activities quite apart from her. In fact, Mr. and Mrs. W. had lived in separate cities for two years of their marriage because, she said, of Mr. W.'s work demands. The precipitating problem that prompted Mrs. W. to seek therapy appeared to be her suspicion that Mr. W. was having an affair. She felt he was becoming increasingly distant to the point that she feared he might soon leave her.

Mrs. W. described her family of origin as a chaotic and unsafe environment in which she had been physically abused. She never knew her father and her mother had died many years earlier. One by one, Mrs. W. had disengaged herself from her family members. She had two aunts whom she described as the only two nurturing figures in her past. She had not communicated with them in over six years following some incident in which she had felt slighted. She has four siblings; although they all lived in the same city, there was only one that she saw or communicated with, albeit on rare occasions.

Mrs. W. was encouraged to keep a daily diary of both past and present feelings toward her interactions with others, including her aunts and siblings. What emerged was a pattern of cut-offs not only from family but also from friends and acquaintances whenever she perceived the slightest indication of rejection or unreliability. She was most concerned about being able to trust and count on others, with an ever-present expectation that she was asking for the impossible. In her attempt to be the self-sufficient person she believed she needed to be, she was obsessive, painstakingly "correct," and at all times very controlling. She sought relationships that were distant in nature in order to feel less vulnerable were they to become the anticipated disappointments that she expected and invariably received, as in her failed marriages. With the material that she herself had created and gathered, she could see graphic examples of a consistent pattern that she could then say she no longer wished to perpetuate.

4. USES

The Interaction Diary can be particularly helpful when one person in the family system has acted to effect a rigid boundary which cuts him off from his family. It can also be utilized with a family that has become isolated through a cultural transition. Each member of the family can be asked to maintain a separate diary of memories of the friends and family left behind. In the case of children too young to remember much, they can record the stories they have heard and the feelings such stories engendered in them. These diaries can then be shared in session to help the family work through feelings of isolation and loss and begin to feel more comfortable with increased interaction with their current environment.

C. The Coat of Arms

1. RATIONALE

This is a technique described by Fulmer (1983) as part of a family life-cycle workshop guide. The family is given the task of working together to formulate and articulate a set of family values. This exercise highlights enmeshment and disengagement issues. In the process of working together on a task, the clinician has an opportunity to closely observe the family's level of interaction, cooperation, support, affect, expectations, rules, roles, and belief system. Family conflicts can arise on different levels, such as across subsystems or along generational lines. Influences of families of origin inevitably appear, whether as an outcome of attempting to emulate what is seen as valuable or in an effort to avoid what are believed to be mistakes of the past.

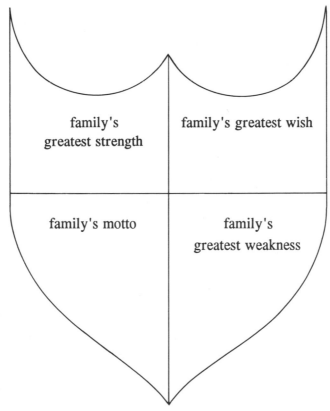

Figure 1. Coat of Arms

2. PROCEDURE

The therapist can help the family get started by assisting it in compiling a list of possible family values, such as achievement in school or in work, reputation in the community, loyalty, unconditional love and positive regard, discipline, sobriety, and home ownership, among others. Using a blank drawing of a coat of arms (see illustration), the family is instructed to fill it in, using the following directions:

> *Work together to devise a Coat of Arms for your family. In each of the four quadrants place symbols (or words) for the following: "The Family's Greatest Strength," "The Family's Greatest Wish," "The Family's Greatest Weakness," and "The Family Motto."*

As the family works on this task, the therapist learns a lot about the family's picture of itself and its philosophy, both as a unit and in terms of individual goals and aspirations. Who participates, who withdraws, who dominates, and who relates most to whom are just a few examples of the kind of information that is quickly evident.

3. CASE EXAMPLE

The R. family, consisting of Mr. and Mrs. R., their son, Jack, age 16, and their daughter, Joyce, age 14, sought therapy after discovering that Jack had been experimenting with drugs. Mr. and Mrs. R. were alarmed and shocked. How could this happen in their family? Neither they nor their families of origin engaged in any kind of substance abuse. They described themselves as a close-knit, upstanding, hardworking, and moral family within their community, and they could not understand how their son could go astray.

Mr. R. was employed as a middle manager with a large utility firm. He was quite ambitious and worked long hours. Mrs. R. was not employed outside the home. Both she and Mr. R. had always agreed she needed to be home for her family. Jack and Joyce earned reasonable grades in school and Mr. and Mrs. R. kept a watchful eye on their activities and friends, hoping to protect them from some of the dangers of society.

Because the parents stressed the point that they had strongly shared values, they were asked to work together in spelling out what those values and beliefs were. After some discussion, the R. family's Coat of Arms was completed. They listed their greatest strength as "family commitment" to a common goal; their greatest wish as "solidarity;" their family motto as "united we succeed," but their greatest weakness was an "inability to express feelings openly."

Here was a family that professed a desire to be as one, but apparently family members had feelings and thoughts they did not feel able to share. In fact, the son's drug usage was seen as his way of attempting to assert his individuality and independence from a "perfect" and self-contained family. This family might be described by Wynne, Ryckoff, Day and Hirsh (1958) as being so caught up in its own mythology that what emerged was a relationship best characterized as pseudomutual. Everyone appeared to be pulling together, sharing the same values and beliefs, but actually they were quite distant from one another, with just the illusion of family unity. For more about family myths, see Chapter 9 of this text. Working together on this task gave the family an opportunity to develop both more actual unity and more differentiation by discussing their values.

4. USES

The Coat of Arms technique can be used with either a family or a marital couple to explore how well the members understand each other's values and goals and to alert the therapist to conflicted as well as nonconflictual areas in those relationships. Family traits, patterns of communication, structure, level of differentiation, degree of openness versus secretiveness, and clarity of boundaries are just some of the areas that can be assessed as the family works on a common task. It can also assist them to discuss and resolve differences as they work for a common Coat of Arms.

III. TIPS AND TACTICS

1. Return Someone's Memory

When working with a family in which one member habitually answered for another, Minuchin and Fishman (1981) used "cognitive indicators" such as "You're helpful, aren't you? You take his memory" (p. 147) to underscore the intrusiveness of family members who speak for one another. The overinvolved family member may be asked to restore the other's memory by letting him speak for himself. When these incidents are highlighted, the intrusive family member becomes aware of the lack of psychological space between himself and the other.

A variation of this tactic, which is less confrontative but nevertheless points up the intrusiveness of speaking for another, is akin to reframing. The therapist might say: "You have been working so hard this evening. Let's see if we can get the others to share by speaking for themselves."

2. Making "I" Statements

To emphasize the need for more rigid boundaries, the therapist can introduce a rule that each family member must speak for himself. This can be done by first asserting that "I" statements are much clearer than "he" or "she" ones, since there is less chance of misrepresentation or misunderstanding when one speaks for himself. Members are also encouraged to take responsibility for ideas and thoughts they express. When Carl announces that Sally does not really like attending therapy sessions, for example, the therapist can suggest that Sally will get an opportunity to express her opinion, but then ask Carl how he feels about attending the sessions, giving him the chance to give an "I" statement and allowing both him and Sally to speak for themselves.

3. Supporting Generational Boundaries

Sherman and Fredman (1986) list nearly a dozen structural moves and strategies to reinforce the generational boundaries in a family and to support the parents' executive function in the home, dealing with their responsibilities for decisions about their children. These include the rearrangement of seating, with parents placed together and apart from the children; the establishment of task differentiation between parents and children; the reinforcement of the need for privacy, for separate parental and child activities; and the need for the parents' need to discipline and make decisions about the children.

4. Draw a Family

Each family member can be asked to draw a picture of the entire family engaged in some activity, such as getting ready for a picnic (Burns & Kaufman, 1970, 1972). Who seems to be in charge? Where is everyone in relationship to each other? Who is working together? Who seems to be either working alone or uninvolved? Not only can family dynamics be graphically demonstrated through such drawings, but, in addition, any differences regarding how they define their relationships can be fully explored.

A variation of this task could be to ask each family member to draw himself as a circle and then place every other family member, also represented as a circle, somewhere on the same page. These drawings can be assessed not only in terms of proximity, but also in terms of size of circles. The therapist would also compare where the drawings overlap and where they greatly diverge.

5. Be an Expert

To emphasize that each family member is unique and to encourage less diffusion, the therapist can help the family members identify each other's strengths and then appoint each person as expert in that area where he is considered most strong. For example, if father is a good handyman but does a poor job of keeping the household bills sorted out, his main responsibility at home will be fixing things—where his expertise lies. The rest of the family depends on father to see that all repairs are made. Maybe daughter is the best grocery shopper in the household because she reads the labels and comparison shops. As the expert, she is then in charge. Of course she can elicit help and even "delegate authority" to her younger brother to go to the store for some needed items, but she is ultimately responsible for selecting the groceries and the family depends upon her to fulfill that task. Such a recognition of expertise encourages separateness and an appreciation of each family member's uniqueness.

REFERENCES

Boss, P. (1980). The relationship of wife's sex role perceptions, psychological father presence, and functioning in the ambiguous father-absent MIA family. *Journal of Marriage and Family*, 42, 541–549.

Boss, P. and Greenberg, J. (1984). Family boundary ambiguity: A new variable in family stress theory. *Family Process*, 23(4), 535–546.

Burns, R. C. and Kaufman, S. H. (1970). *Kinetic family drawings* (K-F-D). NY: Brunner/Mazel.

Burns, R. C. and Kaufman, S. H. (1972). *Actions, styles and symbols in kinetic family drawings* (K-F-D): *An interpretative manual*. NY: Brunner/Mazel.

Carter, B. and McGoldrick, M. (Eds.). (1988). *The changing family life cycle: A framework for family therapy* (2nd ed.). NY: Gardner Press.

Fulmer, R. H. (1983). Teaching the family life cycle: A guide for a workshop using simulated families. *American Journal of Family Therapy*, 11(4), 55–63.

Goldenberg, I. and Goldenberg, H. (1980). *Family therapy: An overview.* Monterey, CA: Brooks/Cole.

Landau, J. (1982). Therapy with families in cultural transition. In M. McGoldrick, J. K. Pearce and J. Giordano (Eds.). *Ethnicity and family therapy.* NY: Guilford Press.

Lewis, H. C. (1985). Family therapy with stepfamilies. *Journal of Strategic and Systemic Therapies*, 4(1), 13–23.

McGoldrick, M. and Gerson, R. (1985). *Genograms in family assessment.* NY: W. W. Norton.

Masterson, J. (1985). Family assessment of the child with intractable asthma. *Journal of Developmental and Behavioral Pediatrics*, 6(5), 244–251.

Minuchin, S. (1974). *Families and family therapy.* Cambridge, MA: Harvard University Press.

Minuchin, S. and Fishman, H. C. (1981). *Family therapy techniques.* Cambridge, MA: Harvard University Press.

Penn, P. (1983). Coalitions and bonding interactions in families with chronic illness. *Family Systems Medicine*, 1, 16–25.

Perls, F. S., Hefferline, R. F. and Goodman, P. (1951). *Gestalt therapy.* NY: Julian Press.

Sherman, R. and Fredman, N. (1986). *Handbook of structured techniques in marriage and family therapy.* NY: Brunner/Mazel.

Webster's seventh new collegiate dictionary (1967). Springfield, MA: G. & C. Merriam.

Wood, B. and Talmon, M. (1983). Family boundaries in transition: A search for alternatives. *Family Process*, 22, 347–357.

Wynne, L. C., Ryckoff, I. M., Day, J. and Hirsh, S. I. (1958). Pseudomutuality in the family relationships of schizophrenics. *Psychiatry*, 21, 205–220.

6

DON'T FORGET THE CHILDREN

"Children can be exposed to horrible influences and great traumas. Usually they survive them very well—they react and then they adapt. Incidents don't affect children as much as patterns do. The patterns under which children grow up will affect them for the rest of their lives."

(Pittman, 1987)

I. INTRODUCTION

A. Discussion

A couple's decision to include children in their lives is often perceived as the final and definitive step into adulthood. The relationship established with the young family member(s) is generally more durable than contractual matrimonial vows. Marriages are dissolved and cohabitors move apart, yet the biological reality of parenthood remains. As Carter and McGoldrick (1980) point out, it is a nonnegotiable reality.

1. CHILDREN CHANGE THE COUPLE DYNAMIC

A child entering a family constellation permanently changes the dynamics of the group. The patterns of interaction move from dyadic to triadic. Usually, the integration of the young member into the family's life-style requires a change in routine. Some autonomy is lost in providing for the needs of the child. Questions arise. Who will assume responsibility for which of the new member's needs? How will the boundaries defining relationships prior to the new arrival be adjusted? How much time is to be reallocated to care for the needs of the new family member? Economic resources may require evaluation and financial expenditures reordered. During this stage, misunderstandings, resentment, and frustration can accompany the reconciliation of individual needs with those of other members and what is best for the group.

As the family grows and develops, new and different demands are placed upon the system. Invariably, discussion, negotiation, and change are required to maintain a sense of stability within the system. Children play an integral part in determining the pattern of the weave in the fabric of family life. Yet, children are often excluded or separated from the family for therapeutic exploration of dysfunctional patterns.

There are reasons for this. Child therapies are largely derivatives of individual psychotherapy. Also, the world of the child is considered to be very different from that of adults. As a result, children manifesting difficulties are generally referred to child specialists (psychologists, social workers, counselors, therapists), who were trained to deal with children outside the family unit and who frequently do not have backgrounds in family therapy.

Adults tend to fancy that their problems do not or have not been allowed to impact upon the rest of the family. As a result, parents may be inclined to believe that their children need not be included in the search for solutions. In some instances, this is a form of resistance.

Marriage counselors and therapists who tend to place responsibility for the family in the laps of the parents do not always feel the need to regularly include children in the therapy. Some family therapists have had limited experience working with children. They feel concerned about losing therapeutic focus when the group responds to a child's spontaneous outburst or inquisitive behaviors. They allow parents to refuse to permit their children to attend therapy sessions.

Working with less than the family unit constitutes working with subsystems of the family unit. This may be beneficial or necessary at times. It may be that two family members need to work on specific aspects of their relationship apart from the rest of the family for part of a session or in a separate session. It is also reasonable for parents seeking sex therapy to expect that their children will not be required to attend sessions. In general, however, the decision to exclude children from family therapy or the family from child therapy overlooks possible advantages that inclusion could bring for the child, the family, the therapeutic environment, and the therapist.

2. REASONS TO INCLUDE CHILDREN IN FAMILY THERAPY

Keith (1986) points out that children's concerns for their parents are about equal to their parents' concern for them. However, the children's concerns are usually not overtly expressed. Children's problems, whether related or unrelated to those of other members in the dysfunctional family, may be overlooked by parents preoccupied with their own difficulties. When recognized, a child's problem may be dealt with in a halfhearted manner by the parents. Suggested or imposed solutions may not be carefully thought out or might be offered out of parental annoyance, if offered at all.

The opposite is also true. Parents may overdramatize and become preoccupied with a child's difficulties to avoid the tensions in the marriage or the self. Such problems are sometimes used by spouses to manipulate each other or the therapist. Parents' comments to the effect that their children are "holding their own" or "taking everything in stride" may be an attempt to cover up any difficulties their children may be experiencing. It might be an attempt to hide what they perceive as additional, unrelated inadequacies.

Excluding children deprives them of the opportunity to work through their difficulties in conjunction with the related events affecting their lives. It also deprives the rest of the family of the opportunity to strengthen family ties by helping younger members understand and participate in the process of change.

Framo (1981) considers the manifested difficulties of the children in a family as metaphoric clues to the nature of the marriage. The presence of the children in a family fills out aspects of the family dynamic which cannot be adequately or objectively described. Relative intensities of responses, how a child looks at or responds to a parent, freedom of movement within the system, posture, who monitors the child, and other nonverbal cues exchanged between parents and children provide significant insights into the family life-style. Children make the family whole and natural. They can help to open the unconscious to facilitate integration of new material by decreasing the rigidity often infused into the system by intensive focus on the perceived problems (Keith, 1986).

Other benefits for the family identified by Keith (1986) include increased permeability of the boundaries of time, persons, definitions, and generations which may enhance the formulation of new perspectives. Alliances, coalitions, seats of power, and responsibility within the family may be more readily apparent when children are included. Younger children also tend to keep both the adults and older children more honest.

Attention to younger members of a family communicates that they have a place and value within the family context. The therapist's interactions can also be designed to model appropriate parenting skills for the parents. The spontaneity of children may lead to new avenues of exploration, increasing the possibilities for change.

A child's innocent behavior can lighten the mood of a session. The presence of children tends to help maintain a more civil tone in the give and take between family members. Decreasing the ferocity and negativity may motivate the search for acceptable ways to communicate anger, frustration, and differences of opinion.

Attention paid to young children by the therapist usually enhances the joining process. The honest verbal and nonverbal reactions of young children can often shorten and improve therapeutic assessment. It is not uncommon for a younger child to be an objective reporter of family interactions in session. For example: When Mr. F. attempted to downplay his actions by saying that he tried to discuss a particular matter, the three-year-old nodded and said, "Yes, Daddy, you shout very loud."

As the exclusion of children from therapy tends to minimize the role and effects of children upon the family system, the converse is also true. To exclude parents/guardians tends to deny direct access to the foundation upon which the child's person is being constructed. In both scenarios, the therapeutic environment bears little resemblance to the realities of home life. This tends to complicate and protract integration of conceptual and behavioral shifts into the systemic patterns of interaction with which the child must live. Exclusion tends to prolong therapy and, without accurate feedback, may doom the therapy to failure.

This chapter provides some techniques and tactics which will facilitate the involvement of children in the family therapy experience. Hopefully these will help make working with entire families more manageable and productive.

B. Definitions

The period of time in one's life during which an individual is considered to be a child can be loosely defined as the interval from birth to maturity, the parameters of which are socially defined by culture and law. Generally, there is a heavy educational component, both formal and informal, attached to this developmental time in life.

The importance of childhood in our society seems to be indicated by the variety of developmental and social stages into which this period has been divided: infant, toddler, preschooler, pubescent, teenager, adolescent, and young adult, for example. Familiarity with the characteristics common to these stages of development is helpful when working with children.

Giacomo and Weissmark (1985) conceptualize a child ". . . as an evolving system that can generate a great deal of variety. . . ." For the purposes of this chapter, "child" and "children" will refer to persons of either sex between birth and maturity. (Another chapter will be devoted to working with the adolescent.)

II. STRUCTURED TECHNIQUES

The central aspect in functional or purposeful living is participation. Participation necessitates engaging in cooperative efforts to solve problems which inhibit healthy growth and development. The three techniques selected for inclusion in this chapter reflect our beliefs in family participation in the solution of problems.

A. *The Team Picture*

1. RATIONALE

Young children, due to their lack of verbal sophistication, are often at a disadvantage when sessions are composed exclusively of verbal exchanges between the therapist and older family members. This may lead to a lack of interest, inhibiting the change process. The use of projective techniques frequently narrows the perceived gap between age groups. Adults may not exhibit much more proficiency in acting, drawing, or painting than their children. This tends to enable all family members to feel that their contributions are of equal value. The utilization of such therapeutic modalities with families can facilitate exploration of attitudes, characteristics, and feelings which are often not revealed through direct verbal communication methods. They can also be a lot of fun.

The Team Picture technique used by Landgarten (1987) is primarily diagnostic in its purpose. A variation (Mills, Crowley & Ryan, 1986) of this technique, Family Drawing, included in the Tips and Tactics section at the end of this chapter, is also used in diagnosis. Landgarten (1987) utilizes the art therapy model in working with families from the initial session through termination.

The Team Picture technique involves three procedures, all of which are easily administered. The tasks focus the family's attention upon the creation of a product. While the family is actively engaged in carrying out these assignments, the therapist is able to observe the family process of interaction. Individual and group assessments by the therapist of functional and dysfunctional characteristics within the system are possible in a relatively brief period of time, often within one session. Taking notes can be helpful. It is suggested that the therapist inform the family that notes will be taken prior to doing so. The information gleaned from observing the family at work helps the therapist choose appropriate strategies and interventions based upon the individual members' and subsystems' resources and structures.

2. PROCEDURE

At the initial session, the family is told that they will be participating in an art activity which is commonly used in therapy to observe the family functioning as a group. The therapist might want to use more formal language such as "standardized method" (Landgarten, 1987) to minimize the possibility of resistance. Family members must be reassured that they will not be judged by the quality of the work. The procedure can be presented as an informal and enjoyable way for the therapist to become better acquainted with the family's unique way of getting things done. The family is told that whatever they produce will be acceptable and helpful.

In explaining what the family is to do, it is important that the therapist not be too specific. The directions are intentionally vague in the area of what to draw and how the drawings are to be executed. Whether the team should work together or separately is decided upon by each team's members without additional direction from the therapist.

For the initial work, the family is requested to form two teams. The therapist places a number of different colored markers on the table. After dividing, each family member is instructed to choose one marker to be used for the three tasks in which they will be involved. After the markers are chosen, extras, if any, are removed and put away.

The first task is then explained: Each team works together on one sheet of paper; they are not to communicate with any family member verbally, by signals of any kind, or through written messages; when each person is finished, he is to stop work and put the marker down. When everyone has finished, communication is allowed. The teams are instructed to name their work and write a title on it.

The second task reunites the family to work on one sheet of paper. The instructions are the same as for the first procedure: The family members are to work together on the one sheet of paper; verbal and nonverbal communication is again banned; each person is to retain the marker used on the previous work. Upon completion, discussion is allowed to determine a title and it is written on the drawing.

For the third task, the therapist instructs the family to produce a single work of art; talking is permitted; each member continues to work with the same marker chosen initially. Upon completion, a title may or may not be attached.

While observing, the therapist might want to keep the following questions in mind. The answers will provide useful insights into the systemic organization and patterns of interaction of the family (Landgarten, 1987).

1. Who was the first to draw and how was it decided that this person would begin?
2. Who began working next and in what order did the other family members begin to make their contributions?
3. Whose suggestions were accepted and whose were rejected?
4. To what degree was each family member involved in the task?
5. Which family members confined themselves to one section of the paper and which utilized more than their share of the paper?
6. Did any member draw over or attempt to delete another member's contribution?
7. Was contact attempted, what kind, and by whom to whom?
8. Was the work done together, one at a time, or in teams?
9. Was a change in style attempted, why, and by whom?
10. How much space did each family member use to make their contribution and in what part of the paper?
11. How much room did each person utilize to make their contribution?
12. What does each member's work symbolize?
13. Who worked independently of the others?
14. Which member(s) initiated?
15. Which member(s) followed/reacted?
16. Did any members respond emotionally at any time during the work? When? Why?
17. To whom, or in which subsystem, does the responsibility for family leadership fall?
18. Could the family's style be considered "cooperative, individualistic, or discordant"?
19. The therapist might ask the family, following the completion of the third task, if what she had observed was typical or atypical of the way the family usually functions.

3. CASE EXAMPLE

The Smiths entered the office with Mother holding eight-year-old Ronnie's hand while talking to her husband. Ronnie was pulling his mother toward the sofa. Father pulled up two chairs, oblivious to Ronnie's efforts, and seemed surprised when Mother and Ronnie sat down on the sofa as he was about to sit on a chair across the room from them. As he arose to move closer, Ronnie slid off the sofa and began to explore the room. Mother and Ronnie looked at the therapist, waiting for the therapist to begin. Both were a little surprised when the therapist began by establishing contact with Ronnie.

The Smiths were having difficulty controlling Ronnie from time to time. They claimed that he was unruly and when he did not get his way was prone to tantrums. He refused to cooperate in the time-out procedure tried by Mr. and Mrs. Smith.

Mother: We don't usually include Ronnie in adult discussion.

Therapist: Thank you for telling me that. As I explained to you on the telephone, however, Ronnie will be involved in the work we will be doing here. He seems to be fairly independent and inquisitive, to your credit as parents. He should do just fine. (To Ronnie) If you could sit with your parents and listen, we all will know what to do when the time comes. Do you think you can do that?

Ronnie: Yes. (Ronnie patted his father's leg as he passed and then crawled up onto the sofa next to his mother.)

Therapist: Do you like to draw or color?

Ronnie: Yes, a little.

Therapist: Well, today I would like to get to know this family better. So, I'm going to ask everyone to do three things together and we will talk about them after we are finished. While you are working, I will be watching and, if you do not mind, I may write a few notes so I will not forget some of the things I might want to say when these projects are finished. Is that okay?

Father: What is it that you want us to do? I do not mind your taking notes as long as they remain in our file.

Mother: I don't mind.

Therapist: Ronnie?

Ronnie: It's okay. What are you going to write?

Therapist: Just some ideas or thoughts that I do not want to forget to discuss later.

Ronnie: Is this like school?

Therapist: A little bit, perhaps, but I am not going to mark your work or give you a Report Card. I am sure that whatever you do will be your best work and that is all I would like. I am sure your work will be very good. Okay?

Ronnie: Okay.

Therapist: (*Explains the first task to the family.*)

Father: None of us are great artists here. I am not sure what we all are doing here. How can we have fair teams, anyway. There are three of us. (*Ronnie moves to his mother.*)

Therapist: I know that you are not an artist. Most clients are not. I do believe, however, that you are talented enough to complete the three tasks we will be working on today. As for the uneven teams, there are no points to be scored and neither team will win or lose. So could you divide up and let's see what can be done? We will talk about it later, if time permits, or at the next session.

Father: Will Ronnie be part of that, too?

Therapist: He will be here.

Father: Well, okay, let's get started. Since Ronnie is over by you, you two can stay together and I'll work alone. You want each team to draw a picture of anything they wish.

Therapist: Right. First choose your marker. Also, remember, there is not to be any talking, writing notes to each other, or any other creative type of communication.

Mother: But what are we to do? He has it easy working by himself. He just does what he wants.

Therapist: Would you like to discuss the teams with your husband before we begin?

Mother: No. I don't mind working with Ronnie. It's just that how can we work together if we can't talk to each other?

Therapist: Well, Ronnie, do you think you can work without communicating with Mother?

Ronnie: I don't know.

Therapist: Would you like to work with Father?

Ronnie: No, this is okay.

Therapist: Well, you and your mother are going to have to do the best you can together, okay?

Mother: We'll try. Okay, no talking, Ronnie.

Ronnie: Okay.

Therapist: Okay. Choose your marker and you can begin.

The family followed the instructions. Father chose the black marker; Mother chose the yellow; and Ronnie chose a dark blue marker. Father began drawing first—a boat on the water with the family (stick figures) smiling in it. Mother and Ronnie's paper was divided by a line drawn by Mother, with Ronnie being allocated less than half of the paper for his drawing. Ronnie began drawing first. He drew the family members, all smiling, standing in their backyard to the right of the pool; the people were all taller than the house but in descending order from left to right, beginning with Father; Ronnie appeared to be proportionally larger than his parents. Mother observed what everyone else had begun before she quickly drew a car with the family inside driving away from a house slightly larger than the car; her drawing did go over into Ronnie's space a little. Later Ronnie drew a line around his work. The therapist jotted down answers to the questions listed above as the family worked. The second and third tasks did not meet with resistance.

The second task resulted in three separate drawings on the paper, which was divided by Father in such a way that each family member had the length of a rectangular section. Ronnie was given about one-fourth of the paper and drew an airplane in the sky being attacked by large flying saucers. Mother took the longest amount of time and drew a picture of herself lying in a hammock reading a book. Father drew what he described as a moose in a meadow.

The third picture was of their home (Mother with help from Father), pool (Father), and garden (Ronnie). The third task was quickly decided upon but took the longest to complete as there was much discussion as to what to include, who was to do what, and how much space to allocate for what was to be included. Ronnie was consulted about the front garden and when he said that it should be included, he was told that he would draw it and the trees and grass around the house. Mother drew the house first, then Father and Ronnie were able to work on the pool and garden respectively, at the same time, with Mother talking mostly to Ronnie about where to draw the garden and the trees in front of the house. When Father was finished, he outlined the house and then commented that it looked better that way. No one agreed or disagreed.

Following the completion of the third task, the therapist asked the family to arrange the pictures and to use the masking tape to affix them on the wall. Two polaroid snapshots were taken with the family's permission; one was given to the family and one was put into their file. Ronnie was cooperative throughout the session, except for the one outburst. The therapist then asked if they had any questions.

Father: Yeah. Why was it necessary for us to divide up the first time? And why weren't we allowed to communicate until the last project?

Therapist: If I am to help you, I need to be aware of how the members of this family get along in a variety of situations. I cannot re-create here all of the circumstances which occur outside, so I chose three. As for the request that you do not communicate, how you interact with each other in such a situation helps me to understand your behaviors apart from what you say.

Mother: So, what can you come up with?

Therapist: This family seems to enjoy the outdoors. Everyone drew pictures of outdoor activities. You also seem to be able to pull things together when you are working together on a task. You appear to enjoy working together more than alone. You also seem to have a lot of strengths which may not be used in helpful ways at home. Could each of you explain where you experienced the most difficulties?

Father did not feel good when he had to work alone, although he chose to do so. He also felt that not being able to talk in working with the rest of the family was frustrating. Mother thought that the family would have had less difficulty if they could have communicated. Ronnie felt that he was not given enough to do in the last picture, as he was allocated a very small part of the overall paper to draw the flowers and trees around the house. He would not draw over the work of his parents; he loudly complained that he could not do his "whole part because Mom's and Dad's house and pool would be covered up." He was told to only do the front garden, trees and grass, and the grass on the side of the house. The rest was done by Mother and Father.

Tentatively, the therapist concluded that the parents spent little positive quality play time interacting with Ronnie in the home. The family appeared to enjoy spending much time out of the house. Ronnie was able to do many things on his own and accepted a nonintrusive position in the system. His tantrums probably occurred when he wanted or needed attention that was not forthcoming from his parents. In subsequent sessions, the hypothesis was confirmed. The specific difficulties were illustrated by the family, but addressed by combining enactments, role playing, and additional art therapy techniques.

4. USES

The division of the family is generally indicative of the alliances existing within the family unit. How the division is accomplished provides insight into the decision-making process and the relative power of each of the members. Limiting each person to one marker allows the therapist to monitor each member's contribution throughout the session. Gestures, facial expressions, and other body language are important contributions to be observed. The number of markers the family is given to choose from is up to the therapist. Limiting the number of markers to the number of family members forces member interaction and, possibly, some negotiation in the choosing process.

From the variety of transactions the family needs to make to accomplish the three tasks given to them, the therapist should be able to draw several significant conclusions about how the family system functions. Following the completion of the tasks or in a subsequent session, the therapist could ask questions to clarify or identify the reasons for the choices made. A tentative working hypothesis should be possible following the administration of this technique. The technique could also be used to check the accuracy of a working hypothesis derived through the use of other methods.

B. Puppet Reenactment

1. RATIONALE

Children are sometimes reluctant to volunteer information in session. They tend to feel more relaxed when involved in play. Frequently, they will agree with other family members' feelings and descriptions out of an insecurity stemming from their feelings about family loyalty and protectiveness, possible retribution from family members, or embarrassment. A child's discomfort may be communicated in a variety of ways. He may feign drowsiness or pretend to fall asleep, act out to divert attention, increase his squirming in the seat, act shy and not answer, respond with an "I don't know" or "I forgot," or become more deeply involved in another activity. Professionals who work with children find that it becomes essential to familiarize themselves with play therapy techniques.

Through play activities, reality can be altered to better fit a child's concept of the way things should or could be. Direct discussion may be too threatening. This can be especially true when negative behaviors of family members are discussed. Given the luxury of suspending reality, a child seems to have the ability to deal with a situation within the imagination or fantasy world he creates. This distance placed between reality and fantasy may offer a protective shield against hurtful influences.

One such means of "discussing" what happened in families with young children is through the use of puppet reenactments. Puppets are associated with play. The use of puppets helps to bypass nonproductive behaviors. They permit children to accommodate their fantasies to the real world. The puppets themselves are nonthreatening and their use allows for more open exploration of family patterns.

Although it may be possible to purchase puppets ethnically appropriate, it is far more productive to have each family member create his or her own. They can be made out of paper bags, paper maché, or other materials. The family discussion(s) and/or production can be assigned for home or carried out in session. It is generally more meaningful when the therapist also has a puppet representative to be used if a situation should arise that involves the therapist.

It is necessary to have the puppets at every session. Leaving them accessible to children provides the opportunity for discussion combined with play. At times, a child will play out a situation being described by parents, and add, perhaps, a few forgotten details, the child's unexpressed reaction, or a different ending. Puppet play can also provide insight into a child's feelings for other family members through observation of the treatment each puppet receives.

2. PROCEDURE

First, the therapist needs to suggest the family activity, puppet making. The family should be informed of the therapist's intentions to use the puppets in therapy. Agreement of all family members is necessary.

The suggestion can be placed within the context of a family fun activity that can be done together or, depending upon the family style, with individuals preferring to work independently and then surprise each other with their completed work.

The production process needs to be discussed. If it is addressed in session, the interactions among family members to arrive at a consensus regarding size, type of puppet, materials to be used in construction, purchasing of materials, scheduling time to work on the project, date of completion, and providing for help, if needed, supply the therapist with much insight into how a family functions. Once the puppets are completed, they may be kept by the therapist, as their purpose is therapeutic: to help understand the events which occur in the home. This also tends to protect the puppets from breaks or tears.

It is best to alert the family to the fact that the therapist would be willing to store the puppets and the reasons why it might be beneficial for her to do so during the initial discussion. However, if the family wishes to undertake the responsibility, it could be therapeutically valuable to trust them to do so, following some discussion as to what that entails. To avoid a child's objection to leaving his puppet with the therapist, it might be suggested that the child construct two, one for home use. After a period of time, the therapist might move to encourage the family to accept such responsibility. Upon termination of therapy, the puppets would be offered to the family.

Once the puppets are ready, the therapist might introduce them into use in the following manner:

Therapist: Let's try out these fantastic puppets. Would you bring out the puppets for us (*addressing the child*)?
Child: (Distributes the puppets)
Therapist: First, let's introduce everybody. (*After introductions.*) Now, what can these puppets tell us about what happened in the family this past week? Let's try to talk and use the puppets to show what happened. (*The therapist might make some logistical suggestions to facilitate the interaction of the puppets and get the family started.*) Where were you Mother? Father? Child? when this was beginning? Maybe it would be better if you moved over there? What do you think? Okay? Lights; camera; action. (*Additional questions might need to be asked to clarify members' actions.*) What were you doing when she did that? Show us with your puppet. Good. Your puppet seems to be falling asleep over there. Is that what you were doing? And what is your puppet doing?

With practice, the reenactments tend to improve. Attention needs to be paid to what each family member was doing even when not directly involved in the interaction being discussed.

3. CASE EXAMPLE

The P. family came for therapy complaining about the runaway behavior of their youngest son, James, age 7, and their difficulty resolving differences. Their older son, Matt, age 11, did not seem overtly affected by the parents' arguments, but he too was concerned about his younger brother's behavior.

It seemed that periodically, James would disappear and return an hour or two later sobbing or with red eyes, for no apparent reason. He would not reveal where he had gone or the reason for his tears, even after being spanked for not telling them. The therapist decided to reenact what had occurred on the past Saturday, using the puppets. The P. family had worked with the puppets for a brief part of two sessions prior to this reenactment to practice using them.

Therapist: Let's see what happens when there is an argument in this family. We can use the puppets to reenact what happened this past Saturday. What do you think?

Mother: Fine with me.

Father: Okay with me.

Matt: I didn't do anything.

Therapist: Would you use your puppet to show what you did while the argument was going on?

Matt: I just stayed in my room and listened to tapes.

Therapist: Could you demonstrate that with your puppet?

Matt: I guess so.

Therapist: Good. And what about you? Could you work your puppet well enough to show us what you did?

James: (*Smiling proudly*) Yeah. I can do it.

Therapist: Very good. Now you awoke on Saturday morning and had plans to work in the garden and then to go to visit relatives in the afternoon. You said that everyone helped out in the garden without any difficulties over who should do the weeding or the trimming or the grass cutting, right?

Father: Right.

Therapist: Let's use this lamp table as the kitchen table. Everyone was sitting around it eating tuna sandwiches. Let's position our puppets around the table as we sat on Saturday. So where did things start to go wrong?

The argument was over something one of the relatives to be visited had said about Mother. As soon as Mother and Father started to raise their voices, Matt moved his puppet away from the table saying, "Here we go again," and sat on the couch. Shortly after he moved away from the table, James stood up and walked his puppet into the waiting room. At the end of the argument, Mother and Father called for James. After they stopped calling, he reentered the room sobbing with his puppet.

Therapist: Where did your puppet go?

James: To the lot. (*Sobbing*)

Therapist: And what did your puppet do there?

James: He cried. (*Began crying*)

Therapist: Why did your puppet cry?
James: Because . . . my mommy and daddy are divorced.

The therapist moved to have Mother and Father reassure James that they were not divorced and that they were disagreeing. He asked several questions about disagreeing and whether it means that they would be divorced soon. When asked why he did not confide in Matt, he said that he thought that his brother did not care that Mother and Father were divorced. Matt reassured him that Mother and Father were not divorced and explained his behavior. James appeared to be very much relieved. It was also agreed that James would join Matt during any future loud disagreements between Mother and Father in front of the children. If Matt was not at home, James could go to his room and watch television.

In subsequent sessions, Mother and Father used the puppets to explore a variety of ways to deal with their differences, without the accompanying hostility. Using the puppets, the children practiced alternative ways to deal with their parents' arguments. They found that it was easier to try alternatives with the puppets than in reenactments with each other.

4. USES

The use of puppets adds a kinetic dimension to the therapeutic process. It provides the family with the opportunity to move themselves into action, suggesting that they are responsible for their behavior. Parents may observe how their behavior affects their children. Children may also observe how their behavior affects their parents.

Following a people or puppet reenactment, try to discuss alternative behaviors and play them out by using the puppets. The physical exploration seems to reinforce the concept that change is possible. It also tends to facilitate integration of the new, functional material. A particular incident can be replayed "better" a second time, following some discussion or a suggestion from a group member. Also, the different members can exchange puppets and play others' roles. Puppets can open doors to the magical realm in which a family's myths and beliefs can be cavorted with and influenced to change.

C. Big Messages in Small Packages

1. RATIONALE

Pittman (1987) feels that there are few truly critical childhood situations, except school phobia, which would require immediate attention. Frequently, parents expect the symptomatic child to generate the means by which his objectionable behavior can be brought under control. If the child is unable to do so, he is punished, but not helped directly. When the punishment loses its effectiveness or the behavior becomes bizarre enough, the parents panic; they have a crisis on their hands and do not know what to do about it. They may now become somewhat hysterical and call the therapist, demanding to be seen immediately.

Often, a child's behavior is the flare in the night signaling parental difficulties in the marriage. Such problems may run the gamut from an inability to negotiate differences or insecurity in the parental role to dealing with pathology or abuse.

Other times, the parents' rush to straighten out what may be perceived as symptomatic of their child's possible abnormality may be a reaction to an isolated incident. A child pulling a fire alarm, throwing small stones across the street and accidentally hitting a passing car, placing a doll in the toilet and pulling the handle which flushes the toilet, or biting the dog might be examples of such behavior. If repeated, they could be indicative of a youngster with dysfunctional interactive patterns. As isolated incidents, however, they may represent childhood curiosity, imitation of something viewed on television, an attempt to imitate a parent's interaction with him, or a fighting fire with fire type of response to a specific situation.

The possibility of neurological or physical difficulties needs to be considered. The instruments of measurement and their interpretations, however, are frequently not reliable enough to accept as the gospel unless the disability has been documented over long periods of time or is readily apparent. Even then, it is possible that the diagnosis has resulted in more restrictive limitations than are necessary. Under most circumstances, it is best to assume that a child's behavior serves a purpose within the family system.

2. PROCEDURE

The therapist first needs to listen to what the panic-stricken parent has to say. Then the sense that the crisis can be handled, but will require time and everyone's cooperation, needs to be conveyed. Although an immediate appointment may be requested, when the therapist attempts to schedule an appointment, recreational activities (music lessons, karate, skating, homework, or television) frequently conflict with the times available.

All members of the household should be included in the first session(s): both parents, stepparents, grandparents, siblings, housekeepers, and any others. In addition, school reports and medical information can provide relevant insights into the parameters of the identified child's problems for a more accurate assessment. Identifying a time convenient for all and obtaining the school records can take anywhere from a day to a week. During this time, the family can begin to organize for their quest for help.

During the initial session(s) Pittman (1987) suggests that the child's behavior be accepted as the identified problem. The conditions needed to define the problem as clearly as possible must be identified. This process requires the therapist to democratize the system. A truce needs to be negotiated so that everyone can feel free to talk. All family members must feel safe from hysterical reactions and possible chastisement during and after the session. At the same time the therapist is asserting authority over the parental or adult subsystem(s), she must not overpower the child. While supporting parental authority, she must defend the child's right to speak.

Once the truce is arranged, the child can be instructed to describe the behavior and explain the reasons for it. The parents and significant others in the session are directed to listen to the child and to fathom his feelings. The parents are then requested to stop the behavior. The child is instructed to do what his parents tell him.

The therapist does not instruct the parents as to what might stop the objectionable behavior, but discourages the use of threats and punishment. There is no need to inform the parents of the necessity for them to change to become more effective parents. Such a suggestion could promote resistance to the changes which will have to be made.

Frequently, a child may suggest ways to control or stop his objectionable behavior. Sometimes the child will admit that the behavior is childish, but says it is common or normal for kids his age. Is it possible for parents to forget what it is like to be a child? Perhaps some parental expectations and goals are too heavily imbued with adult attitudes that, if met, could have the effect of skimming off those qualities which make childhood so special and entertaining for adults. Age-appropriate behaviors of children can also be disconcerting to adults from time to time.

Requesting that the parents understand before attempting to control the behavior increases the chances for success. Acceptance of this responsibility generally leads to change. Other issues are brought to the fore in the process of effecting change. These may involve difficulties between spouses or among siblings, or intergenerational problems. Most childhood crises are quickly resolved. Systemic changes take more time, however, with the different family members and subsystems often moving at different rates.

Pittman (1987) indicates that with improvement the therapeutic intervals can be increased, leading to termination. The child may be given the responsibility for determining when his attendance is needed as long as the behavior does not manifest itself. He might also determine the timetable for termination.

3. CASE EXAMPLE*

J was 11 years old and obese. He had the lowest grades in his class in all areas. His nickname was "whale." Both parents were obese. J's father was powerless and incapable. There was little else in J's mother's life other than arguing with the school about J. The school was adamant about therapy for J. An evening at home after dinner was described as follows: 1. Mother and Father would plead with J to do his homework. 2. J would refuse and cry. 3. Mother would bring food and father would give up and watch television. 4. Older brother (15 years old) would tease J until he cried. 5. Mother would intercede on J's behalf. 6. J would take his food and watch television with his father.

The plan that was put into operation put father in charge of overseeing J doing his homework for one hour each evening. If the homework was not finished, they would exercise for an equal amount of time and then complete it. Dinner would be served only when the homework was completed. If father did not do his part, mother would direct her comments to him and not to J.

Over the course of the next two weeks, the family was following the plan and feeling positive about their efforts. J's father, however, was having difficulties with the exercising; he was unable to continue for the hour. He would begin sobbing, J would begin sobbing, and mother would argue with the therapist or the school to go easier on her son. When older brother attempted to fill in for father, mother interfered; the teasing commenced; J cried; father cried; therapist persevered. Mother was convinced to return to school herself and became too busy to become involved with the plan. J began doing the homework, but did not turn it in to his

*Reprinted from *Turning Points: Treating Families in Transition and Crisis*, pp. 172–173, by Frank S. Pittman, III, M.D., by permission of W.W. Norton & Company, Inc. Copyright © 1987 by Frank S. Pittman, III.

teacher. Older brother, who replaced father as exercise partner when needed, threatened to beat J up if he did not turn in the work. J began doing the homework and exercise alone. Older brother became involved in other activities, but promised to resume in the same capacity should the need arise in the future.

4. USES

This technique allows the family to maintain its style in the solution of the problem(s). In situations where the difficulties occur under some circumstances but not others, all that may be required is for someone, usually a person outside the nuclear family—a grandparent, teacher, therapist—to indicate where the difficulties are and interact to interfere with the pattern giving rise to the difficulty.

In families where the dysfunctional patterns comprise the family style or approach to life, change is the most difficult. A family member who has somehow found a different way can play a significant role in effecting the necessary change from within.

The technique places the therapist in the driver's seat from which to address a wide variety of problems which manifest themselves during childhood within families of varying levels of stability. With severely dysfunctional families, the therapy is more difficult. One requirement for this technique to be effective is at least one active, functional person capable of impacting upon the problem, other than the therapist. If that person is not available, the first job of the therapist is to work to produce one.

III. TIPS AND TACTICS

1. Establish Personal Contact

Establish contact with the child by greeting him at the beginning of the session. A simple "Hello" will serve to communicate the therapist's availability. It is best not to overdo the initial contact. For some children, too much eye contact can be threatening (Keith in Combrink-Graham, 1986). The child will signal when he is ready to accept interaction with the therapist.

The therapist must also be available to acknowledge a child's attempt to establish contact. This may come in the form of a smile, a verbalization, a tap or pat, a wrinkling up of eyes, nose, and mouth just prior to turning away, or a reaching out to touch something the therapist is wearing.

Saying hello to three-year-old Allen at the very beginning of the first session did not produce a response from him. He explored the room, sat on his parents' laps, interacted with his brothers and sister somewhat, and sucked on his fingers. The therapist said good-bye, complimented him at the end of the session, and told his parents that they could bring some of his toys the next time.

Allen was again greeted at the beginning of session two. A toy was brought and he spent about half of the time in play sitting at the therapist's feet and rubbing against her legs. The therapist gently mussed his hair as she continued talking to another family member. The compliment and good-bye was freely given at the end of the session. With each session, additional contact was made until three or four sessions later there was a garbled verbal greeting from Allen. Things continued to improve afterwards.

2. Family Drawing

This drawing technique is a variation of the Team Picture technique described in the Structured Techniques section of the chapter. It could be used with any family in addition to or instead of the technique included in the above section. The reason for its inclusion is that it may be more effective when one is dealing with family members who insist on working independently.

Each person is given three sheets of paper and a few markers. They are instructed to draw three scenarios. The first is to represent the family problem. The second is to depict the problem solved, fixed, or "all better." The third is to show how the first picture can become the second picture. Following these instructions, the therapist suggests that each person "enjoy discovering something important" for himself as he works.

When all members have completed each art task, the work is shared and discussed. Similarities and differences need to be acknowledged and spoken about. The relative sizes of family members depicted, the amount of space the pictures occupy on each sheet of paper, the existence of "unspoken alliances," and the significance of the colors used can provide significant clues regarding the family system.

3. Use Toys

Most therapists who deal with children agree that toys are helpful tools to facilitate communication. The toys in the waiting room might reflect the items popular with children. Inside the therapy space, however, the toys should include items that could provide insight into the concerns in the child's life: dolls representing family members, a dollhouse, crayons, paper, and puppets, for example. Observing the child's play need not require that the therapist interact directly with the child.

4. Describe Actions or Feelings

Keith (1986) feels that directing questions to children can alienate them. It is far better to describe what they are doing than to question their actions or feelings: "You are smiling," perhaps followed by "You are happy about what your sister said," instead of "Are you smiling because you are happy about what your sister said." Once a relationship is established, the therapist might try making a mistake to encourage interaction: "You are smiling. You are unhappy about what your sister said." Children often enjoy catching and correcting the mistakes of adults.

5. Establish Therapist-Child Relationship

It is important to establish a relationship directly with children. This may be accomplished with talk, play, teasing, flattery, or by setting realistic limits and requiring compliance. An honest reprimand need not be taken negatively by children (Keith, 1986).

6. Interact on Child's Level

To improve contact with children, one can find it helpful to interact on the child's level. This usually requires that some time be spent squatting or sitting on the floor, talking or playing with a child (Chasin & White, 1989; Keith, 1986; Zilbach, 1986).

7. Use Reinforcement

Positive and negative reinforcement can be effectively used to shape behavior in session, especially with children who are difficult to manage (Anderson & Stewart, 1983). A smile, a hug, a flattering remark, a compliment, a star on a chart, or a tangible reward can go a long way with some children to change behaviors. This may enable feelings to be explored and family goals to proceed more evenly.

8. Discuss Significant Childhood Events

Include discussion of events which play prominently in childhood experiences, such as holidays, birthdays, family get-togethers, and religious events. Questions about how the family celebrates special occasions can provide as much insight into family life as discussions concerning the family problems. At the same time, these topics are of interest to children and will encourage their participation (Zilbach, 1986).

9. Celebrate in Session

Celebrate a birthday or a holiday in session. The process of preparing for these events provides a variety of opportunities to move families in the direction of functional changes in their patterns of interaction (Zilbach, 1986).

10. Utilize Stories About Family Problems

Have parents tell their children stories which relate to family problems (Wachtel, 1987). These can be told in session or at home. One crucial element is that the stories told be realistic in nature and based at least in part upon actual experiences. They can be about the parents' or other relatives' adventures as children or with children. They can be about adults' dreams or problems. They can be about animals. All occurrences in life do not have happy endings. The goal is to expose the child to a variety of feelings and experiences in some way related to the child's family.

Such stories frequently touch upon topics and feelings that the telling parent has not fully resolved. The activity allows the parent to work through his own issues in the telling. Structurally, the interactive patterns must shift to make time for the telling, move the parental focus away from the child while providing the child with a different kind of attention, and involve the parent and child in a mutually gratifying situation from which a new understanding can develop.

11. Model Parenting Skills

There is some disagreement about whether the therapist should parent the children in therapy (Keith, 1986) or leave the responsibility with the parents (Anderson & Stewart, 1983). In chaotic families or families in which parenting skills are identified as problematic, the therapist will need to be more involved with parenting. Many parents are capable, however, of handling their children. When a therapist interacts with children, it is worthwhile to bear in mind that their actions are being observed by the parents. In effect, therapists model parenting behavior whether or not it is intended. Generally it is better to coach parents in parenting unless the behavior is directed personally at the therapist. The object is to improve the skills of the parents and not to prove that the therapist is a better parent than the parents (Sherman, 1988).

12. Use a Cotherapist

Have a cotherapist in session to observe and, if invited, to interact with the child(ren) when not directly involved with the rest of the family group in session (Chasin, 1981; Keith, 1986).

13. Furnish Office Appropriately

Furnish the office with items comfortable for adults and children. Pillows, movable chairs, and beanbag chairs make the therapeutic environment more conducive for involving all family members (Chasin, 1981).

REFERENCES

Anderson, C. M. and Stewart, S. (1983). *Mastering resistance: A practical guide to family therapy.* New York: Guilford Press.

Carter, C. A. and McGoldrick, M. (1980). *The family life cycle: A framework for family therapy.* New York: Gardner Press.

Chasin, R. (1981). Involving latency and preschool children in family therapy. In A. S. Gurman (Ed.), *Questions & answers in the practice of family therapy* (pp. 32–35). New York: Brunner/Mazel.

Chasin, R. and White, T. B. (1989). The child in family therapy: Guidelines for active engagement across the age span. In L. Combrink-Graham (Ed.), *Children in family contexts.* New York: Guilford Press.

Combrink-Graham, L. (1985). Treating small children. *Family Therapy Networker, 9*(3), 21.

Framo, J. L. (1981). The integration of marital therapy with sessions with family of origin. In A. S. Gurman and D. P. Kniskern (Eds.), *Handbook of family therapy,* New York: Brunner/Mazel.

Giacomo, D. and Weissmark, M. (1985). Treating small children. *Family Therapy Networker, 9*(3), 21.

Keith, D. V. (1986). Are children necessary in family therapy? In L. Combrink-Graham (Ed.), *Treating young children in family therapy* (pp. 1–10). Rockville, MD: Aspen Publications.

Landgarten, H. B. (1987). *Family art psychotherapy: A clinical guide and casebook*. New York: Brunner/Mazel.

Mills, J. C. and Crowley, R. J., in collaboration with Ryan, M. O. (1986). *Therapeutic metaphors for children and the child within*. New York: Brunner/Mazel.

Pittman, III, F. S. (1987). *Turning points: Treating families in transition and crisis*. New York: W. W. Norton.

Sherman, R. (1988). Unpublished lecture on parenting. Queens College of the City University of New York.

Wachtel, E. F. (1987). Family systems and the individual child. *Journal of Marital and Family Therapy, 13*(1), 15–25.

Zilbach, J. A. (1986). *Young children in family therapy*. New York: Brunner/Mazel.

Additional Resources

Burns, R. C. (1982). *Self-Growth in families: Kinetic family drawings (K-F-D) research and applications*. New York: Brunner/Mazel.

Forehand, R. L. & McMahon, R. J. (1981). *Helping the non-compliant child: A clinician's guide to parent training*. New York: Guilford Press.

Lankton, C. H. & Lankton, S. R. (1989). *Tales of enchantment: Goal oriented metaphors for adults and children in therapy*. New York: Brunner/Mazel.

Schaeffer, C. E. & O'Connor, K. J. (Eds.) (1983). *Handbook of play therapy*. Somerset, NJ: John Wiley & Sons.

7

WINNING OVER
THE ADOLESCENT

"For almost every child, adolescence means one thing above all else: he wants to prove he is no longer a child. . . ."

(Adler, 1931)

I. INTRODUCTION

A. Discussion

1. ADOLESCENCE DESCRIBED

Adolescents strive to be recognized, to belong, and to control their lives. Knights in shining armor are they all, male and female, seeking various degrees of autonomy within their domain. Their exploits can severely test established relationships, boundaries, and limits worked out with both family and friends. Teenagers flirt with danger as they pit their talents against those they encounter, friend and stranger alike. Today's ally may become tomorrow's rival, only to be called upon 48 hours later to join a new foray into the growing-up process.

Lacking the experience, knowledge, and time required for coagulation of what is generally referred to as wisdom, many adolescents will joust at the drop of an offhanded comment, the rolling of an eye, or a simple reminder concerning a task to be completed. Many tempt fate and put their very lives on the line by experimenting with harmful substances or following through on a challenge.

Pittman (1987) calls this period "the time of normal psychosis." It is a time when family equilibrium must be maintained to forge the adult who will emerge from the maturational gauntlet. In primitive societies, childhood ends with the onset of adolescence. The young adults are expected to take their places alongside their elders in the community, responsible for themselves and whatever possessions they are given or manage to acquire. In modern Western society, this is not the custom (Lowe, 1983).

2. EFFECTS OF ADULT INFLUENCE

The argument has been made that the adolescent's psychotic normalcy is a condition fostered by adults seeking to maintain control. Adler (1931) suggests that "The more parents try to prove he is a child, the more he will fight to prove the opposite. Out of this struggle, an antagonistic attitude develops and we then are provided with a typical picture of 'adolescent negativism'." Pearl (1978) writes that teenagers need to be useful and will be, if not to society then to themselves.

Every adolescent does not experience the kind of internal conflicts for which parents are advised to prepare as the teenage years of their children approach. Many maintain fairly stable relationships with their parents and tend to refrain from assailing the community with actions indicative of a lack of respect for social institutions and policies (Gallatin, 1976). They go to school, work through their problems, and live their lives without the acute contrariety with which the teen years tend to be associated.

3. SIX TYPOLOGIES

Pittman (1987) describes six troubled adolescent typologies, linking them to parental life-styles: "(1) underground adolescents, (2) sociopathic adolescents, (3) rebellious adolescents, (4) adolescents marked for failure, (5) imperfect adolescents, and (6) rescuing adolescents." The characteristics of each are summarized below.

1. The undergrounders seek independence from parental involvement in their lives. Usually, the parents are involved in their own lives and do not have the time or feel the need to become involved in their child's world. There is little interaction between parents and child.

2. The sociopaths are society's rule breakers. This kind of behavior is usually sanctioned and complemented by the parental subsystem's behavior pattern. In most cases, the child learns this behavior from the parents, who

take pride in circumventing or breaking rules themselves. Excuses are made and lies are told to protect their youngster.

3. Rebels challenge parental authority outright. Their quest for independence, however, is a cover for their dependency needs. The social order is safe. As soon as the punishment is meted out, the resistance folds. The parents of such children tend to fear their own freedom and work hard at establishing restrictions for themselves. Their rebellious adolescent sons and daughters are seeking the means to justify their conforming to the family style.

4. Children who do not like themselves are marked for failure. Usually this begins in childhood, often a result of a variety of observable deficiencies—obesity, a physical handicap, a lack of coordination, retardation, visible deformities, or poor hygiene. At times, these children are embarrassments to their parents and other family members. They are frequently depressed and feel they have nowhere to turn. Their acting out or involvement with deviant subcultures is one way to obtain attention and acceptance.

5. In families where competition is keen, expectations soar higher with every accomplishment. The values and range of acceptable behaviors are expected to be rigidly adhered to regardless of changes in the social environment or the actual abilities of the adolescent. Here, conditions are ripe for the diagnosis of imperfections. Teenagers who are raised in such environments tend to have little trouble out in the world. Their shortcomings are perceived and considered problematic only by members of the family, including themselves.

6. In troubled marriages, it is frequently the adolescent who attempts to save the family. A sacrificial knight, the teen develops symptoms to call attention to the difficulties in the marriage. The usual reward is indignant chastisement by the lord and lady of the manor.

As the adolescent explores personal issues concerning identity, social competence, teenage narcissism, and separation (Fishman, 1988), the family may need to deal with the resulting impact on established responsibilities, changes in the homeostatic interactions expected within some relationships, and challenges presented by the new information gleaned from wider communal exposure (Carter & McGoldrick, 1980). How these issues and behavior changes are handled by the family of origin and the social institutions with which the adolescents interact impact heavily upon the teenager's expectations of therapy and the therapist.

B. Definitions

Adolescence is generally defined as the period in life between childhood or puberty and adulthood. It has its origins in the Latin "adolescere," meaning "to grow up." An adolescent, then, would be one in the process of growing up.

The word "teen" is derived from the Old English "teona," meaning "injury" or "grief" (Webster's Seventh, p. 906) and damage or trouble (World Book Dictionary). Webster's (p. 906) cites two archaic definitions of "teen": "MISERY, AFFLICTION."

The word "teens" is commonly defined as those numbers from 13 through 19. Accordingly, today, the word "teen" tends to refer to someone between 13 and 19 years of age, an abbreviated form of the word "teenager." Interestingly, it is often used as a synonym for "adolescent."

II. STRUCTURED TECHNIQUES

Introduction

1. THE BASICS

Underpinning the current research are what Fishman (1988) calls the "Essential Techniques." These are general categories of interventions which provide the therapist with directionality. They are goal-establishing, but do not address specialized problems. Often, a combination of these techniques will lead to a design that will match the needs of families with adolescents. Very briefly summarized below, they include the following:

a) *Establishing boundaries*—The therapist engages in the process of appropriately positioning family members within subsystems.

b) *Enactment*—The therapist identifies significant dysfunctional patterns, stages and encourages the family members to dramatize the identified patterns, and intervenes until functional patterns emerge.

c) *Unbalancing*—The therapist purposely joins a family member or subsystem for a period of time to foster exploration of different aspects of the interactive family system.

d) *Reframing*—The therapist offers the family a different interpretation of their reality to move the members to seek alternative paths to change their dysfunctional patterns.

e) *Identifying Abilities*—The therapist facilitates the use and recognition of individuals' areas of competence in the search for acceptable change in the family system.

f) *Energy*—The therapist engages in the process of modulating the "degree of feeling in the room" to promote an understanding of the "therapeutic message."

2. NEEDS TO ADDRESS

The therapy for families with adolescent members needs to include roles of substance for the teen. The therapist, if she expects to effect systemic change, must address the young adult's needs within a frame acceptable to the other family members. In addition, the techniques employed to facilitate change need to move the individuals comprising the family unit in the direction of meaningful modes of social interaction. The following specific techniques can be used with most families.

A. The Family Council

1. RATIONALE

This technique is adapted from Grunwald and McAbee (1985). The majority of adolescents choose to attempt to run the gauntlet adult society lays out for them. In many cases, this results in perpetuating reliance on immature behaviors and institutionalizing the childish treatment against which most young adults rail as they move along. The usual authoritarian nature of adult patterns of interaction with teenagers tends to deprive the adolescent of the knowledge and skills needed, when they come of age, to function effectively in our democratic, adult society.

2. PROCEDURE

The intent of the Family Council technique is to provide the context within which all family members can democratically plan and execute the family business. It is important for the therapist to outline the parameters within which the family will need to function once they agree to participate in this ritual. A regular meeting time and place must be agreed upon. It is also necessary for all family members to agree to the free exchange of ideas and feelings in an atmosphere of mutual respect, without fear of retribution later. Although all family members are council members, attendance is not compulsory if the members agree to accept the council's decisions in their absence.

Each member is to be allowed the right to propose items for every Council meeting's agenda. Items can include individual or group concerns and activities that involve family resources: chores and responsibilities, family outings, allowance, privacy, and behavior. In addition, the communication of feelings, experiences, and recognition for achievements can add a positive and uplifting spirit to such council meetings.

The meetings are conducted by a chairperson, who should be rotated among those capable of carrying out this responsibility. When a family member other than a parent is chairperson, parents cannot have the right to override the chair's decisions. Democratic principles are adhered to and minutes may be taken. Unanimity with regard to a course of action is preferable to a majority vote, however. All must agree to abide by the council's decisions once made, including the intended spirit. Changes can be negotiated at subsequent meetings.

In therapy, the family's experiences are described and discussed. The therapist initially needs to focus upon the fostering of the process, stepping in as a consultant when difficulties arise.

Some additional considerations for the family to deal with in the organizing of the Family Council could be (Grunwald & McAbee, 1985):

1. The length of the meetings;
2. How much time each family member is allowed to speak;
3. What to do about members who do not adhere to agreements worked out by the Council;
4. Setting short- and long-range goals;
5. How to avoid turning the Council into a complaint resolution board.

That all of the members understand and agree to a set of basic rules is essential. The family also needs to be cautioned that the first few meetings may not be as fruitful as what might be expected.

3. CASE EXAMPLE

In the session segment below the therapist reinforces the importance of everyone's participation.

Mother: Well, we managed to get through our first meeting.
Therapist: Yes.

Mother: Yes and everyone had a chance to talk and say what was on their minds. I must admit, I was surprised at what my son had to say about school. I don't know if I can believe all that he says. I don't know.

Son: But that's the way it is, Mom.

Therapist: I am impressed.

Mother: You are?

Therapist: I am.

Mother: At what?

Therapist: At you and your son. Your son was trusting enough to talk about an issue over which he and the family are at odds. You respected that trust by listening to what he had to say.

Father: We all listened and we all talked. But we didn't decide on anything.

Therapist: You spoke.

Father: I told him how disappointed I was about him. . . .

Therapist: So you used the family council as a forum to gently tongue lash your son.

Father: I didn't really think of it that way. He brought up the subject and I thought I'd let my feelings be known about it. He took it all well, though, I got to say. But, as my wife said, we didn't get to decide on anything. Nothing's really changed.

Therapist: I hear you. (*To Daughter.*) Did you participate?

Daughter: Yeah, said some things I don't really remember now. Ask one of them.

Therapist: (*To Daughter.*) Maybe you were uncomfortable this first time.

Daughter: Yeah, I didn't think the meeting was going right. Most of the time we spent talking about my brother.

Therapist: You felt that your brother didn't deserve that much of the family time.

Daughter: Well, no, but we should have talked about other things more.

Therapist: How did you inform the other council members of your feelings?

Daughter: I just didn't say much.

Therapist: (*To Daughter.*) The council needs members like you who don't just go along with the drift of things. You can help the others, I think, if you speak your thoughts and feelings when your turn comes.

Daughter: (*Shrugs shoulders.*)

Therapist: I see. (*Long pause.*) You said that you listened to your brother and mother.

Daughter: Yes. I did. I said a few things about how it was difficult to believe some of his excuses for not doing things sometimes. He once told me that. . . .

Therapist: Seems like a good first meeting to me. How could this council have been more effective? The chairperson last.

In subsequent sessions other process elements were encouraged. Important items addressed later in the session were the need for an agenda and how to move from discussion to formulating a resolution for action. Tabled until the next session was how to negotiate different points of view regarding the same problem.

4. USES

The Family Council provides a safe environment within which family members can come together to exchange information, express feelings and ideas, identify areas of agreement and disagreement, and plan for the future. It is useful within many contexts and with a wide variety of families. The technique facilitates role differentiation, boundary identification, and the structuring of subsystems within the family. Members' reports concerning family interactions during meetings can provide information about behaviors not always observable in session. The technique is also adaptable to many family therapy approaches.

B. Contracting

This technique is based upon contracting as described by Rutherford (1975).

1. RATIONALE

One of the rights of an adult is to negotiate the terms of one's contract. Accompanying this right is the responsibility of living up to the negotiated terms of the agreement. Mediated solutions can be perceived as imposed and, as such, may encourage a search for ways to circumvent the terms of such agreements. If an agreement is imposed by adults, a teen's self-perception of status as "child" can lead to denial of responsibility for living up to the terms as a form of rebellion. Inclusion in the formulation of the terms of a solution to an adolescent's situation tends to promote a greater degree of compliance.

Contractual agreements should be short, covering only easily attainable goals at first. This maximizes the success factor. Below are two contract outlines that cover a wide range of applicable concessions. Separate formats and stipulations are given for parent and adolescent. This is most accessible for easy reference. In practice, each contract would include rights and responsibilities of both generations.

2. PROCEDURE

Rutherford (1975) identifies 10 items needed to establish an effective behavioral contract:

1. Specify the behavior(s) to be dealt with in the contract. In addition, identify the precursors and the resultant behaviors.
2. Organize the contract to include the date(s), time(s), expected behavior(s), amounts or extent of consequences, and names of all parties signing and involved with the contract.
3. Negotiations should be conducted by the principal parties entering into the contract to ensure equitable treatment.
4. Wording must be positive to promote compliance. Positive reinforcement for compliance with the contractual terms also needs to be included.
5. When the target behavior is new, the shaping process needs to be spelled out in the contract. Specify in the agreement if the behavior exists within the family members' patterns of interaction.
6. The presence of a mediator can facilitate negotiations when changes in behaviors on both sides are necessary.
7. All parties should sign the contract.
8. The effect(s) of successful and nonsuccessful fulfillment of contractual obligations needs to be included in the document.
9. Accomplishing the changes stipulated in the agreement should result in the providing of the reinforcement specified. Smaller encouragements may be included in the contract for the accomplishment of the necessary changes leading to the desired result(s).
10. The movement to adolescent suggested behavioral changes and consequences needs to be made at the first opportunity. The more active the involvement of the teen in the process, the better the chances that the effects will be carried over into other areas of the teen's life.

In addition, there must be included a statement addressing the occasional difficulty in the fulfillment of contracted responsibilities. For example: (a) If, for any reason, a family member is unable to fulfill an obligation, a change may be negotiated with another family member; or (b) If a family member is sick or physically unable to fulfill responsibilities, an equitable distribution of those chores will be made. Payback will not be necessary unless the condition persists for a period of two weeks, at which time the family will meet to negotiate possible changes in responsibilities.

3. CASE EXAMPLE

The Smiths initiated therapy to avoid the perceived necessity of having to administer physical punishment to control their teenage son and daughter. They demanded respect and obedience from their children; they felt that they were being taken advantage of due to the adoption of a lenient attitude when the children were younger. The children felt that their parents had become overbearing and unrealistic in the expectations for them; they described the parents as "slave masters." Specific areas of conflict centered around chores, clothing, and allowance.

The therapist initiated discussions to explore the feasibility of entering into a contractual family agreement which would address those issues. Involving the adolescents during this initial exploratory phase was the primary focus of the therapist. The concept was examined in session and accepted. Following further discussion in therapy, all agreed that it would be best if the parents would enter into negotiations with each of their children separately. The family began their negotiations with the goal of working out arrangements which would promote harmony and strengthen the family unit.

Once the areas of dispute were identified, the therapist provided the format for the agreement. She suggested that the family attempt to negotiate a separate contract for each problem area instead of negotiating a comprehensive document containing the terms of agreement on every issue. During the first meeting, the therapist was asked to mediate differences of opinion. She refused, offering instead to suggest criteria for the evaluation of the relative importance of one's position. Questions were suggested, such as: Which will bring the family closer? What would I ask for if I were in his shoes? Can I live with this? Can I afford this? What will I be receiving in return? How important is this to my life-style? Are my needs really more important than his on this issue?

The contracting process was easily mastered by the family. Following an initial success, a more comprehensive contract was negotiated, which, at termination, was the following:

Contract

DATE: March 17, 1990

We acknowledge that this contract was entered into freely, without coercion. The terms stipulated below represent the fruits of the parties' negotiations, during which all were given the opportunity to speak and be heard with regard to each of the items listed below. Our signatures represent our willingness to abide by these terms.

I. Alice and Rick agree to do the following:

A. *Chores*

1. Dust and vacuum one's bedroom once a week.

2. Straighten one's room prior to going to sleep daily; especially hang clothing in the closet or fold and put it in the appropriate drawer.

3. Assist in cleaning the rest of the house every other week, on a rotational basis—Rick one week, Alice the following week.

4. Walk the dog after dinner, on a rotational basis—Alice one night, Rick the following night.

5. Clear the table and put the dishes into the dishwasher every fourth night on a rotational basis with our parents.

6. Help with the maintenance of the garden and exterior of the house as requested by mother or father once a week.

B. *Allowance*

1. Considered as compensation for doing chores.

2. To cover carfare to and from school, entertainment, the purchase of some articles of clothing, and savings.

3. Amounts: Alice—10 dollars per week. Rick—12 dollars per week.

4. Allowance will not be decreased if part-time jobs are taken, with parental consent, unless negotiated in a separate contract.

C. *School*

1. Alice and Rick agree to attend regularly, unless sick.

2. Rick and Alice agree to complete homework and studying prior to going out with friends or watching television, unless parental permission to do otherwise is requested and granted. Rescheduling homework and study time is to be worked out prior to making such a request.

3. Alice and Rick agree to respect teachers: will not answer back, will follow instructions. Any difficulties will be brought to parents' attention before any action is taken, when possible, and afterward if not possible.

4. Rick and Alice agree to inform teachers, supervisors, guidance personnel, and parents of difficulties in subject areas or with other students.

5. Alice and Rick agree to share with parents written communications from school personnel.

D. *Clothing*

1. Rick and Alice agree to inform parents of anticipated needs.

2. Alice and Rick agree to provide parents with pictures or descriptions of current styles prior to going to the stores when clothing is needed.

3. Rick and Alice agree to consider sale items.

4. Alice and Rick agree to purchase articles of clothing out of savings or pay the difference when purchases are considered too expensive by parents.

5. Rick and Alice agree to refrain from purchasing clothing displaying messages, pictures, or symbols objectionable to other family members. If in doubt, they will inquire. Objectionable purchases will be returned within the refund time limit set by the store from which the clothing was purchased.

E. *Conduct*

1. Alice and Rick agree to refrain from vulgarity.

2. Rick and Alice agree to eat meals with the family, unless permission from parents to do otherwise is requested and granted prior to the meal to be missed.

3. Alice and Rick agree to accompany parents on visits to relatives when notice is given by one parent at least one week in advance or, in emergency situations to be determined, in consultation with all family members, when possible. When not possible, Alice and Rick will make the visit in an emergency situation at the request of one parent.

4. Rick and Alice agree to leave telephone numbers and other pertinent information regarding their whereabouts when away from the house longer than the typical school day; on weekends, when away longer than four hours.

5. Alice and Rick agree to call every five hours or as agreed in private discussion, when away from home.

6. Rick and Alice agree to adhere to the tenets of this contract in the absence of either mother or father or both.

7. Alice and Rick agree to follow the directions, if any, left for them on the answering machine in the absence of their parents. Disagreements with instructions are to be brought up at a family meeting when parents return and adjustments, where appropriate, will be negotiated and made.

II. Parents agree to do the following:

A. *Privacy*

1. Mother and father agree to knock on children's doors and announce intention to enter prior to so doing.

2. Mother and father will respect adolescents' request to delay entry into room.

3. Mother and father agree to refrain from searching adolescent's room or clothing without cause and in the absence of the adolescent. Both parents must agree and inform the party of the reason prior to the search.

B. *Transportation*

1. Mother and father agree to drive Alice and Rick to softball practice and games, library, dentist, as necessary, and to friends' homes once a week.

2. Father agrees to purchase bicycle for Alice.

3. Mother and father agree to permit Rick to use the car two nights a week.

C. *Financial Arrangements*

1. Father agrees to pay full allowance on time weekly, when deserved.

2. Mother and father agree to pay for all essential clothing items: socks/stockings, undergarments, shoes, sneakers, pants, skirts, dresses, shirts/blouses, jackets, coats, ties, scarves, hats.

3. Mother and father agree to pay for all school supplies, trips, and other special school events. Social events will need to be discussed at least one week prior to the event or as soon as possible prior to attending the event if prior knowledge of the event is less than one week.

4. Mother and father agree to pay for piano lessons for Rick and music lessons for Alice if interest is expressed and discussed.

5. Mother and father agree to pay telephone bills, except for long distance calls made by Alice or Rick and their friends.

D. *Conduct*

1. Mother and father will schedule time for family discussion when convenient for all members of the family.

2. Mother and father agree to set aside time for activities with family members individually and as a group.

3. Mother and father agree to refrain from use of vulgarity.

4. Mother and father agree to stop physical abuse or punishment, unless physically threatened themselves.

5. Mother and father agree to consult with Rick and Alice prior to planning an outing or vacation.

6. Mother and father agree to leave telephone numbers and other pertinent information on the bulletin board if they expect to be away from the house for a period longer than their workday; on weekends for a period longer than five hours.

7. Mother and father agree to call home periodically when away from home for a full day or longer, at least once a day.

III. If any member of this family cannot carry out his/her responsibilities, as agreed to in the above contract, he/she will be required to arrange for someone else to fill in for him/her. We agree to negotiate fairly, openly, and honestly.

The contract was signed by each family member. Implementation difficulties of individual items were resolved and renegotiations, when necessary, occurred between subsystems prior to the compilation of this contract. A few other issues were resolved in subsequent sessions. In follow-up contacts with the family, it was determined that the contract continued to guide the family. It was amended with regard to allowance, car use on the weekends when Alice obtained a learner's permit, and chores, which had to be redistributed when Rick left for college.

4. USES

The intergenerational contracting technique provides the adolescent with pragmatic opportunities to exercise control over his life. The budding adult is exposed to the burdens and rewards of negotiation. Each contractual agreement that meets with success will enhance their relationships with their parents. Contracting provides a graphic framework within which specific problems can be identified and solutions negotiated in a nonjudgmental, democratic environment.

C. The "Winners Bet" With Adolescents (Williams & Weeks, 1984)

1. RATIONALE

The "Winners Bet" is a paradoxical technique. Such interventions have been found to be especially useful when one is dealing with oppositional and resistant clients. Designed to accomplish the opposite of that which is suggested, they can be very effective in dealing with adolescents who manifest oppositional behaviors.

A brief summation of Papp's (1983) three ingredients for the implementation of a successful paradox bears reviewing here:

1. The problem is reframed in a positive manner. A case is made for the maintenance of the behavior as having a beneficial impact upon the family. Worried anxiety becomes a means of obtaining time to relax, impatience an expression of confidence, intolerance a high level of expectation.

2. It is requested that the frequency of the behavior increase. The client is instructed to consider the possibilities of each family member having difficulties at least three times a day. At the very first sign of anxiety, everything needs to stop for 30 minutes of relaxation; when a family member is late, even by one minute, pacing and grumbling is to commence and not stop until the individual arrives and thanks the pacer-grumbler for demonstrating the high level of confidence that the other

individual would arrive on time; when any rule is broken, the breaker is to be scolded for breaking the rule and, in return, the breaker is to find some overt way to thank the scolder for upholding such a high level of expectation.

3. When change is reported, the therapist needs to communicate concern for the possible consequences: "I don't know what will happen if there is a change in this behavior. I can only say that there may be problems should you stop. It probably would be better for all concerned if you continue with what you were doing." The family has to *convince the therapist* of the need to abandon the patterns of interaction in which the family is engaged.

2. PROCEDURE

The therapist structures the winners bet to provide for the continuation of the dysfunctional behavior. The therapist suggests or strongly recommends the continuation as being in the best interest of the family. If the adolescent chooses to be oppositional, the position he must assume is that of giving up the behavior. Should the teen continue the behavior, as advised, he is put in the position of listening to the authority figure. The therapist must win. This intervention often works best when delivered as a bet or a challenge to the adolescent. If the therapist chooses to bet, the stakes must be meaningful to the adolescent.

3. CASE EXAMPLE

A single parent came for therapy complaining that the behavior and language exchanged between her two teenage sons in the house were unacceptable to her. She had tried a variety of ways to convince them to behave differently. She had reached the point at which she felt that physical force would need to be employed if she wished to maintain control.

The boys thought that their mother was too strict and rigid. They felt that she was out of touch with teenage behavior. They resented having to give up time on the weekend to come to therapy. Her boys also said that their friends behaved in a similar manner when they arrived home from school. They didn't like her shouting at them and the threats she had made to punish them more severely if they wouldn't do as she said.

The therapist obtained a fairly detailed description of the boys' after-school and their mother's after-work behavior pattern. The boy's behavior and work in school were good based upon teacher reports on their Report

Cards. She inquired about the boys' friends and their homes and parents. Toward the end of the third session, she explained to the family that she felt that there were many things the family members wanted to work out with each other and that the after-school interactions were a good area to begin the work. The family agreed.

The therapist then suggested that adolescence is the stage of development during which letting off steam is to be expected. She went on to say that she thought that what they were doing was healthy and from all reports good for their academic work in school. She then bet that if they would continue the behavior until they had to retire for the night, that they would feel better in the morning and improve their grades in school. In addition, she recommended that they begin in the mornings, before school, instead of waiting until after school.

The therapist explained to their mother that if the boys were denied the freedom to cut up outside of school such behavior might begin during the school day. The mother agreed that such a situation would be worse than the present one.

At the next session, the mother reported that her sons had calmed down quite a bit. The boys denied that any major change in their behavior had occurred. The therapist responded with a loud sigh of relief immediately following the boys' denial and reiterated her concerns about a normal adolescence and their grades should the behavior not continue. She then moved the focus to other issues. At the end of the session, she reminded the boys that she would like them to increase their cutting-up behaviors. The behavior continued to decrease and ceased to be a family issue. Their grade averages and school conduct remained as they had been prior to the intervention.

Another case in which the winners bet was effective involved Mr. and Mrs. M. and their 12-year-old daughter, Sue. The M. family came to therapy embroiled in a variety of conflicts concerning parenting. Their daughter had begun to experiment with lipstick and nail polish to improve her appearance. Mr. and Mrs. M. felt that this was the beginning of an adolescent rebellion which had to be nipped in the bud. They prohibited her from leaving the house with lipstick on her face or in her possession and would search her for both lipstick and nail polish before they allowed her to go out. She retaliated by refusing to engage in conversation at the dinner table, disobeying the house rules, and neglecting her responsibilities.

Following some discussion during the next sessions, the therapist suggested that perhaps Mr. and Mrs. M. were reluctant to let their baby begin to grow up. Sooner or later, Sue would be allowed to use lipstick, mascara, and a variety of other makeups. The therapist suggested that Mr. and Mrs. M.

allow her to use the lipstick and nail polish as long as she also applied all other types of makeup with it. The other kinds of makeup, if properly applied, would decrease the glaring effects of the lipstick and nail polish alone.

After some negotiation, Mr. and Mrs. M. and their daughter agreed to a trial period of one month. The therapist bet Sue that by the end of the month she would enjoy every aspect involved in the wearing of makeup: the challenge of choosing and matching colors, shopping for different types of makeup and the appropriate applicators, making new friends, sitting in front of the mirror applying her makeup early in the morning and removing it every night before going to bed.

The therapist also bet that if she learned to apply the makeup properly, her parents would become so accustomed to her wearing makeup that they would have no qualms about extending their permission to do so. The therapist cautioned Sue, however, that if she appeared without makeup, her parents could have reason to think that maybe she was losing interest and might renew efforts to attempt to convince her to stop and be their baby girl again.

By the end of the month, Sue announced that she had decided to stop wearing makeup. She said that it was too time-consuming to apply every morning and she felt out of place when she was with her friends. She did not like the kind of people with whom she was beginning to find herself spending time. She requested that she be allowed to wear some makeup when she went to a party.

The therapist cautioned her to think over what she wanted to do and to consider the consequences. What would she say to her newly acquired friends? What would she say to her old friends? How would they take her decision? The following week Sue attended session without makeup and continued to do so through termination.

4. USES

The winners bet provides the adolescent with a means to evaluate specific oppositional behaviors, as long as the behaviors to be encouraged are not life-threatening. Frequently, it is the ability to make decisions about themselves for themselves that is the crux of the matter. Once this is granted, a more objective evaluation of the behavior can be made by the teenager.

The therapist needs to evaluate the circumstances carefully prior to implementation. Certainly, the paradox must be tailor-made for the adolescent recipient of the bet or challenge. However, the therapist cannot lose sight of the possible objections which might be raised by other family members upon hearing that the continuation of the behavior is the recommendation of the expert. The rationale presented by the therapist must be reasonable or, at least, minimally acceptable to the other family members. Sometimes the therapist may need to rely upon past successes or the joining which has occurred in previous sessions to gain the needed cooperation from the family.

III. TIPS AND TACTICS

Leveton (1984) compares "working with adolescents . . ." to "working with people engaged in a struggle for freedom and independence." Teenagers play upon systemic and individual weaknesses in their attempts to open the system up to make room for their growth. If the families cannot handle the problems created by their child's maneuvers, an impasse between subsystems or individual members can develop. Energies then turn toward developing symptoms as a means of advertising for a resolving agent. The therapist needs to overcome the impasses so that resolution can occur.

Opening new avenues for exploration can ameliorate the struggles and keep the therapy moving. The following tactics provide the therapist with a variety of frames within which the family members can work to redesign family patterns.

1. Withhold Responding

At times the teenager may attempt to provoke the therapist as authority figure. This testing behavior requires no active response from the therapist. It is best to listen attentively to what is being said. Advisements, judgments, agreements, or interpretations would be "counter-therapeutic" (McHolland, 1985). The therapist could acknowledge that she had heard what the adolescent had said and move on to something or someone else.

2. Skirting the Whirlpool

In working with teenagers, family members often request that the therapist intervene on behalf of one member or subsystem before she has had an opportunity to evaluate the needs of the entire system. Unconcerned parents or foreign-born parents being taken advantage of by their children through the withholding of information or the providing of misinformation may also tempt the therapist to form a coalition. It is important for the therapist to be aware of any personal bias and the reasons for it. However, Leveton (1984) and McHolland (1985) note that unbalancing the system before adequate joining with all family members has been accomplished generally leads to the failure of the therapy.

To skirt the whirlpool, the therapist might respond by saying: "I'd like to help, and I will try, but I have to do it my own way. That means trying to get you and the folks talking together more successfully. I will try to help you to make room for yourself and say what you think. I will try to get them to really listen. But I'll be doing the same for them—trying to get you to listen to their side, also. First, I want us all to get a clear picture of what's going on. Then, later, we can talk more about what to do" (Leveton, 1984, P. 174).

3. Use Positive Statements

Positive statements can break blaming or accusatory communication patterns (Nelson, 1983). A statement of one's feelings or thoughts without an accompanying value judgment conveys respect for differences at the same time that it communicates the existence of a difference of opinion or value. The point is to move family members to say what they want or feel without attacking others for wrongdoings.

For example: Mr. B. was interrupted while reading the newspaper. "Dad, I need a lift to Cathy's house. You're just sitting around doing nothing, so how about dropping me off?" The first statement was positive. The follow-up was accusative which, combined with the interruption, resulted in an argument. A simple "Could you drop me off?" would have served Mr. B.'s daughter better.

4. Doubling

Either the therapist or another family member can double for an individual (Leveton, 1984). The person doubling represents the hidden agenda or the underlying feelings of a family member. The double communicates the things the other person may be thinking or feeling, but not saying. It is possible for a family member to have more than one double. For example:

Family member: I want to be closer to you.
Double: I am dependent on you.
Double: I am being rebuffed by you.

A variation might require the double to respond by asking the question the family member's statement implies:

Family member: I want to be closer to you.
Double: Do I?
Family member: Yes, I feel I need you.
Double: Am I dependent upon you?
Family member: Yes.
Double: Can I do anything on my own?
Family member: Yes, but I like to know that I have your approval.

Another variation could be to request the double(s) to respond with extreme interpretations:

Family member: I want to be closer to you.
Double: I think you hate me!
Double: I want you to pay more attention to me.
Double: I love you more than I feel comfortable saying to you.
Double: I want to replace the twin beds separated by a night table with a king-size bed.

Doubling presents a family member with another's interpretation of the motivation behind statements made. This technique tends to quickly focus attention upon central issues. Frequently, intense and emotional experiences evolve. When this occurs, the therapist needs to allow time to aid the family member in the integration of the new information.

5. Active Fantasy (Leveton, 1984)

Most people, especially adolescents, would agree that things could always be better. If only my parents would leave me alone, if only my daughter would come straight home from school, I should have spent more time with my son when he was younger, and I should just chuck it all to do what I really wanted to do for a long time are examples of some of the wishes clients have made in session. Such wishes are the first step toward fantasizing.

Once the area of concern is identified, the therapist can move to encourage exploration through the use of questions. For example: What if upon awakening tomorrow your parents informed you that they would leave you alone from then on? What would be different? What would you think? Could you describe your feelings? How would your situation improve? Would this cause you any difficulty? What would your relationship with your parents be like then? How would this change affect school? socializing? television watching?

The therapist could ask the family member to close his eyes, visualize the activities of the day, and describe the fantasy to the family. A variation might be to ask all the family members to close their eyes and visualize what their day would be like if one family member's fantasy were to come true. They could then take turns relating what they envision would result from the change. A discussion of their hypothetical imaginings could result in uncovering new potential directions for change. The Active Fantasy technique helps to increase creativity in the search for options.

6. Wilderness Therapeutic Experiences

Mason (1987) uses a series of wilderness adventures as the milieu within which therapeutic issues are explored. When integrated into the therapeutic process, experiences such as rock climbing, canoeing, or backpacking can bring significant impact upon familial patterns of interaction. The therapist may or may not accompany the family on their adventure. If the therapist chooses to do so, daily discussions of the therapeutic issues would be possible. If not, the therapist may ask the family members to keep daily journals.

Preparation for the wilderness experience is carried out under the guidance of professionals. There are organizations which can put therapists in touch with groups which provide such services. Mason specifically mentions Outward Bound as such a program. A new environment, accompanied by the increase in the anxiety level which tends to accompany such ventures, opens the system to be more receptive to the possibility for change.

A highly efficient, controlling mother may have to rely upon another family member to steer the canoe. A weak, ineffective father may demonstrate his ability to carry the heavier pack of supplies for the family. A self-centered teenage daughter may be given the responsibility of belaying her father, mother, or sibling(s). An oppositional son experiences entrusting his life to a father who vehemently opposes his values as he rappels over the edge of a cliff.

In session, the therapist continues to work through the family's perceptions, thoughts, and feelings, using the activities as a backdrop for possible changes in dysfunctional systemic patterns. It is important that the adolescent(s) be given full participatory status.

It is suggested that the specific activity be fitted to the family's metaphorical perception of itself: climbing, paddling, or walking through life. If a family perceives itself as mushing along, dogsledding might be the appropriate therapeutic adventure.

Mason (1987) matches the family with the type of activity, the specific program, and the location for the experience. She finds that the concreteness of the adventure, which requires the family to call upon their intellect, emotions, and physical capabilities, provides the family with a wholistic experience. This tends to increase self-awareness, a sense of cooperative effort to accomplish a goal, and intimacy.

7. Bibliotherapeutic Experiences

The term "bibliotherapy" means treatment through the use of books. The use of bibliotherapy to facilitate exploration for solutions to problems, like the wilderness experience, can be integrated into other approaches to family therapy. Poems, short stories, plays, and films can be used in a similar fashion. The term "literatherapy" is used to cover the therapies involving the use of any of the variants of literature as the primary treatment modality (Rubin, 1978).

Spache (1978) describes the values of bibliotherapy as providing a family or a family member with the knowledge that the problem(s) being faced have been dealt with by others and that solutions exist. In addition, a deeper self-awareness, understanding of human behavior, and information concerning the world outside the individual's community can be obtained. Another by-product of the process is to expose the reader(s) to problems which may be down the road or which have not been identified as such. Within this context, such newly discovered difficulties are accompanied by at least one solution.

For the adolescent, appropriate books or stories can fulfill emotional and psychological needs, provide information about adolescent problems, and acquaint the youngster with a variety of social interactions within the community. Four requirements from the reader are needed for this tactic to be successfully employed. The reader must possess: (1) the ability to read the material; (2) the ability to identify with characters in the story or story elements; (3) the ability to empathically connect with the character(s); and (4) the ability to identify similarities and differences between personal needs and motivations and those of the character(s) (Spache, 1978; Rubin, 1978).

Screening families or individual family members prior to the introduction of the intervention can minimize unsuccessful results. Questions include: "What kinds of activities does this family enjoy doing together?" "Do you think that movies/television/books/poems can impact in a significant way upon someone's life?" "In school, what kind of reading is required?" "What types of reading matter are of interest to you?" "Has anyone in this family enjoyed a poem they had read; would you tell us what it was about?" "What difference(s) has material you have read made in your lives?" Such screening provides the background information necessary to ascertain which material would be most appropriate for the particular family or individual.

It is important that the therapist read the literature prior to recommending it to clients. It is also helpful to keep records of appropriate materials and clients' reactions to the works. The following is a limited list of materials recommended by Rubin (1978):

—Fitzhugh, Louise. *Nobody's Family Is Going To Change* (New York: Farrar, Strauss, and Giroux, 1974). A book about a Black, middle class family's difficulties with expectations, it covers a variety of issues in a humorous manner.

—Gill, Brendan. "Truth and Consequences." *Fifty-five Stories from the New Yorker* (New York: Simon and Schuster, 1949). A short story dealing with the relationships between a mother and her son and his girlfriend.

—Heide, Florence Perry. *The Key* (New York: Atheneum, 1971). A book of three short stories about family relationships in unusual situations.

—Klein, Norma. *Mom, The Wolfman, And Me.* (New York: Pantheon, 1972). A humorous, up-front novel about a single mother, her daughter, and the mother's live-in male friend.

—Klein, Norma. *Taking Sides.* (New York: Pantheon, 1975). A sensitive book about divorce and alternative life-styles.

—Stafford, William. "Fifteen". In A. Adoff (Ed.), *A City in All Directions,* p. 66. (New York: MacMillan, 1969). Poems.

—"The Son." A 10-minute film about generational alienation. New York: McGraw-Hill.

In addition, William Golding's *Lord of the Flies*, a novel about the organization of a society of youngsters without adult guidance, is useful with families experiencing intergenerational problems with boundaries and structure. *Ordinary People* is a powerful movie concerning a family's difficult adjustment to the death of the oldest son. For additional materials relating to specific client situations, it is helpful to maintain a working relationship with the local librarian.

Bibliotherapy is best used with other therapies (Rubin, 1978). The therapist might introduce the bibliotherapeutic intervention through the screening process over a period of time or by saying: "Some of the difficulties this family is experiencing have been obstacles which many families have been faced with. That's why many writers have attempted to address these issues in literature. Although I do not expect that your perceptions, thoughts, or feelings are identical to those of literary characters, perhaps reading about how similar difficulties have been handled could provide us with some additional insight into the problem(s) being experienced in this family. How would you feel about reading and discussing a pertinent piece of literature?"

Should the family members show interest, the therapist could then introduce the material, discuss acquisition, and outline a reading or viewing schedule. If the family declines to employ that modality, the therapist can obtain information concerning the lengths the family is willing to go in search of solutions to their difficulties.

An alternative to having the material read at home is to read the material aloud and immediately discuss it in session. This can be especially effective when working with a play. Roles can be assigned by the therapist or chosen by the family members; they can also be changed at different points in the reading. Rubin (1978) has found that psychodrama and sociodrama techniques tend to complement bibliotherapeutic interventions.

REFERENCES

Adler, A. (1931). *What life should mean to you.* New York: Putnam.

Barnhart, C. L. and Barnhart, R. K. (Eds.) 1985. *The World Book Dictionary* (p. 2155). New York: Doubleday & Company.

Carter, E. A. and McGoldrick, M. (1980). *The family life cycle: A framework for family therapy.* New York: Gardner Press.

Fishman, H. C. (1988). *Treating troubled adolescents: A family therapy approach.* New York: Basic Books.

Gallatin, J. (1976). Theories of adolescence. In J. F. Adams (Ed.), *Understanding adolescence: Current developments in adolescent psychology* (pp. 30–53). Boston: Allyn & Bacon.

Grunwald, B. B. and McAbee, H. V. (1985). *Guiding the family: Practical counseling techniques.* Muncie, IN. Accelerated Development.

Leveton, E. (1984). *Adolescent crisis: Family counseling approaches.* New York: Springer Publishing.

Lowe, R. (1983). Adolescents and their families in counseling. In O. C. Christensen and T. G. Schramski (Eds.), *Adlerian family counseling: A manual for counselor, educator, and therapist* (pp. 249–278). Minneapolis, MN: Educational Media Corporation.

Mason, M. J. (1987, Spr.-Sum.). Wilderness family therapy: Experiential dimensions. *Contempory Family Therapy: An International Journal, 9*(1–2), 90–105.

McHolland, J. D. (1985, Sum.). Strategies for dealing with resistant adolescents. *Adolescence, 20*(78), 349–368.

Nelson, J. C. (1983). *Family treatment: An integrative approach.* Englewood Cliffs, NJ: Prentice Hall.

Papp, P. (1983). *The process of change.* New York: Guilford Press.

Pearl, A. (1978). Toward a general theory valuing youth. In A. Pearl, D. Grant and E. Wenk (Eds.), *The value of youth* (p. 18). Davis, CA: International Dialogue Press.

Pitman III, F. S. (1987). *Turning points: Treating families in transition and crisis.* New York: W. W. Norton.

Rubin, R. J. (1978). *Using bibliotherapy: A guide to theory and practice.* Phoenix, AZ: The Orynx Press.

Rutherford, R. B. (1975). Dealing with runaway behavior through behavioral contracts. *Federal Probation, 39*(1), 28–32.

Spache, G. D. (1978). Using books to help solve children's problems. In R. J. Rubin (Ed.), *Bibliotherapy sourcebook.* Phoenix, AZ: The Orynx Press.

Stafford, W. (1969). Fifteen. In A. Adoff (Ed.), *A city in all directions* (p. 66). New York: MacMillan Company.

Webster's seventh new collegiate dictionary (1965). Springfield, MA: G. & C. Merriam Company.

Williams, J. M. and Weeks, G. R. (1984). Use of paradoxical techniques in a school setting. *American Journal of Family Therapy, 12*, 47–58.

Additional Resources

Arnold, L. E. & Estreicher, D. (1985). *Parent-Child group therapy: Building self-esteem in a cognitive-behavioral group.* Lexington, MA: Lexington Books.

Friedman, A. S., Sonne, J. C., Barr, J. P., Boszormenyi-Nagy, I., Cohen, G., Speck, R. V., Jungreis, J. E., Lincoln, G., Spark, G. & Weiner,

O. R. (1971). *Therapy with families of sexually acting out girls.* New York: Springer Publishing.

Okun, B. F. (Ed.) (1984). *Family therapy with school related problems.* Rockville, MD: Aspen Systems Corporation.

Robin, A. L. & Foster, S. L. (1989). *Negotiating parent-adolescent conflict: A behavioral family systems approach.* New York: Guilford Publications.

Szapocznik, J., Kurtines, W. M. & contributors (1989). *Breakthroughs in family therapy with drug abusing and problem youth.* New York: Springer Publishing.

Todd, T. C. & Selekman, M. D. (1991). *Family therapy approaches with adolescent substance abusers.* Needham Heights, MA: Allyn & Bacon.

8

INTIMACY
The Dance Around Closeness and Distance

I. INTRODUCTION: THE DREAM AND THE REALITY OF INTIMACY

Our culture currently assigns great importance to intimacy as an essential ingredient of love, friendship, and family relations. The mass media constantly portray the human longing for intimacy. Encounter groups, marriage enrichment groups, workshops, and self-help literature promise help in developing intimacy with others. There is also an abundant professional literature on the subject, only a handful of which will be referenced in this chapter. As economics provides less of the rationale for maintaining marriages and having families, personal factors become more important.

A. Definitions

The American Heritage Dictionary of the English Language (1970) defines intimacy as:

> 1. Marked by close acquaintance, association or familiarity. 2. Pertaining to or indicative of one's deepest nature. 3. Essential, innermost. 4. Characterized by informality and privacy; secret . . . A close friend

or confidant. 5. Very personal; private; secret. Intimate comes from the Latin "intimare" meaning to put in.

Waring (1988) defines intimacy operationally as a composite of eight critical elements (p. 23):

". . . 1) affection—the degree to which feelings of emotional closeness are expressed by the couple; 2) expressiveness—the degree to which thoughts, beliefs, attitudes, and feelings are communicated within the marriage; 3) compatibility—the degree to which the couple is able to work and play together comfortably; 4) cohesion—a commitment to the marriage; 5) sexuality—the degree to which sexual needs are communicated and fulfilled; 6) conflict resolution—the ease with which differences of opinion are resolved; 7) autonomy—the couple's degree of positive connectedness to family and friends; and 8) identity—the couple's level of self-confidence and self-esteem."

Waring & Reddon (1983) and many others have constructed instruments for measuring intimacy, each based on somewhat different but overlapping definitions of the operational behaviors involved. Fredman and Sherman (1987) and Touliatos, Perlmutter, and Straus (1989) list and describe such instruments.

Waring (1988) further claims that: "The behavioral aspect of intimacy is predictability; the emotional aspect is a feeling of closeness; the cognitive aspect is understanding through self-disclosure; and the attitudinal aspect is commitment" (pp. 38–39).

The feeling in intimacy is one of closeness and trust that one can safely share the innermost parts of oneself with another. The behavior involves making one feel safe on the one hand and willingness to share and entrust oneself on the other hand. These are two separate sets of complementary role behaviors.

We usually seek a reciprocal exchange of intimacies to assure our safety. However, it does not have to be so. Therapists, clergy, Shamans, and others may not equally share back. The trust lies in the position occupied by the receiver. Sometimes a child confides in a parent, or one spouse in another, or one friend in another without reciprocation. This may be acceptable or else a source of difficulty in the relationship, with intimacy not continuing beyond an initial exchange.

B. Ideal Characteristics

Ideally, to create a safe climate, the receiver needs to be attentive, aware, and sensitive to the other. He needs to listen carefully and signal that the other is being heard. He has to give time for this to happen without showing impatience. He shows caringness and is open to what is being said without being defensive, argumentative, or right. He is sympathetic without losing the boundary between self and the one who is sharing. He distinguishes between when direct help or a good listener is asked for by the sharing one. He does not respond with a game of "can you top this" by putting forth his feelings, pain, joy, or experience as greater than those of the initial sharing one. He respects the differences between them and what the sharer is experiencing and acknowledges the experience. Acknowledgement does not necessarily mean agreement. Therefore, he does not deny the other's feelings. Of course, the therapist, supposedly, is the ideal intimate receiver.

Ideally, the sharer is open and able to convey in word and body language what he wishes the receiver to know about him. He communicates directly; avoids double messages, hints, and untruths; and is open and honest. He indicates clearly to the receiver whether he wants only to be heard, or to get sympathy, or to obtain some form of direct help.

Social interest is at the heart of intimate behavior. One must be able both to put forth the self and to care about the other. To express intimacy requires social and communication skills and the ability to negotiate differences.

C. Issues in Therapy

It is axiomatic that people are different. Each has different values, expectations, styles, myths and territorial needs. Following are a few examples of the consequences of some of these differences for intimacy that come up in therapy.

1. SYMBIOTIC ATTUNEMENT

Usually the sharer wants the receiver to be "tuned in" and know what is wanted and needed. Having to describe it verbally spoils the sense of intimacy and engenders feelings of disappointment, often leading to conflict.

2. INTENSITY

Unless the sharer expresses his feelings in an intense or dramatic way, the listener may discount its importance and not attend; or else he may refuse to attend unless the feelings are expressed "calmly."

3. BEING VS. DOING

It appears in our culture, up to the late 1980s, that, modally, women favor intimacy as the kind of sharing described above (*being* together), while men are more prone toward experiencing events together, especially sexual intercourse (*doing* together). This difference is a common source of conflict observed by the authors in their practice. Further, men seem to be more competitively socialized than women, making them less trusting of sharing themselves. They fear it might be used against them (De Angelis, 1989; Gilligan, 1982; Pogrebin, 1987).

4. CONTROL

Some people withhold themselves in order to maintain control over a relationship. They may also use withholding as a form of spite in a family conflict or to establish a boundary of personal independence. Parents and other adults often share little but question children much (see the Non-Demand Communication exercise on pp. 169–171). Others use a great deal of sharing in order to control the relationship and keep a "safe" focus on the self. There are also those who want so badly to be genuine and authentic that they engage in "emotional diarrhea," spilling everything to anyone who will listen, thus proving their genuineness.

5. TERRITORIALITY

Each person, as well as each culture, has a different sense of physical and emotional space. That which is too distant for one may be suffocating to the other. Closed doors may be an insult in one family and open doors an abomination in another family. The rule in one family may be, out of respect for the individual, to wait to be told. In a second family, this can be a grave sign of uncaringness, the rule being to inquire vigorously (see the Intimacy Sculpture exercise, pp. 166–168). Jealousy is a form of possessiveness in which you belong to me and must stay close and constantly prove fidelity and loyalty and tell me everything. Jealousy is a powerful control mechanism. (See Barker (1987) for a full discussion of jealousy in marriage.)

6. PRIVATE LANGUAGE OF INTIMACY

Each person within his private logic, personal needs, and priorities develops his own language of intimacy. It may be being with, sharing with, doing with, doing for, understanding or being understood, comforting or being comforted, being told what to do, maintaining a quiet or passive physical presence, or moving in and out of one's wavelength. It may be physical closeness, warm-positive expressions, encouragement, making demands, or being needed. The priorities are most typically derived from what was most positive in the family of origin growing up or what was most importantly missing. The problem is that unless intimacy is exchanged in the private language of the individual, it will have little of its intended impact.

For example, mere physical presence may feel very cold to someone who wants to talk or do things together. Further, we qualitatively rate interactive behavior in terms of its impact and value to us. For one of the authors, on a scale of 1–10, with 10 the highest, holding hands while walking together may be a 7 for him and only a 2 for his partner. Unfortunately, a hundred 3s do not equal one 10 (see the Experiencing and Expressing Love Exercise, pp. 171–175).

7. WANTING TO CHANGE THE OTHER

Often, people who care about each other are very eager to change the other one. If only you would change, everything would be better. Trying to change another may create conflicts and blocks to intimacy. On the other hand, people do operate within complementary relationships and teach and learn from one another in effective relationships. For this learning to happen, there has to be a deep respect for the differences. Paradoxically, for me to get you to change when we are engaged in a repeating pattern leading nowhere, I must first change my own behavior to elicit a different response in you. Greenberg and Johnson (1986) stress the importance of enabling couples to access and express their emotional experiences as a prerequisite to helping each other change the nature of their intimate relationships.

8. BEING OF SEVERAL MINDS

There are those who want closeness, but fear and reject it when it is offered. Examples are those who fear alternately being absorbed or abandoned; those who were physically, sexually, or emotionally abused; and those who fear loss of control. Such persons invite others to be close and then push off, unable to tolerate the closeness. This behavior is a very confusing double message.

9. SEXUAL INTIMACY

Sexual intercourse is sometimes confused with intimacy. If the behavior also includes the sharing of selves and a feeling of closeness and joining, then sex may be intimate. Rape is not intimacy. Depersonalizing a partner as an object to satisfy a physical need does not lend itself to intimacy.

Obstacles to intimacy can occur when there is a lack of agreement relative to being sexually active or passive and what activities are acceptable and pleasurable. Fear of performance, loss of power (being leveled or made subservient in the relationship), and fear of being absorbed (losing oneself) all create a sense of guardedness and block intimacy.

Additional obstacles are anger or lack of attraction toward one's partner, reminders of abuse and incest, guilt that sex is dirty, and differences in sexual desire and appetites. There is a developing literature on sex as an addiction. Similarly, gender issues in sexuality are being more frequently discussed (Walters, Carter, Papp, & Silverstein, 1989; Lerner, 1988; Carr, 1988; Kantor & Okun, 1989). Hof and Berman (1986) provide new methods for using the genogram to assess and work on issues of sexual intimacy.

10. COMMON BLOCKS TO INTIMACY

Fears of sharing, becoming dependent, losing control, losing face, and losing personal integrity inhibit intimacy. A need to be the strong, invulnerable one leads a person to be very cautious about entrusting oneself to another. Misunderstanding and miscommunication are probably very common blockers. Projecting one's own meanings onto another and attributing them to the other is a major source of misunderstanding. Being negative, critical, always right, or disinterested in others is also an effective deterrent to intimacy (see The Couple Conference and Family Meeting exercises on pp. 175–179 and Chapter 2, The Art of Encouragement).

Following are techniques drawn from various theoretical schools that assist people to change beliefs about intimacy, practice new skills, and change their patterns of interacting to improve intimacy. Those techniques appropriate to a given theoretical model can be adapted to and organized into a strategy consistent with that theory, the model, and the specific case.

II. STRUCTURED TECHNIQUES

A. *The Intimacy Sculpture*

1. RATIONALE

The purpose of the intimacy sculpture is to dramatize the physical and emotional closeness or distance required by the members of a couple, family, or group. Sculpting is a sociometric technique frequently used by Adlerian, strategic and structural family therapists and psychodramatists. (For some examples, see Duhl, 1983; Papp, 1982; Sherman & Fredman, 1986.) This particular variation was developed by Sherman and has been widely demonstrated publicly, but not previously published.

By definition, intimacy is very much involved with the degree of closeness or distance that is comfortable for the participants. But how close is close enough or too close? It would be unusual for each member to want the same degree or style of being close or to want to be close every time other members do. There is, therefore, considerable negotiation and, sometimes, conflict around the closeness/distance dimension of a relationship, which is at the heart of the intimate experience.

Sculpting gets past usual verbal defenses and allows the brain to conceptualize the relationship in a new way by setting up a physical representation of an interpersonal dynamic. The participants visually and kinesthetically experience the relationship in this new way and can begin to revise it symbolically through the sculpting rather than by talking about it or living it in the usual unresolving ways.

2. PROCEDURE

The therapist invites the couple to try something new. "Would you please create a sculpture by placing yourself and your partner physically in relationship to one another in a way that best represents at present how that relationship is in general both physically and emotionally. I know you are sometimes closer and sometimes more distant, but sculpt what is most typical, what the relationship really feels like to you right now." If they don't understand, model three examples. "With your permission, may I touch you and show you some examples? Some experience themselves like this (*place the couple facing one another about six inches apart*). Some think it's like this for them (*place them holding hands standing side by side and facing front*). And some are like this (*place them in an embrace face to face*). Of course, there are many other possibilities. Now would you (*selecting the one who appears to be the more powerful member*) be willing to create the first sculpture?"

The positions are carefully noted by all. Then the partner is invited to create his own sculpture after being told that it can be a different experience for him than for his partner. This sculpture, too, is carefully noted by all. The differences and similarities of how each experiences the relationship are then discussed. They are each asked to put a caption on both sculptures. Differences in experience and feelings are framed by the therapist as differences in perception and style.

The couple are then asked to sculpt in turn their ideal relationship. Again, they are requested to put a caption label on both sculptures. Differences are framed as differences in need and life history rather than as more or less loving. They are then asked to negotiate NONVERBALLY a sculpture that both can accept and live with in a reasonable way.

The therapist may end the exercise at this point, depending on an analogical impact to bring about change. Or the therapist can continue by discussing in concrete terms what each can do operationally to create that degree of closeness and intimacy just agreed upon. They are then each asked to commit to doing one to three things between now and the next session to develop that level of intimacy.

The same procedure can be used between parent and child with minor changes in vocabulary. If only one person is present, the sculpture can be made with pillows, office furniture, office supplies, or the therapist serving as the other person. Similarly, in working with a couple, their children or parents can be included in the sculpture by the use of whatever is available in the office. Letting them choose is particularly interesting as a projective device. Who is represented by the scissors or by the wastebasket?

3. CASE EXAMPLE

Laura and Joe are in conflict after seven years of marriage. Laura complains that Joe shows no warmth and chooses to spend little time with her. Joe complains that Laura is always criticizing him and says that of course he loves her. He buys her birthday and anniversary presents and they are together all weekend. Joe and Laura agree in their sculptures of the existing situation that they are too far apart. He pictures them as holding hands, side by side, at arm's length. As Laura describes them, she has her hand on the back of Joe's shoulder and he is turned away from her. Her caption is "The cold shoulder." Joe's caption is "A safe distance."

Ideally, Joe wanted to hold Laura around her waist, side by side. Laura would have liked a close embrace, face to face. They nonverbally negotiated facing each other in a "V" shape, arms around waists. The therapist validated their individual differences as normal and based upon personal history and needs. She told them that to make it together they might want to figure out ways that each could get more of what he or she needs. They agreed that Laura will operationally step back and give Joe an hour to himself each night and time to play tennis on weekend mornings without complaint. Joe agreed to be "present" with Laura when he is present. He will talk with her, make plans for recreation together, and assist in a list of household chores.

At the following session, each reported that the other had made some effort to carry out the agreement and that each had fallen back to old patterns on occasion. The prior week's task was reaffirmed with the comforting idea that habits are difficult to break and falling back is inevitable, but that they were on a pleasing track and could continue with increased effectiveness. The family of origin history of the need and myths about closeness and intimacy were discussed during this session. It was helpful for each to see where he or she came from historically in relation to intimacy and to take responsibility for his or her own feelings, beliefs, and behavior as they affected the relationship.

4. USES

This technique can be used with couples, parent and child, and families to assess their interaction with respect to closeness and distance. It uncovers the strong emotional charge connected with their differences in style and need and their individual myths about closeness. It validates and normalizes their differences, thereby reducing the emotional charge. It can enable them to identify what a mutually more favorable degree of closeness or distance might be.

B. Non-Demand Communication Ritual

1. RATIONALE

This technique was taught to one of the authors in a personal communication by Arthur Stein (1972) to encourage intimacy between parent and oppositional child. It works equally well for couples. Implicit in virtually all communication is both information and a command (Watzlawick, 1978). The command is an expectation of some type of response from the receiver. When the receiver is taking an oppositional stance toward the sender, the response is likely to be some form of resistance or hostility by withholding or acting out, increasing the negative feelings in the relationship. The object is to enable the participants to come closer in a friendly way while respecting the boundary between them.

To achieve this, the therapist asks one compliant member to share the self ritually with the oppositional person, without expecting any response. This is also particularly useful where there are pursuer/distancer relationships.

2. PROCEDURE

The parent or the initiating or pursuing member of the couple is asked by the therapist if he/she would like to get closer to the other or befriend the other. The negative effects of command communications in this relationship are described. If the person agrees that he would like to try something new, the therapist proceeds to explain a ritual which befits the situation.

"Each night at the child's bedtime, sit at the corner of the bed and for 5–15 minutes share information about yourself—your childhood, family, dreams, experiences that day, concerns. Do not speak about the child or ask any questions of the child. Do not criticize or complain about the child. *Do not expect the child to respond in any way.* When you are finished sharing, say goodnight and leave. (*The ritual can be a daily walk, or snacking at the kitchen table, or any other convenient time and way.*)

"At some point within one to four weeks the child (or partner) will share something with you by interrupting or just before you leave. Just listen or acknowledge what you hear or be sympathetic. Do not criticize, inquire more deeply, or offer advice unless specifically invited to do so. If in doubt about being invited, ask. This is a test of your trustworthiness to be a confidant. Pass it and continue to pass it until there is a natural flow of sharing between you. Tell me now when and how you will implement this. Next session tell me in detail how it worked out."

At the next session the therapist reinforces any progress made and helps to refine and continue the ritual.

3. CASE EXAMPLE

The T. couple presented with marital discord and a 14-year-old son who was oppositional at home and doing poorly in school. Whenever the parents made a demand upon him, the son would either lock himself in his room or leave the house. He absolutely forbade his parents from asking him about school or homework. Among the techniques and tactics used with this family was the Non-Demand Communication Ritual. The child felt oppressed by parental demands and resisted in part to maintain a sense of his own identity and independence in a very enmeshed family in which all members wanted to "get out from under" the oppression of demands.

Father and mother were each committed to engage in a nondemand ritual with their son, father at bedtime and mother at snacktime. During the first week, each managed only one experience (a tentative toe in the water, expecting rejection). There was indeed a feigned rejection with little energy put into it. Encouraged by the therapist, each created two such encounters of longer duration during the second week. They noted no change in the boy's behavior, but he didn't appear quite so hostile in demeanor.

The third week, mother engaged three times and father twice. This time, the parents noted that there was definitely less fighting and less tension in the house. By the fifth week, the son shared a problem with mother about school. Forewarned by the therapist, she just listened and this was the beginning of a greater sharing of information by the son. This sharing continued to improve over the next three months.

The technique helped to reduce the demands made on the boy, increase individuation in the system, and increase intimacy while reducing enmeshment. It became easier to be friends than enmeshed opponents.

4. USES

This exercise helps to bring individuals together as appropriate sharer of self and safe receiver of what is shared. Because there are no demands, a great deal of respect is exhibited toward the receiver and the receiver is not overwhelmed or overburdened. This reduces defensiveness and hostility.

The technique can be used with individuals, couples, and families and can be prescribed in parent education groups.

C. The Experiencing and Expressing Love Exercise

1. RATIONALE

This technique was designed by Robert Sherman and the underlying ideas were described in Sherman (1983) and in Sherman and Dinkmeyer (1987). It was designed to help participants identify their own private languages for both expressing love and feeling being loved. Much loving is extended between people without having the intended impact because it fails to join with the other person's framework of meanings and values about being loved.

If my best way of showing my love is to serve the person I care about, while her most important way of being loved is to be given respect and independence, then conflict is inevitable. She is likely to feel put down and made dependent by my wish to do for her and will therefore reject my ministrations. This will make me feel rejected and unloved. In turn, she shows her caringness by giving me space and independence even though I want her to be appreciative and to show her appreciation by being physically warm and affectionate. Both partners are loving and in conflict because they do not understand each other's language of loving. Similarly, the loving parent who constantly disciplines the child "for her own good" is rejected by the child who feels discounted and put down rather than loved and encouraged.

The technique is based upon Adlerian concepts of subjective perception, private logic, and individual life-styles within which individuals strive to teach those they interact with how to behave to meet their personal needs, goals, and expectations. If I see myself as a leader, then I expect you to follow me. The development of social interest and social feeling allows each to become more sensitive to and more caring of the needs of others and the common good.

There are four major assumptions. (1) A person creates a philosophy of life based upon his subjective perception of the world: "Everyone is out to get me." "As long as I am pretty, people will love me and take care of me." "If I work hard, I can get ahead." Based upon his particular philosophy, the person selects goals to strive for through which he may attain some significance and belonging. He organizes his behavior around these goals; this is his life. (2) A person chooses to be loved in ways that were present and highly valued in childhood and/or in ways that were painfully missing. (3) People generally show they are loving to others in ways similar to those in which they prefer to be loved by them. (4) The quality or intensity of loving and being loved is dependent on the subjective priority and needs of each person. Thus, on a scale of 1–10, with 10 the highest, I may rate being loved by my wife a #10 when she holds me and tells me she loves me, a #4 when she puts a fresh flower on my desk, and a #2 when she buys me a shirt. Unfortunately, a thousand 4s do not equal one 10 in my experience of being loved.

We further "feel" loved more through a favored sense modality than through others: aural (told and heard), visual (shown and done for), kinesthethic (touched and touching), olfactory (perfume, cleanliness, sweat, breath), and taste (licking, sucking, food, and, symbolically, taste in things).

A failure to communicate love in a mutual language creates distance rather than intimacy. Helping each to recognize and appreciate the language of the other, to expand one's own vocabulary, and to join with the other's language of loving is the objective of this technique, thereby enhancing intimacy among participants.

The technique can be similarly used to enhance intimacy by substitution of such words as closeness, anger, appreciation, or fun for the word love in the technique.

2. PROCEDURE

The participants (couple, family, friends, class, or group) are asked if they would like to better understand how they love and show caringness to others and how they would prefer others show love and caringness to them. In working with a couple or a family, this might follow a descriptive statement such as: "There seems to be a lot of love here and yet it is not being received, one from the other. Perhaps we could explore what is happening to all that love." Once they agree to explore together, they are asked to make themselves physically comfortable and relax. They are then asked to respond to the following series of questions by writing their responses or by the therapist writing the answers of the members of a small group responding in turn:

"How will you know if another person is being loving to you? What does the other person have to do? We are not talking about philosophy. What does the other person actually have to do? Think of a number of things that make you feel loved. For example, do you expect the other person to listen to you, do things for you, anticipate in advance what you want?

"When you finish, could you please note which are the first, second, and third most important ones.

"Could you now please identify what you do to show others that you are being loving. Again, not philosophically, but what do you actually do?"

The therapist has each reveal and discuss his or her responses. Each statement must be clarified in operational terms. A statement that "I want to be heard" is probed with a question like "How will you know if you are being heard? What does the other person have to do?" The answers are compared and contrasted to validate that each is loving and trying to show it. Then point out how they misunderstand or miscommunicate.

The participants can be given assignments to better connect in each other's language, thereby increasing satisfaction, trust, and intimacy. To encourage agreement and compliance, the therapist indicates that "We do not communicate the same way to everyone since we are all different. If we want to be successful, we target our communication to get the results we intend. Having different styles and priorities is not a sin; it is inevitable between any two people and part of the excitement between them."

If the therapist wishes to examine the life-style qualities, assumptive values, loyalties, or old business underlying the language of loving, the exercise may be continued.

"Could you please relax again. Could you please imagine yourself as a child growing up. What were the most important pleasing things about loving in your family? What did people actually do that was very loving that you would always want in your life? Please identify the three most important among them.

"Could you now please notice what important things about loving were either negative or missing in your family that you wish were there and you wish were now in your life? Please number the three most important in order." The answers to those two questions are now discussed, compared, contrasted, interpreted in relation to each other and to the responses given for the first two questions. Similar comparisons and contrasts are made for the answers among the participants so as to identify similarities and possible sources of conflict. These data and observation of the ensuing interactions are utilized to formulate other techniques for change through challenging myths revealed, revising roles in the relationship, teaching skills, or encouraging social interest.

3. CASE EXAMPLE

Arnold (age 57) and Sue (age 48) came in for couple counseling after three years of living together. Both previously had been married and divorced and had four young adult children between them, all in college or on their own. Arnold complained that Sue was very critical of him and was too focused on her own children. Sue complained that Arnold never talked with her or shared himself with her. We can hypothesize that for greater intimacy Arnold wants to be approved and Sue needs to hear and be heard. Fighting maintains a safe boundary between the two stepfamilies, but also inhibits the couple from becoming the unit they want to be. He can't come close when she criticizes (disapproves) and she can't hear or be heard when he distances and disconfirms what she says.

The exercise revealed Arnold's need to belong, be approved, and be accepted. People are to do this by praising and thanking him, spontaneously doing things for him, and being loyal to him by making him important in most social or competitive situations. He loves by doing for others, by providing financially for them, and by giving others space to do what they want and giving them praise. He does not reveal his own vulnerabilities or ask for help because this might lower his esteem in the eyes of others. There was much fighting in his family growing up and he felt least adequate as the youngest of three children. It was hard to feel that he belonged and was accepted. He enjoyed being praised when he did special things for mother.

Sue noted that she feels loved when people make her #1 and do things for her. But most important is that the other person listen to her, approve what is heard, and share personal feelings and experiences with her. To be loving, Sue shares her feelings, experiences, and skills, is understanding of others, and watches them carefully to see what help they need. Sue is the elder of two sisters. Mother and the girls would often have intimate talks and share most things, which made her feel important and loved. As the eldest, she was mother's confidant. Father was more distant. He was critical of the girls and "stingy" with his time. He appeared uninterested in what was going on in Sue's life. She could never get his love and attention.

There is a direct relationship between old business in the families of origin and this couple's pattern of seeking and giving love. Each in his or her own way is seeking attention and approval to replicate what was enjoyed in the family of origin or to somehow make up for what was missing. Their styles are different. In discussing their mutual needs for love, each became more aware of his or her own style and pressures and became more understanding and tolerant of the partner's. Each committed to engaging in more of the partner's higher priority ways of being loved. Such interactions were practiced in session. This exercise was then followed up by additional techniques to improve communication skills and enhance intimacy.

4. USES

The Experiencing and Expressing Love Exercise can be used diagnostically to identify where and how loving communication is breaking down and the differences in style and needs among the members of the group. It can identify elements in the marital or parent-child contracts that are going unmet or unnegotiated, leading to distrust, distancing, or invasion of boundaries. It is also helpful in assessing the complementarity among roles and the myths and old business being attended to in those roles.

The process assigns positive intention to and validates each participant and creates a positive climate among them. Each person is attended to and made significant in his or her own right with recognition of his or her personal needs. Thus, appropriate separation-individuation is being brought about. At the same time, the needs of every other one are identified and acknowledged, thus developing social interest and concern about the other person. The members are cooperating in the exercise and learning thereby to constructively cooperate with one another. They are taught new techniques for communicating and loving in a wider, less rigid vocabulary that has a deeper, more meaningful impact. They learn to give up myths that are no longer relevant.

The exercise can be used in premarital education or counseling programs, parent education groups, and professional training groups. By changing the operant word from loving to appreciation, recognition, significance, anger, or any other appropriate word, one can readily adapt the exercise for human relations groups, organizational or business team-building groups, or any group dealing with some form of alienation.

The process is encouraging to its members and creates a feeling of safety and trustworthiness which facilitates intimacy and teaches specific communication skills through which intimacy can occur.

D. The Couple Conference and Family Council*

1. RATIONALE

The couple conference and family council are formal meetings held on a regular basis by the couple or the family. They are methods designed to increase and improve communication. The technique is particularly prescribed by Adlerian family therapists and follows the principles of that

---

*Reprinted with permission from R. Sherman and N. Fredman's *Handbook of structured techniques in marriage and family therapy* (1986), pp. 151–154.

theory. The meetings operate on the basis of democratic methods by providing all with equal opportunity to participate. Dreikurs and his associates popularized the idea (Dreikurs, 1948; Dreikurs et al., 1959; Dreikurs and Soltz, 1964; Dreikurs, Gould, and Corsini, 1974; Corsini and Rigney, 1970; Dinkmeyer, Pew, and Dinkmeyer, 1979; Manaster and Corsini, 1982).

Most couples or families caught up in a power contest around a symptomatic conflict tend to engage in little other communication. Each experiences not being heard, understood, or acknowledged by the other(s). In a typical interaction, one speaks, the other interrupts and takes off on one point and adds his own agenda. The first picks up on one point and goes off in another direction. Instead, during the conference, each is instructed to pay strict, uninterrupted attention to the other(s). Just being heard all the way through has a powerful effect on those so engaged.

According to Manaster and Corsini, there are four purposes to conducting a family council:

1. To allow free communication among family members.
2. To avoid emotional showdowns and violence in the family.
3. To teach children and parents democratic means of settling differences.
4. To operate an orderly and peaceful home. (1982, p. 231)

The family council is based on the philosophy that democratic methods introduced into family life will encourage respect among all members, increase cooperation because all have a voice in appropriate decision making, increase interest in and feeling for one another because all are involved, and help develop a sense of group identity while clearly recognizing each person's individuality, contribution, and value.

The therapist prescribes the conference and/or council as a homework task. She carefully instructs the members in detail about the rules for conducting it at home or another designated place. It becomes a particular couple and family ritual. Adlerian couple and family educators regularly prescribe it as a developmental enrichment process as well as a remediation technique.

2. THE COUPLE CONFERENCE PROCEDURE

Once the therapist has ascertained that there is a need for improvement in communication between the couple, she suggests that it might be a good idea for the couple to schedule a regular fixed time, place, and frequency per week to meet together. During that time they are to be totally and exclusively there for one another without external interruption. Once the idea is accepted, the couple then discuss and agree upon a mutually convenient time when they are willing and able to be at their best with one another, rather than when they are totally depleted. They also agree to abide by the established rules, which are written down and handed to the couple. These can be varied by the therapist to suit the couple's specific needs. Typical rules are:

1. They will meet at the agreed on fixed times and place between now and the next therapy session and will not allow external interruptions. (A minimum of one such meeting a week.)
2. One spouse will begin and have a fixed time, usually half an hour, to speak or be silent, having 100 percent of the partner's attention for the entire half hour. She can communicate feelings, dreams, plans, hurts, desires, needs—anything she wants. The partner is not to interrupt. During the half hour, the partner is to pay close attention, listening and watching carefully. He is not to smoke, move about, or do anything to distract from the process. Exactly at the end of the time, the spouse stops.
3. The partner then briefly (three minutes) indicates what he has heard his spouse say and mean and acknowledges her position without attacking it.
4. He now begins his half hour with the spouse carefully attending to him. He can communicate anything he wants.
5. The spouse now has three minutes to acknowledge that she has heard and understood her partner.
6. The discussion is to end exactly on time.
7. The items discussed are not to be introduced again until the next conference.
8. The couple comes back to the next session and reports on what happened. The therapist uses the material in the session, reinforces the rules, and repeats the prescription.

It should be emphasized that the couple conference is not a problem-solving technique. Its purpose is to open up communication, increase constructive intimacy, and at least partially defuse the power play.

3. THE FAMILY COUNCIL PROCEDURE

Once the therapist has concluded that the family council will be a useful way for this family to improve their communication and their decision-making capability she introduces the idea to the parents or to the family as a group. She anticipates with them that it will be difficult to implement since it is different from their usual manner of discussing issues and solving problems, but that it provides them with some new options for improving their family life style. She may choose to encourage them by pointing out that up to now the family has demonstrated excellent skills in cooperation by agreeing to fight together and these same skills can be applied to learning to agree together.

The therapist next describes the rules of the council.

1. Set a definite regular time and place for the meeting so there are no interferences or interruptions.
2. The council is to include the entire family, but no one is forced to attend. An absentee must agree to abide by the decisions arrived at. Every effort is made for everyone to be present at every meeting.
3. Decisions made during the meeting cannot be unilaterally broken or ignored. They can be renegotiated at a subsequent meeting.
4. Everyone can propose agenda items. Some families keep a sign-up sheet in a high-traffic place like the refrigerator door, so that agenda items can be written down immediately when they come to mind.
5. The agenda is anything that concerns the welfare of the children, family outings, decisions that affect the family as a unit. Parents do not invite a six-year-old to help decide whether they should invest in real estate or a money market account or whether or not he chooses to go to school. The parents may seek certain agreements from the children such as cooperation in taking care of family chores, rules about being home at a certain hour, behavior with visiting friends. The children may have issues concerning privacy, more independence, more flexibility around chores, and television viewing time. The children may seek assistance in resolving disputes among themselves. Some items may have to do with sharing feelings, hopes, achievements, experiences, and they may require no decisions. The chairmanship of the meeting is rotated among the family members who are capable of leading. This person exerts whatever leadership and authority are required. The parents do not sit as *The* authorities. The usual rules for conducting any democratic meeting are followed. However, it is better to achieve a unanimous, negotiated consensus than a majority vote.
6. All must participate in carrying out the decisions agreed upon, both in spirit and word. Hairsplitting is not acceptable.
7. Both parents and children need to feel that they have a genuine voice

and what they express will be heard, accepted, and seriously considered. A certain degree of good humor and ability to laugh at human foibles rather than at people is a helpful addition.
8. The meeting is held to overcome problems, not to attack people.

The family is cautioned that the meetings may not be productive until everyone learns how to use the council as an effective vehicle for their concerns.

The family returns for the following sessions and reports their experiences. These are discussed. The material generated is used by the therapist in the session. She then reinforces the rules, helps the family work out some of the problems in execution, and encourages them to continue with the meetings.

4. USES

These procedures provide the therapist with the opportunity to teach democratic techniques and social and negotiating skills which will be practiced at home. They convert the agreement to fight together into an agreement to negotiate and share together. They generate agenda items for the next therapy session with a clear notion of where the members are stuck, the disputants all wanting their own way. The therapist is able to point out that disputing someone else's way is just a difference of opinion and not a rejection of another person—or a hateful act. By encouraging more equality within families, we may be able to achieve greater equality in society at large.

III. TIPS AND TACTICS FOR DEALING WITH INTIMACY ISSUES

The following tactics can be adapted for use with either couples or families.

A. Setting the Stage

1. *Assign good intentions.* The tactic of encouraging the clients to assign "good intention" to one another's behavior because they do care for each other, as well as checking the meaning of the communication before jumping to conclusions, can dramatically reduce fighting caused by misunderstanding. Clients are taught to ask, "Is this what you mean?" "Is this what you like?" "What do you intend that I should feel about

this?" Tone of voice and body language are important in such questioning. It has to be friendly and interested, not annoyed or sarcastic. The therapist has the clients practice these tactics in session as they share feelings with one another.

2. *Teach and practice psychoactive listening.* Clients are encouraged to listen carefully and to acknowledge what they heard and understood. If correct, the communication was received and the speaker feels truly heard. If corrected, this avoids distortions. Again, corrections are made in a friendly way. Otherwise, they are experienced as a criticism, put-down or defense. Correct understanding does not mean that the receiver liked the communication or agrees with it. But in the process they are also learning each other's language.

3. *Enjoin the members to take an "I" position to bring about change.* The injunction of the "I" position in therapy is that you speak for yourself and you can change only yourself. This really contradicts the concept of transactions. Each of us constantly seeks to influence and to order the world. If a repeating pattern of conflict emerges, then we are not being successful in bringing about the desired order or changes. At that point, it is imperative that I change my own behavior in order to induce a complementary change in the other. Paradoxically, then, I can change you by changing myself, my role, my stance, thus breaking the existing pattern and eliciting new behavior from you. This construct is explained to the clients and they are enjoined to take responsibility for changing themselves. For example, suggest to the client that he/she may say, "I feel upset and neglected when you come home late and don't call," rather than, "You are mean and inconsiderate or you would be home on time."

4. *Reframe differences among the members as positives.* Assist the members to redefine their differences as differences in style, expectations, and beliefs occurring as a function of individual differences rather than of uncaringness, unlovingness, or desire to harm. Differences provide excitement in the relationship and opportunity for growth through learning from one another or synthesizing new options through negotiation.

5. *Label each person a "good-hearted teacher."* The therapist can point out what each tries to teach the other with the apparent symptomatic behavior. For example, the therapist turns to the first and asks, "Is it possible you are trying to teach your partner that he/she needs to be more independent, that he/she is not neglected or abandoned and can manage well even if we don't spend a lot of time in deep, personal talk?" Then turn to the second and inquire, "Is it possible that you are trying to teach your partner that he/she needs to be less self-protective and is not going to be overwhelmed

and lose his/her selfhood by sharing more of his/herself and by showing more interest in me and other people?" The therapist can ask what would make these things difficult or dangerous to learn? What does it remind them of in their families of origin? Explore the issues that emerge.

6. *Explore gender expectations and resentments.* If gender does play a part in the differences in style, then the therapist may wish to explore gender expectations. An exercise such as, "As a Man (Woman) I must . . ." and "As a Woman (Man) I Could . . ." may be useful. Each is asked to complete each half of the statement over and over again: As a man I must *provide for my family*, as a man I must *protect my family*, etc., while as a woman I could *bear children, cry, spend more time relaxing*, etc., until the patterns of expectations, dreams, and resentments unfold. The patterns can then be discussed in terms of the interactions they elicit. The couple can be asked: "Are these the interactions desired? What changes would be preferred? Are these the ways you would like to express your mutual masculinity/femininity as a man/woman/couple of the 90s?"

7. *Assist the members to identify and spell out their feelings and beliefs about territoriality* relative to space, objects, privacy, body, experiences, feelings, and ideas. Focus on the areas of territoriality that bring them into conflict. A clear awareness of where each one stands is usually beneficial in reducing feelings of personal rejection. For example, "My difficulty in being touched is not directed against you, it is just something unpleasant for me." Help them to accept their differences and agree to work on some compromises and agreements to eliminate the conflicts through negotiation. (See also Chapter 12, Defusing and Redirecting the Power Play.)

8. *Construct an intimacy genogram.* Some family-of-origin work may help to discover the context of the intimacy issues in family-of-origin patterns or unfinished old business. The genogram (McGoldrick & Gerson, 1985) is a good technique for such an exploration. The genogram is a chart which diagrams each member in relation to all other members of the multigenerational family system. Answers to questions about intimacy and territoriality can be incorporated into the chart. The clients can then see visually how their current situation is affected by the structure of their earlier family life. (For an example of how to construct a genogram see p. 56–60.)

9. *Construct a family floor plan (Coopersmith, 1980).* This is a technique designed to visualize how family members "own" and use physical space in the home and the rules and relationships among them. One or all members of the family are asked to draw a floor plan of their home growing up

and/or of their current home. While the person is drawing, the others watch and the therapist poses questions such as:

"Is or was there a particular room where people gather?"

"Are or were there rooms you could not enter?"

"Do you or did you have a special place in this house?"

"Can you let yourself be aware of how issues of closeness and distance, privacy or the lack of it are experienced in this house?"

The technique allows the clients to identify, clarify, and negotiate their varied expectations and styles. It allows the therapist to work either on increasing closeness or establishing appropriate boundaries.

10. *Examine language and style in expression of emotions* to improve mutual understanding and deal with differences that create conflict. Use a variation of the Experiencing and Expressing Love Exercise (see pages 171–175) by substituting the phrase "experiencing or expressing intense or very important emotions" for experiencing or expressing love. The four questions asked of the clients and discussed will then be: 1) How do you know when someone is expressing very intense, important, or strong emotions to you? 2) How do you show to others that you are feeling very intense, important, or strong emotions? 3) What pleased you about the way intense emotions were expressed in your family in which you grew up? 4) What was most negative or missing for you in the way intense emotions were expressed in the family in which you grew up? Discuss and compare the answers. It will help the participants gain a better understanding of their differences as differences and not as uncaringness. They may then be more willing to expand their respective vocabularies to include more of what is important to the other. The therapist assists them to practice the changes agreed upon as a consequence of the exercise both in session and at home.

B. Increasing Empathy and Closeness

1. *Teach attending behavior.* "Do you care for this person? How do you show your caringness? Do you want to care for him/her in a way that pleases? People who care usually pay very close attention to each other. That is, they watch and listen closely and look behind the words and appearance for what they mean and what is really intended at the core or bottom line." This is explained in words, metaphors, and examples best understood by the client so that empathic behavior can be taught. "For example, can you please close your eyes. Please describe what the other person is wearing? Do you recall the look on his/her face? What do you think that look means?" If the client is able to accurately do this, then the therapist com-

mends him and says, "So you do know how to tune in. What stops you from doing this or letting the other person know that you are doing it?" Explore this. If the client has difficulty, the therapist says, "Fine, now open your eyes and pay careful attention. Have you got it now? Please close your eyes and describe the same things."

If the client is having difficulty or is resistant, the therapist can inquire: "What are you thinking about when we are going through this?" Explore: "Is it possible that you are concerned about yourself and what is happening to you? If so, it would be impossible to pay attention to the other person when you are thinking about yourself or something else. You have to get out of the way or put yourself aside in order to think about the other person. Are you willing to do that? If not, what stops you?" or "What would be the risk for you in doing that?"

2. *Prescribe "Caring Days" and/or "Positive Exchanges"* (Jacobson & Margolin, 1979; Stuart, 1980; Sherman & Fredman, 1986). Each person is asked to surprise the others by deciding on three nice things to do for the other(s) each day or each week and by doing them without revealing what is being done. The others must pay attention and discover what the nice things are.

3. *Challenge waiting vs. asserting* to get a passive or dependent person to become more directly active. Use some variation of the following ideas. "Do you know what people who sit and wait are? They are waiters and they wait and wait. How long do you want to wait?"

"Do you observe people who are very successful in life? Do you notice that such persons tend to be assertive and go after the things they want? People who wait tend to be dependent on others and then resent the others for not taking good care of them. Do you want to be a winner who gets what he/she wants or a dependent person who is likely to lose out a good part of the time?"

"Without complaining or criticizing, can you tell the other person now in a positive, constructive way what you would like?"

4. *Prescribe the "Sherlock Holmes" exercise* to improve mutual attentiveness and reduce distorted perceptions. Invite the members to play "Sherlock Holmes." "See how sharply and accurately you can each observe and predict the experiences of the others by carefully noting their expressions like a look, a posture, a tone of voice, or the timing of the event (give other examples pertinent to the case). Record your observations, assumed meanings, and predictions in a notebook. See if you can detect when the other person(s) is being loving, angry, frustrated, happy, pleased or pleasing, tired, energized, taking, giving, withholding (again use examples most per-

tinent to the case). Report to each other what you observed at the end of each day just before bedtime. Just acknowledge to each other, yes, that is what was happening, or I see it differently. Explain the differences. The conversation ends there. You are not to fight over whose perceptions are the more accurate. Notice how often you agree or disagree." The therapist follows up next session to see what they did and discuss the results.

A few examples of differences in perception are discussed in terms of intentionality—what the person was actually experiencing, what he/she was trying to convey, what he/she did, and how the other(s) perceived it. What did the receiver(s) project from themselves in giving meaning to the event and what predictions were made based upon the meanings assigned. What other meanings could be assigned to the same behavior? They can practice this activity as an in-session task.

5. *Prescribe role reversals* to increase empathy. The members are asked to place themselves in the shoes of another and to really get into that place and be the other. Then they work on a problem between them, trying accurately to be the other and experience what it is like (Sherman & Fredman, 1986).

6. *Set up the animal/object sculpture* to increase empathy and reorganize the closeness/distance operations between family members. Each person is asked to identify the other(s) as an animal or an object in relation to the difficulty between them and then identify the self as an animal or an object in the same situation. The therapist suggests that they imagine the situation and notice exactly what kind of animal or object each is: big/small, cold/warm, active/passive, etc. Then the therapist requests that they imagine a scene in which they are relating to one another. Exactly what is each one doing as the scene unfolds.

Next, the members share their fantasy. They are each asked if they are surprised about the other's perceptions and fantasy and their own place in it. They can then physically sculpt the relationship or even enact the sculpture (Duhl, 1983; Papp, 1982). The questions that follow might be; "How does this animal or object feel? What does it believe? What does it need? How can this animal or object make it with the other one? Can we now sculpt or enact that scene?"

7. *Have couple or family plan to experience common interests together.* If closeness is experienced as doing together, the therapist can focus on identifying common interests, helping members to schedule time and to plan during the session things that will be done together. These can be classified under the rubric of working together or of having fun together. The therapist follows up at the next session to see what happened.

C Adjusting the Distance and Intensity

1. *Legitimate the need for distance.* If there is reluctance to change, the therapist might indicate that the consequence of their behavior is to create distance between them. Apparently, they need to maintain this behavior in order to keep a comfortable distance. She explains that sometimes people believe that they want more closeness than they are really comfortable with. She might also add that they may wish to explore what actual degree of distance and closeness works well for them, thereby creating a positive goal. The Intimacy Sculpture described earlier in this chapter may be useful in that work.

2. *Balance off the drama and emotional intensity* by creating a compliance/defiance paradox (Papp, 1983). The less intense person is told that "If you want to help the other member to be less dramatic, I know something that will probably work, but it will be very hard for you to do. If you really want, you can do the following: When your partner is very dramatic, join him/her and play even more dramatic. Play very excited, worried, joyous, or whatever the other is manifesting and demand more details. He/she will know you are playing with him/her and will probably get angry and then calm down. But you want to be careful that you don't squash her joy. Joy is very precious." Tailor the instructions to the person and situation. The less intense person will learn to let go and be more dramatic and the more intense one will observe some of the effect of exaggerated feelings in the behavior of the other, thereby becoming less dramatic.

3. *Stop the pursuer from pursuing and distance the distancer.* If the interaction revolves around a pursuer/distancer process, it is best to encourage the pursuer to take a more independent course of action by doing more on his/her own, or even to change the rules of the game by becoming somewhat neglectful of the distancer. Perhaps the distancer will then want more closeness and take some initiatives to maintain the complementary balance of the relationship. Usually, the pursuer does not believe that this can happen, so it is offered as an experiment. The prescription can be set up paradoxically with the pursuer to take on the role of distancer and become unavailable. The therapist may also be able to obtain the same results by effecting an agreement between the clients: the pursuer will stay back and give more space and the distancer will commit to take more initiatives toward the partner.

4. *Create dramatic labels for dysfunctional role behavior.* Metaphors can be devised as a form of simple paradox to exaggerate and dramatize the behavior and to put it in an absurd light. For example, the person who

overtly attempts to be the controlling one might be referred to as the inspector general, the watchperson, the judge, the righteous one, or the tragedy king or queen. The systemic piece is presented in a statement such as: "If you are the watchperson, then everyone else needs to be watched. They are either very inadequate/unreliable or very needy. If that is so, you are performing a most difficult task. Are they really so inept or out of control? Which of your needs or fantasies need to be protected by this role?"

5. *Balance off critical, aggressive, or controlling behavior.* Paradoxically, instruct the person who feels criticized or controlled to simply say, "Thank you. I'll be glad to consider that. Can you tell me more about that? Please help me with these other things as well." Usually, the controlling person gets the message, even though not pleased about it. It is hard to fight with someone who says thank you.

There are a number of methods the therapist can use to instruct the client in the one-down position to stop aggression. a) Tell the client to say, "Stop attacking me. If you don't stop I will leave until you are calmer and we will discuss this later." By disengaging, the client stops the attack and serves notice that he cannot be treated that way. b) Tell the client to say, "I'm sorry you are so upset." Then hug, hold and comfort the other. It is hard to attack in most instances when you are being loved. c) Tell the client to respond with humor, but without sarcasm. It is hard to be angry when you are laughing. d) Tell the client to agree with the command but then exaggerate it and/or make a counter demand: "Yes, it is a good idea to plant the new rose bushes today, but let's do all the gardening now. We have to turn over all the flower beds, fertilize the lawn, and cut down that overgrown tree, as well as plant the rose bushes. You start with the tree." Everyone wins in this scenario, which establishes equality between them. e) Reveal the command/passive-aggressive response pattern by telling the client to say yes to the other and not do it. When the other becomes angry, tell him that you will say yes to his command to avoid the fight, but will not do it because you were not asked for your cooperation and he did not care how you felt about it. Such an intervention makes overt the covert pattern and sets the stage for negotiation.

6. *Confront the combatants.* The therapist can confront each of those in conflict. Say to the one demanding change: "You seem to want your partner to change to accommodate to you. You have decided that your belief is the correct one and all must do it your way. Is it possible that that may be a bit arrogant?" Or, "Did you get these ideas from a higher authority?" Or, "Is it possible that what you have learned and favor, based on your perceptions and background, is only one way to look at this?" Or, "Do you realize

that in taking this stance you put yourself in a superior position and your partner in an inferior position in which he needs to fight you to become more equal?"

Say to the resistant one: "You act as if this person is your enemy out to destroy you or your integrity. Is it possible that you are so busy protecting yourself that maybe this change, or some part of it requested by the other person, would be very much to your advantage? What would it really cost you to make this change?" Or, "Is there something that you would want in return for doing what the other is asking for?"

The confrontation uncovers some of the underlying mythology that fuels the fight. It also assigns to each responsibility for his own behavior and creates a climate more favorable for compromise and cooperation.

7. *Apply the incest taboo to a couple at impasse* when one is critically demanding and the other is overtly or passively resistant. Interpret to the couple that perhaps they have created a reciprocal one-up/one-down relationship of a critical parent and a rebellious child. Is that the kind of relationship they want? The therapist might also note that it is really hard for a couple assuming the roles of parent and child to also be lovers since in our society there are strong incest taboos. If they agree, it may then be possible to make a deal and shift roles and behaviors.

REFERENCES

Barker, R. L. (1987). *The green-eyed marriage. Surviving jealous relationships.* Glencoe, IL: Free Press.

Carr, J. B. (1988). *Crises in intimacy. When expectations don't meet reality.* Pacific Grove, CA: Brooks/Cole.

Coopersmith, E. (1980). The family floor plan: A tool for assessment and intervention in family therapy. *Journal of Marital and Family Therapy.* 6: 141–145.

Corsini, R. J. and Rigney, K. (1970). *The family council,* Chicago, IL: Rudolf Dreikurs Unit of the Family Education Association.

De Angelis, T. (1989). Men's interaction style can be tough on women. *A.P.A. Monitor.* November, p. 12.

Dinkmeyer, D. C., Pew, W. L. and Dinkmeyer, D. C., Jr. (1979). *Adlerian counseling and psychotherapy.* Monterey, CA: Brooks/Cole.

Dreikurs, R. (1948). *The challenge of parenthood.* New York: Meredith.

Dreikurs, R., Gould, S., and Corsini, R. J. (1974). *Family Council.* Chicago, IL: Henry Regnery.

Dreikurs, R. and Soltz, V. (1964). *Children: The challenge.* New York: Hawthorne.

Duhl, B. S. (1983). *From the inside out and other metaphors.* New York: Brunner/Mazel.

Fredman, N. and Sherman, R. (1987). *Handbook of measurements for marriage and family therapy.* New York: Brunner/Mazel.

Gilligan, C. (1982). *In a different voice.* Cambridge, MA: Harvard University Press.

Greenberg, L. S. and Johnson, S. M. (1986). Affect in marital therapy. *Journal of Marital and Family Therapy.* 12:1, 1–10.

Hof, L. and Berman, E. (1986). The sexual genogram. *Journal of Marital and Family Therapy.* 12:1 39–47.

Jacobson, N. E. and Margolin, G. (1979). *Marital therapy.* New York: Brunner/Mazel.

Kantor, D. and Okun, B. F. Editors. (1989). *Intimate environments. Sex, intimacy and gender in families.* New York: Guilford.

Lerner, H. G. (1988). *The dance of intimacy.* New York: Harper.

Manaster, G. J. and Corsini, R. J. (1982). *Individual psychology.* Itasca, IL: Peacock.

McGoldrick, M. and Gerson, R. (1985). *Genogram in family assessment.* New York: Norton.

Morris, W. Editor. (1970). *The American heritage dictionary of the English language.* Boston: American Heritage and Houghton Mifflin, p. 686.

Papp, P. (1982). Staging reciprocal metaphors in a couple group. *Family Process.* 21:453–467.

Papp, P. (1983). *The process of change.* New York: Guilford.

Pogrebin, L. C. (1987). *Among friends.* New York: McGraw-Hill.

Sherman, R. (1983). Power in the family: Adlerian perspectives. *The American Journal of Family Therapy* 11:3, 43–53.

Sherman, R. and Dinkmeyer, D. (1987). *Systems of family therapy: An Adlerian integration.* New York: Brunner/Mazel.

Sherman, R. and Fredman, N. (1986). *Handbook of structured techniques in marriage and family therapy.* New York: Brunner/Mazel.

Stein, A. (1972). Personal communications.

Stuart, R. (1980). *Helping couples change.* New York: Guilford.

Touliatos, J., Perlmutter, B.F., and Straus, M. A. Editors. (1989). *Handbook of family measurement techniques.* Newbury Park, CA: Sage.

Walters, M., Carter, B., Papp, P., and Silverstein, O. (1989). *The invisible web. Gender patterns in family relationship.* New York: Guilford.

Waring, E. M. (1988). *Enhancing marital intimacy through facilitating cognitive self-disclosure.* New York: Brunner/Mazel.

Waring, E. M. and Reddon, J. (1983). The measurement of intimacy in marriage: The Waring Questionnaire. *Journal of Clinical Psychology, 39,* 53–57.

Watzlawick, P. (1978). *The language of change. Elements of therapeutic communication.* New York: Basic Books.

ADDITIONAL RESOURCES

Allred, G. H. (1976). *How to strengthen your family.* Provo, UT: Brigham Young University Press.

Bank, S. P. and Kahn, M. D. (1982). *The sibling bond.* New York: Basic Books.

Beavers, W. R. and Hampson, R. B. *Successful families. Assessment and intervention.* New York: Norton.

Beck, A. T. (1988). *Love is never enough.* New York: Harper and Row.

Chasin, R., Grunebaum, H., and Herzig, M. (1990). *One couple, four realities.* New York: Norton.

Connecting skills questionnaire and workbook. (1990) Interpersonal Communication Programs. New York: Littleton.

Crosby, J. F. Editor. *When one wants out and the other doesn't. Doing therapy with polarized couples.* New York: Brunner/Mazel.

Dinkmeyer, D. and Carlson, J. (1984). *Training in marriage enrichment* (TIME). Circle Pines, MN: American Guidance Service.

D'Attilio, F. M. and Padesky, C. A. (1990). *Cognitive therapy with couples.* Sarasota, FL: Professional Resource Exchange.

Dinkmeyer, D. and Carlson, J. (1983). *Systematic training for effective parenting of teens.* Circle Pines, MN: American Guidance Service.

Dornbush, S. M. and Strober, M. H. Editors. (1988). *Feminism, children, and the new families.* New York: Guilford.

Fincham, F. D. and Bradbury, T. N. Editors. (1990). *The psychology of marriage.* New York: Norton.

Gordon, L. H. (1988). *A laundry list of marital mishaps, marital knots and double binds with a dialogue guide.* Falls Church, VA: PAIRS Foundation.

Hendrick, C. Editor. (1989). *Close relationships.* Newbury Park, CA: Sage.

Hendrick, C. (1988). *Getting the love you want. A guide for couples.* New York: Henry Holt.

Hudson, M. and Bidwell, R. E. *Assert with love.* Kansas City, KS: High

Consciousness Games. (A board game to develop intimate communication.)

Jacobson, N. S. and Gurman, A. S. Editors. (1986). *Clinical handbook of marital therapy*. New York: Guilford.

Keith, P. M., Braito, R., and Breci, M. (1990). Rethinking isolation among the married and unmarried. *American Journal of Orthopsychiatry*. 60:2, 289–297.

Kern, R. M., Hawes, E. C., and Christensen, O. Editors. *Couples therapy: An Adlerian perspective*. Minneapolis, MN: Educational Media Corporation.

Leverte, M., Cooper, J. A., and Smith, M. (1981). *Encouragement*. Doylestown, PA: TACT.

Marlin, E. (1990). *Relationship in recovery. Healing strategies for couples and families*. New York: Harper and Row.

Meth, R. L., Pasick, R. S., et al. (1990). *Men in therapy. The challenge of change*. New York: Guilford.

Moultrup, D. J. (1990). *Husbands, wives and lovers. The emotional system of the extramarital affair*. New York: Guilford.

Napier, G. Y. (1988). *The fragile bond*. New York: Harper and Row.

Pittman, F. S. (1989). *Private lies. Infidelity and betrayal of intimacy*. New York: Norton.

Rosen, J. (1988). *Going ape. How to stop talking about your relationship and start enjoying it*. Chicago: Contemporary Books.

Smalley, G. and Trent, J. (1989). *The language of love*. Pomona, CA: Word, Inc.

Solomon, M. F. (1989). *Narcissism and intimacy. Love and marriage in an age of confusion*. New York: Norton.

Wynne, L. C. and Wynne, A. R. (1986). The quest for intimacy. *Journal of marriage and family therapy*. 12:4, 383–394.

Ulrich, D.N. and Dunne, H. P., Jr. (1986). *To love and work*. New York: Brunner/Mazel.

9

ONCE UPON A TIME
Family Myths

I. INTRODUCTION

It is difficult to discuss family myths without also describing such phenomena as rules, roles, rituals, metaphors, and symbols. However, to the extent possible, this chapter will attempt to focus primarily on family myths.

A. History of Myths

In an exhaustive study which explores the origins and functions of myths as well as the means through which they are interpreted, Day (1984) examines myths from the 7th century B.C. to the present day. He notes how Aeschylus, Sophocles, and Euripides used mythological themes not only to explore the basic character of man and god, but also to explain their relationships. Those elements of a myth that he deemed important were that many people believed it to be valid despite the fact it could not be scientifically proved; that it was symbolic, representing a spiritual and psychic rather than an external reality; and that it was sacred and timeless, set in the "long ago." He notes that "all tales oft-repeated tend to improve and inflate quite wondrously" (p. 18).

Thus, myths are certainly not a new concept. However, exploring their purpose and utilization within the context of family dynamics and family therapy is relatively new. One of the first such explorations was undertaken by Ferreira (1963) in investigating how family myths function to maintain or bring about homeostasis within the family.

B. Definitions of Myths

Pillari (1986) defines myths as "fairly well-integrated beliefs that are shared by all family members, concerning their role and status in the family. Although these beliefs may represent reality distortions, they are usually unchallenged by the family members" (p. 6). She notes that such myths can be either negative or positive and may contain such elements as folklore, legend, taboos, superstitions, rituals—whatever is necessary to keep the family together.

Madanes (1990) refers to family myths as "legends," stories, sometimes disputed and sometimes shared, that are told repeatedly. She maintains that the stories are somewhat vague and difficult to either verify or contest, but that the meaning and its relevance to the one relating it rather than its actual content are what is more important. She suggests that whenever a client seeks therapy he is looking for a more "comfortable" version of his life, which the therapist can help him discover through either reframing or challenging his original story or legend.

Goldenberg and Goldenberg (1980) emphasize the negative aspects of family myths and refer to them as persistent "shared distortions." They go on to define them as "ill-formed, self-deceptive, well-systematized beliefs held uncritically about themselves" (p. 65). Falicov (1982) refers to myths as the family's "official party line" (p. 152) that is supported by the culture.

What all definitions of family myths have in common, then, is the sense that they are shared beliefs, usually spanning generations, which may or may not be rooted in reality but which serve an important, albeit frequently negative, role within the family as they help to shape the family members' interactions and relationships among themselves and with the world.

C. Types of Family Myths

Pillari (1986) writes of seven different types of family myths. The first is the myth of "harmony" where, despite the family's insistence that they are and always have been happy together and are perfectly in tune with one another, such is not truly the case. They use dissociation, conflict avoidance, and somatization to gloss over hostilities and disagreements. Stierlin (1973) adds that, despite the sense of boredom, depression, and misery that a perceptive observer can very quickly pick up within minutes of being around such families, they seem to believe, and want others to believe as well, that they are happy and "harmonious."

Pillari's second myth is that of the "family scapegoat" who is seen as the source of all familial problems and thus becomes the recipient of all the family's anger. Scapegoating has long been a familiar concept in family therapy. Most commonly, the person selected for that particular role is a child, but the entire family participates in the process. Just as family members, especially the parents, might displace their conflicts onto this child, the child endeavors to keep the family together by taking on the designated role, which can range from being crazy to being socially deviant.

The third myth identified by Pillari is that of "catastrophism," which cautions that the only way a family can avoid dire and tragic consequences, such as a member's total helplessness or death, is to accept certain restrictions. This myth can be seen in families who believe that to tell grandmother of a grandchild's "disloyalty" through intermarriage, out-of-wedlock pregnancy, failure at college, or any number of so-called family disgraces will "send her to an early grave."

Pillari's fourth myth is that of "pseudomutuality," which states that good families always agree, with family arguments occurring only within bad families. These "good" families proudly describe themselves as never arguing or fighting. Goldenberg and Goldenberg (1980) also write about these families, pointing out that pseudomutuality (a concept often attributed to Wynne) is a family myth that is often evident in dysfunctional families. The family members, while emotionally distant, attempt to convey a close and understanding relationship. Disagreement, independence, and the development of individual identities are discouraged in an attempt to establish the myth of mutuality and to dispel a sense of meaninglessness and emptiness that often occurs in dysfunctional families. Change and growth are to be defeated.

The fifth myth is one of "overgeneralization" in which each family member is given a restricted role that carries with it a set of expectations across all circumstances. If a family member is considered the incompetent one, regardless of what he does, there is something wrong with his behavior. The case of Billy, which follows, vividly illustrates this myth.

Billy, a young man seen by one of the authors in family therapy with his mother and grandparents, was viewed in such a way by his family. He had at one point, after much work on the part of the hospital team, become involved in a vocational rehabilitation program and proudly announced during a family therapy session that he had packaged so many pieces of plastic eating utensils that day. His grandfather quickly criticized his achievement, stating that the amount of work completed seemed so small. As soon as Billy explained that he had packaged many more than any of the other clients, his mother commented that packaging utensils was a meaningless job.

The myth of "togetherness" is the sixth one Pillari describes; it warns that because people outside the family are untrustworthy, the family must always stick together, regardless of their problems. He points out that this myth is central to the dynamics in incestuous families. It is also evident in less dysfunctional families.

Rose, also seen by one of the authors, is a 38-year-old divorced mother of a 6-year-old son. Her mother lives in another state, and Rose calls her almost daily—sometimes as frequently as three times in one day—to discuss all aspects of her life in great detail. Even when she is feeling very angry with her mother over something that has occurred between them, Rose quickly represses such feelings and responds in her daily calls as though nothing unpleasant or unsettling has transpired between them. Rose is uncomfortable talking to any of her friends because her mother has always told her that people cannot be trusted. In therapy, she has worked on issues of distrust and oversuspiciousness toward others, but that did not prevent her from nearly going into a state of panic when the man she had been dating for several months asked for her car keys so that he could bring the car from two blocks away to the restaurant they were leaving in order to prevent her from getting soaked in the rain. At that moment, she was convinced he would steal her car.

The last myth defined by Pillari is that of "salvation and redemption" which calls for someone outside the family to come in and save it. This savior can be a wealthy benefactor, a new member (for example, a newborn child expected to bring the couple together, or the entry of a stepparent), or perhaps a family therapist expected to "cure" an identified person within the family. In some families, the redeemer might even be a horse or a winning lottery ticket counted on to bring into the family the answer to all their problems, undoing all the present and past pain and suffering the family might have experienced.

Another family case seen by one of the authors is that of Wally, a 66-year-old retiree. His wife is an alcoholic. Throughout his life he had had high hopes of striking it rich and living "on easy street." While overtly denying that she had the same expectations, his wife, too, had bought into Wally's dreams. Over the last several years, the hopes of both Wally and his wife have dimmed as his opportunities have faded and she has become increasingly dependent on alcohol. The one hope they hang onto is that one day he will win a million dollar lottery. The myth is that with that "windfall" all their troubles will instantly end. In the meantime, they are failing to make meaningful life changes while they "wait for Godot."

Goldenberg and Goldenberg (1980) list 20 myths that are specific to marriages and that are typically viewed as ways in which marital happiness is achieved. In looking at each of those myths from a family systems perspective, however, they point out some of the fallacies and pitfalls inherent in them. An example of those myths is one that states that marital partners should be unselfish and unconcerned with their own needs. A problem with such a myth is that neither self-absorption nor selflessness is desirable in the extreme. People need personally satisfying, sharing relationships rather than ones in which they are regarded merely as appendages to others.

D. Functions of Family Myths

Goldenberg and Goldenberg (1980) suggest that myths serve several purposes for families. Myths can define the family, perhaps showing it to be more upstanding, moral, kinder, or helpful than other families; or myths can distinguish between individuals within the family, such as one side of the family being industrious and the other side lazy. These distinctions might well be misstatements and distortions, but they are generally accepted by the entire family as "truths." What a family believes about one of its members can set up expectations that continue from one generation to the next.

One of the authors saw Pat, who has an aunt whom the family has labeled "crazy." Pat describes herself as physically looking and sounding exactly like that aunt. It is no coincidence that Pat and the rest of her family consider Pat to be emotionally fragile and "nervous." As Goldenberg and Goldenberg (1980) point out, this explanation then becomes "the basis for explaining all interactions involving that labeled person" (p. 69). Indeed, whenever Pat does or says something that is at variance with her siblings' opinion of how she should behave, they quickly dismiss it as a manifestation of her being "off," although Pat functions as well as if not better than they—a reality they might all need to examine were they to abandon this myth.

Stierlin (1973) suggests that family myths serve two major sets of functions. One set is defensive in nature, enabling intrafamilial distortion of reality to defend against pain and conflict. The other set served by family myths is protective in nature, providing a boundary between the family and out siders such that the real family dynamics remain unclear to everyone. As Stierlin explains it, the two sets of purposes are interrelated, as a family can continue to believe its image distortions only so long as those outside the family do not understand and challenge those distortions.

Pillari (1986) comments on these defensive and protective functions as well. Occasionally, individual family members might become aware of the distortions in the familial image, but such perceptiveness is generally short-lived. All members contribute to and attempt to preserve the myths.

Imber-Black, Roberts, and Whiting (1988) have written extensively about family rituals and their use as therapeutic interventions. They define rituals as "coevolved symbolic acts that include not only the ceremonial aspects of the actual presentation of the ritual, but the process of preparing for it as well. It may or may not include words, but does have both open and closed parts which are 'held' together by a guiding metaphor. Repetition can be a part of rituals through either the content, the form, or the occasion. There should be enough space in therapeutic rituals for the incorporation of multiple meanings by various family members and clinicians, as well as a variety of levels of participation" (p. 8).

The rituals that families perform are frequently an outgrowth of the family myths. For example, a family myth might be that a couple in love should always understand and know what each other's needs and wants are without being told. Such a couple may find itself repeatedly arguing about inconsequential petty incidents when the real issue is that each feels abandoned and unloved because the other fails to comply with an unspoken wish that cannot be uttered because that would "spoil" it.

On the other hand, rituals can also be used as a means to critically examine family myths. Palazzoli, Cecchin, Prata, and Boscolo (1978) often prescribed rituals to families as a way to destroy family myths, some of which had existed in a family over generations. These authors define the family ritual as "an action or series of actions, usually accompanied by verbal formulas or expressions, which are to be carried out by all members of the family" (p. 95). They present a vivid example of a myth which stated "all for one and one for all" and was transmitted down three generations, ending with the depression and suicidal attempt of a 15-year-old girl. The purpose of the ritual prescribed to that family was to allow them to break the rule inherent in that myth, thereby allowing the family free rein to explore the problems heretofore covered over, hidden or repressed by the myth.

Boszormenyi-Nagy and Spark (1973) caution the family clinician to be aware of certain societal and cultural myths that might impede family growth. One such myth is that people can be considered completely independent and disconnected from their family of origin. While it is desirable for people to accept responsibility for themselves, they cannot be understood outside the context of their familial relationships. By the same token, the myth that nuclear families can be "self-contained" entities ignores the invisible and unresolved loyalties that inevitably connect them to their extended families. Intense emotional ties and family loyalties are the glue that cement family myths and allow them to be continued unquestioned through the generations. Boszormenyi-Nagy and Spark note: "Just as that which is symptom or psychopathology in the individual can mean implicit loyalty, therapeutic change or improvement, while consciously welcome, on a deeper level often implies invisible disloyalty to the family of origin" (p. 370). Thus, to directly challenge the family's loyalty or myth, the therapist risks the family's abrupt termination of treatment. Pillari (1986) also addresses the issue of loyalty when she describes some family myths as being sacred and taboo. The loyal family member respects the sacred myth.

Cultural issues and myths were examined by Friedman (1982) in looking at the "myth of the shiksa." Friedman attempts to put to rest a Jewish myth that has survived for over a thousand years. This myth states that non-Jewish women (shiksas) attempt to lure Jewish men away from their religion and their families and thereby eventually destroy their culture. In pointing out the fallacy of such a belief, Friedman not only shows how similar myths exist wherever cross-cultural marriages exist, but also how family process rather than culture is more likely to determine the power of myths. He discovered ". . . that in any family, but particularly in easily identifiable, ethnic families, to the extent the emotional system is intense, members confuse feelings about their ethnicity with feelings about their family" (p. 506). Friedman cautions that culture and environment not be permitted to absolve families' responsibilities for the way in which they function and he puts forth a reminder that not all families from the same background, or even individuals from the same family, behave in the same manner.

Anderson and Stewart (1983) propose that an effective way for therapists to deal with the initial resistances of families feeling threatened by therapy is to invent a myth, with the expectation that a family will more willingly accept therapy for someone else or when they feel there is a rationale that does not require them to admit they have a problem. Thus, if the therapist fails to challenge but does not explicitly agree with the family's myth that therapy is only for the sake of the child, for example, they might be more willing to come in for treatment.

Lewis (1985) describes how myths can be problematical for stepfamilies, especially since most family myths apply to either first-married or tradi tional nuclear families. She believes that, despite current changes in attitudes, family configurations other than that of the traditional first-married nuclear one are viewed as "second best" and that all too frequently families unsuccessfully attempt to reach the first family ideal while saddled with negative images of alternative family styles. She lists several problematical myths such as, "(a) stepparents should love their stepchildren just like (and perhaps better than) the biological parents; (b) motherhood and fatherhood are the exclusive domain of biological parents; (c) children should be loyal to one mother and one father only; (d) the stepfamily should compensate for all the deficits of the first family; and (e) stepchildren should be pitied for 'losing' a parent" (p. 14). These faulty beliefs create additional burdens on families already struggling with the enormous task of structuring a complex system.

Of course, this discussion of family myths would be incomplete without a recognition that not all family myths are negative or impede the growth of its members. Positive myths, which carry high expectations for achievement, well being, decency, and mutual support can encourage and motivate family members when they truly believe "we're all winners" and "we shall be successful," whatever their criteria for success may be. Nevertheless, most of the myths that come to the attention of and require intervention from family therapists are described by Stierlin (1973) as those myths that "appear to safeguard the family members' entrenchment and involvement with each other. Instead of being windows through which a therapist may look into a family's interior, they are rather like painted walls around ghetto buildings, distracting and/or amusing while they keep the onlooker safely outside" (p. 123).

II. STRUCTURED TECHNIQUES

A. *Finding Alternatives*

1. RATIONALE

McMullin (1986) discusses how irrational thoughts can be weakened when such thoughts are constantly bombarded with counterarguments. These counterarguments, or "counters," as he calls them, can range from a single word such as "rubbish" or "ridiculous" to describe the irrational thought to a sophisticated philosophical statement. The important elements are that the counters are forceful, logical, realistic, and stem from the clients' own values and experiences.

The technique as described here is based on McMullin's "alternative interpretation," which posits that clients' first interpretation of an event is not only usually the worst but also the interpretation most resistant to change. An example of a bad first interpretation might be that of a client who experiences a panic attack and believes he is going to die. To be able to counter such an irrational belief with alternative interpretations can be enormously helpful. In much the same way, dysfunctional myths in families are irrational interpretations of some event—no longer questioned—that happened once upon a time. Finding viable alternatives to explain that phenomenon can release families to experience different expectations and thereby behave differently.

2. PROCEDURE

The first step would involve a thorough exploration of the myth, accumulating all of the details: when it was first noticed, by whom and under what circumstances; how often it occurs; who seems most affected by it and how; how each family member copes with and reacts to it, and so on.

Once the family has scrutinized all of the implications of the myth as they currently understand it, they are then asked to consider alternative explanations or counters. It is much more effective for the family to develop their own counters rather than to attempt to adopt a list provided by the therapist. The more counters the better. These counters are developed over a period of several weeks.

As the family develops their list of counters, they are instructed to set aside their first impression of events connected with their myth and to use the logical counters. Practice over a period of time will not only cause a suspension of judgment and reevaluation automatically, but also weaken the dysfunctional myth.

3. CASE EXAMPLE

Mrs. Q. requested therapy because of her 15-year-old daughter's behavioral problems. During the initial interview, Mrs. Q. described her dismay that her daughter, Maria, had recently lied to her, and she feared that this was the beginning of a destructive pattern. The incident had occurred a couple of weeks earlier. Mrs. Q. had come home early from work and saw several of the girls who attended Maria's high school. She asked why they were not in school and they informed her that they had a half day off because of teachers' meetings. When Maria arrived home, she said she had just come directly from school. Her mother confronted her, and she then admitted she had spent a couple of hours at a pizza shop with a boy from school.

The picture of Maria that unfolded was that of a well-behaved, hard-working student who did well in school. She was not allowed to date, nor was she permitted to hang out after school in the afternoons with her girlfriends because "they attract boys." Mrs. Q. and her boyfriend drove Maria to school every morning. She was well protected. What soon emerged from the sessions was that Mrs. Q., and her mother before her, had been an unwed teenage mother. Now, Mrs. Q. was determined that her daughter would not follow what for her seemed an almost inevitable path. The family myth was that teenagers cannot stay out of "trouble," so Mrs. Q. felt it her obligation to take full responsibility for her daughter's behavior and to shield her until adulthood. She attempted to do that through the establishment of rigid boundaries which her adolescent daughter was just beginning to resist.

Mrs. Q.'s initial interpretation was the worst one possible: that her daughter's rebellion against her overprotectiveness spelled doom via teenage pregnancy. After exploring all the circumstances surrounding Maria's grandmother's pregnancy, as well as Mrs. Q.'s, Mrs. Q. was helped to explore and eventually come up with alternative interpretations of Maria's behavior: that Maria had lied about her pizza "date" because she did not want her mother to worry unnecessarily; that Maria was a normal 15-year-old who was curious about boys; that Maria wanted to be like the other girls and have a boy be interested in her; that Maria, unlike her mother, enjoyed a warm supportive home environment and need not misinterpret sexuality for emotional caring, and so forth.

As Mrs. Q. became more adept at finding other interpretations for Maria's behavior, she could also begin to see that alternatives other than a teen pregnancy were available for Maria as well. The futility of expecting she could successfully shield Maria completely from any heterosexual contact was also explored, with the idea that Maria needed to know how to appropriately handle any such contact that was bound to occur.

4. USES

This technique can be effective with individual clients, as well as with families. Any faulty or irrational beliefs, dysfunctional myths, poor self-image, phobic behavior, or low self-esteem, to name a few problems, can be countered and subsequently resolved through the process of challenging the initial, inappropriate interpretations.

B. *Twice Upon a Time: Rewriting the Past for the Future*

1. RATIONALE

One way to intercede and break the cycle of a dysfunctional myth is to rewrite the past (and what now appears to be an inevitable future) to reflect how the family would ideally want their future to be. Families get a second opportunity to interpret past events and can then work toward making corrected versions come true in the future. This technique is an adaptation of an activity developed by Wise (1983) to examine not only how people are recipients of tradition but also how they can contribute to and create their family traditions.

2. PROCEDURE

The family is encouraged to explore in detail what has emerged as a family myth. An example might be a family struggling under the myth of male underachievement and currently faced with an adolescent son's lack of academic success. The family is asked to give all the details that it can remember about the men who never made it: how their failure to reach potential was manifested, what lost opportunities resulted, and how it might have affected the current generation.

After thoroughly exploring how all of those missed and failed opportunities might have affected their life today, the therapist should ask the family how, in the best of all possible worlds, their future prospects would be if all those men—Dad, Uncle Joe, Grandfather Jim, Cousin Jake—had reached their full potential. Would the family be nationally recognized as astute lawyers, wizard accountants, unbeatable salespersons, among other possibilities? The focus of the problem should be the inability of those men to break through and achieve according to their actual potential rather than an assumption that they were incapable of achievement. Therefore, the current emphasis should look at what the family can do now, in the present, to interrupt and break through that vicious cycle to see that their newly fantasized future becomes a reality.

3. CASE EXAMPLE

Mr. and Mrs. K. began marital counseling 18 months after their marriage, which had occurred shortly before the birth of their child. The couple agreed that they were beginning to feel they had little in common except the baby whose conception had prompted them to marry. Mr. K. complained that his wife was "too slow" intellectually, while she accused him of being hypercritical and perfectionistic. A sensitive issue for both of them was Mrs. K.'s lack of a high school diploma.

Mrs. K. described her family of origin as indifferent to education. She was, for example, permitted by her parents to drop out of high school at age 15. In fact, her mother gave her written permission to do so. Not only did her parents fail to encourage her and her siblings to attend school, but there was an assumption that the children could not be educationally successful. Neither parent had graduated and that was "just the way it is in our family."

Mrs. K. conceded that she would feel better about herself if she had a high school diploma. Aside from being embarrassed about not having one, she feared that employers, to whom she invariably lied about her education, would find out and fire her. However, Mrs. K. feared that achieving a high school education was beyond her ability. She had no facts to substantiate this belief. She had neither been assigned to special classes as a child nor been classified as learning disabled. Since she had not applied herself to her studies, it was not surprising that she had not learned to master the material. It was not that she lacked the capacity to obtain a high school education, but rather that she had lacked the opportunity because of faulty beliefs and assumptions.

Mrs. K. was encouraged to imagine how her current life situation and her future might be different if her parents and her older siblings had obtained high school diplomas. She pictured her family urging her to achieve and saw herself with a degree from a two-year college working in a professional capacity. Once she dared to see that as a wish, further discussion and planning ensued regarding how she and her husband could work together to reach her goal.

4. USES

This technique can be utilized in situations where clients have unrealistic fears and anxieties about tackling goals and projecting into the future. It first allows them to fantasize and dream and then offers a challenge with a realistic plan with which to attain what once seemed unreachable. Rewriting the past blocks the self-fulfilling prophecy and creates a practical, creative alternative.

C. Accentuate the Negative: A Paradoxical Approach

1. RATIONALE

Frequently, although families have turned to therapy for help, they are very resistant to accepting whatever help is offered. Homeostasis, referred to earlier in this chapter, is threatened when an attempt is made to introduce change. A paradoxical instruction to a family communicates a contradictory message that calls both for change and for no change simultaneously: "One asks people to stay the same, within a framework of helping them change" (Haley, 1987, p. 79).

Corey (1991) states that paradoxical interventions place clients in a double bind. If they follow the prescription, they exhibit control over the symptom and mastery in their life; if they rebel against the prescription, they must give up the symptom, which also places them in control. The key is to ask the family to not only continue to believe in the myth and thereby engage in the problematic behavior, but to also dramatically exaggerate or increase the behavior. This technique has also been referred to as prescribing the symptom. If the paradoxical prescription is successful, the family will rebel against the therapist and decrease the behavior.

2. PROCEDURE

Paradoxical interventions are not easy to devise. The therapist is conveying several different messages. For example, she is saying that she is concerned and wants to help. However, in telling the family to continue their behavior, she is also indicating that she is not sure the family can change. The family should not feel that the therapist is insulting, nor that she believes them to be beyond hope.

Before a prescription can be formulated, the therapist needs to clearly understand and isolate the symptom. If it is a compulsive behavior such as handwashing or checking the knobs on the gas range, the therapist can dramatically increase the number of times the patient must engage in the behavior. If a family has focused on one member as the carrier of a symptom, they can be urged to focus in on that symptom in an exaggerated way.

3. CASE EXAMPLE

Mr. and Mrs. N. entered couple therapy because they were experiencing severe conflicts centered around Mr. N.'s 10-year-old son, Freddie, from a previous marriage. Mr. N. wanted custody of his son and Mrs. N., who had initially agreed to that plan when Mr. N. had proposed it several years earlier, was now extremely reluctant to accept such an arrangement. Mr. N. felt betrayed by his wife. She felt neglected by her husband whom she saw as totally emotionally wrapped up with this son.

Of great significance in this family is Mr. N.'s family history and the myth of the nonexistent father. His father deserted him when he was a toddler and his mother was ineffectual and neglectful. Mr. N.'s mother had also been brought up in a fatherless household. Mr. N. had never resolved his feelings of being abandoned and "discarded" and believed that without his total presence in the life of his son, his son would be an ineffectual and unhappy individual.

Attempts to get Mr. and Mrs. N. to detriangulate Freddie and to look at other conflicts between themselves that also prevented them from being able to resolve issues around Freddie were to no avail. Freddie remained the focus. The therapist then explored the myth of the unavailable father and how Mr. N. saw himself in this light. He insisted he could never desert his son and gave that as his reason for wanting total custody. He was commended for being so loyal and concerned, but then the therapist wondered if he was really concerned enough given all the terrible things that could happen to a fatherless boy. Mr. N. was asked to list all his worst nightmares about what might befall his son were he not to gain total custody. Mr. N. saw his son as an adult selling newspapers on the street. The therapist urged him to go on by asking: "Is that the worst that could happen?" Eventually, he saw him homeless and destitute. By the time he reached the point of imagining his son as having some incurable disease, he recoiled by saying: "This is ridiculous. Freddie won't die if he's not with me!" At this point Mr. N. was able to talk with his wife about possible options, including how he might be a positive influence in his son's life even if they were not living in the same household.

4. USES

Paradoxical interventions usually clarify rather than cure problems within the family (McMullin, 1986). Often, paradoxical techniques are not used until after therapists have tried more conventional procedures. Embracing

change is especially difficult in rigid family systems; thus, paradoxical procedures can be most useful in those cases (Sherman & Fredman, 1986).
This technique can be used when one is dealing with depression, insomnia,
phobias, and anxiety disorders.

Corey (1991) lists several situations in which paradoxical procedures
would probably be ineffective or even irresponsible, such as crisis situations,
suicide, homicide, violence, abuse, or excessive drinking.

III. TIPS AND TACTICS

1. Collect Proof to Support Irrational Beliefs

One young woman complained that her family had always been highly
critical of her and had never been helpful. She saw herself as always having struggled alone. She was asked to keep a daily log for one month of
each contact with her family—parents and siblings—with an analysis of
what was not helpful about the interactions. It did not take long for her
to see that her "proof" disproved her claim of "always." While there were
a few instances of critical remarks, the vast majority showed caring and
support.

2. Gentle Challenging

Lewis (1985), in looking at myths and stepfamilies, finds that directly
challenging some of their myths can also serve to directly educate the families as well. She proposes that questions such as: "What makes you think
your child cannot benefit from having intimate relationships with four caring
adults instead of just two?" (p. 15) be asked. One mother who had
remarried, as had her ex-husband, was challenged with a similar question
about her two young sons. After exploring what a typical week was like
for her sons, who were the focus of a lot of positive attention, she stated:
"I can't feel bad for them; they have it really good!"

3. Prescribe a Task

This strategy was illustrated in a case presented by Lewis (1985) in which
she worked with a newly formed stepfamily. The husband and wife each
had a young daughter from a previous marriage. As the daughters tried to
adjust and showed evidence of grieving over their parents' divorces, the new
couple worried that their current marriage might be harmful to the girls.

One way they tried to reassure their daughters was to assure them that they would always be treated equally and without favoritism. Knowing that to be impossible, the girls constantly tested them and accused them of not treating them the same.

Lewis assigned a task to the parents. It was around Easter time. They were to prepare two identical Easter baskets, with jelly beans, for the girls. The beans were to be exactly the same by number and color. Upon receiving the baskets, the girls were to compare each bean, color by color, to ensure that their parents had properly executed their task. This task helped the parents realize that neither their efforts to achieve sameness for the girls nor their allowing the girls to be in charge of the family was a viable solution to resolving remarriage adjustment issues.

4. Invent a Fairy Tale or Fable

McMullin (1986) suggests that fantasy through stories, fables, and metaphors can communicate complex subtleties and assist in cognitive restructuring. The therapist can either fabricate her own stories, draw upon the experiences of unidentified clients, or use published literature. The fairy tale reframes or reinterprets earlier experiences or dysfunctional beliefs that families have. The fairy tale should incorporate positive feelings and provide direction, a kind of "bridge" between the old dysfunctional belief and a new more positive one. It can be written prior to the session, read to the family and then given to them to take home. It should not be explained to the family, but rather they should be given the opportunity to work together on its meaning. If the fairy tale is made up spontaneously during the session, it should be audiotaped so that the family can review it at home.

5. Reevaluate the Family Myth

Often a couple in marital conflict present with the current perception that nothing in their marriage has been good. When encouraged and able to remember some positive events and feelings, the couple can experience their marriage in a less painful way. It can also enable them to feel better about themselves. To have entered into and remained for whatever length of time in a totally negative relationship conjures up a much poorer self-assessment than to realize that there was a point when things were good and to try to think about what went wrong rather than about what was never there.

6 *Give a Generic Prescription*

The concept of family myths connotes a certain amount of rigidity—members are not allowed to become independent of one another and identify with others. Family members must all, in Stierlin's (1973) view, adopt the party line. They are like those who staunchly insist that brand-name aspirin must be more effective than acetaminophen, NF, its generic equivalent. In an effort to loosen the rigidity that binds families into a collusive relationship that accepts the limitations set forth above and the distortions and misstatements as though they are immutable facts, families can be encouraged to generalize their myths.

They need to begin to accept the fact that in all families, parents get angry at their children, for example, and that such feelings neither mean that they do not love their children nor that they are bad parents. They are not unique. This is not an X family problem (brand name), but one that is true of all families and generic to being a family. Thus, the family's beliefs can be normalized.

7. *Cleaning the Attic*

Wise (1983) devised an exercise to ferret out and reevaluate family traditions that have been discarded. It is as though they were stored in an attic just collecting dust. He suggests that some of those customs or beliefs are family treasures which with some dusting off or minor repairs might provide some measure of satisfaction.

An example of a family that might have discarded a treasure is one which fails to celebrate birthdays, anniversaries, and other milestones. This might stem from earlier unpleasant occurrences accompanying such events, such as an alcoholic parent whose unpredictable behavior convinced the family to avoid celebrations which could prove embarrassing. The family can be instructed to list family traditions that it once enjoyed, either in their nuclear family or family of origin, and to think about the meanings those traditions had and how they could be reintroduced into the family. Thus, this can become a family that can gather together for a good time without expecting a calamity.

REFERENCES

Anderson, C. M. and Stewart, S. (1983). *Mastering resistance: A practical guide to family therapy.* NY: Guilford Press.

Boszormenyi-Nagy, I. and Spark, G. M. (1973). *Invisible loyalties: Reciprocity in intergenerational family therapy.* N.Y.: Harper and Row.

Corey, G. (1991). Theory and practice of counseling and psychotherapy (4th ed.). Pacific Grove: Brooks/Cole.

Day, M. S. (1984). *The many meanings of myth.* NY: University Press of America.

Falicov, C. J. (1982). *Mexican families.* In. M. McGoldrick, J. K. Pearce and J. Giordano (Eds.). *Ethnicity and family therapy.* NY: Guilford Press.

Ferreira, A. J. (1963). Family myth and homeostasis. *Archives of General Psychiatry, 9,* 457–463.

Friedman, E. H. (1982). *The myth of the shiksa.* In M. McGoldrick, J. K. Pearce and J. Giordano (Eds.). *Ethnicity and family therapy.* NY: Guilford Press.

Goldenberg, I. and Goldenberg, H. (1980). *Family therapy: An overview.* Monterey, CA: Brooks/Cole.

Haley, J. (1987). *Problem-solving therapy.* (2nd ed.) San Francisco, CA: Jossey-Bass.

Imber-Black, E., Roberts, J. and Whiting, R. A. (1988). *Rituals in families and family therapy.* NY: W. W. Norton.

Lewis, H. C. (1985). Family therapy with stepfamilies. *Journal of Strategic and Systemic Therapies,* 4(1), 13–23.

McMullin, R. E. (1986). *Handbook of cognitive therapy techniques.* NY: W. W. Norton.

Madanes, C. (1990). *Sex, love, and violence: Strategies for transformation.* NY: W. W. Norton.

Palazzoli, M. S., Cecchin, G., Prata, G. and Boscolo, L. (1978). *Paradox and counterparadox: A new model in the therapy of the family in schizophrenic transaction.* NY: Jason Aronson.

Pillari, V. (1986). *Pathways to family myths.* NY: Brunner/Mazel.

Sherman, R. and Fredman, N. (1986). *Handbook of structured techniques in marriage and family therapy.* NY: Brunner/Mazel.

Stierlin, H. (1973). Group fantasies and family myths—Some theoretical and practical aspects. *Family Process,* 12(2), 111–125.

Wise, G. W. (1983). *Where do you fit into your family's traditions?: Five-*

minute lesson plan. Columbia, MO: Child and Family Development Office, University of Missouri.

ADDITIONAL RESOURCES

Bagarozzi, D. A. and Anderson, S.A. (1989). *Personal, marital, and family myths: Theoretical formulations and critical strategies*. NY: W. W. Norton.

Goldenberg, I. and Goldenberg, H. (1991). *Family therapy: An overview* (3rd ed.). Pacific Grove, CA: Brooks/Cole.

10

WHO'S THE FAIREST OF THEM ALL?
Treating Cross-Cultural Conflicts

I. INTRODUCTION

Examining cultural issues in family therapy is a multifaceted and compli-
cated undertaking. There are so many angles from which to approach this
very essential, but all too often ignored, factor in therapy. One can think
of similarities and differences between the therapist and the family being
seen or one can consider differences within a family and how those differences impact on the family's ability to function, or both factors can impact
simultaneously.

Culture provides the language and framework through which people come
to understand their experiences. It outlines not only opportunities but also
constraints. Cultural patterns change and evolve constantly. People deal with
several cultures simultaneously—their corporate culture, their school culture, their cultural heritage. Each has a specialized language and unique
ways of coping with and interpreting the world.

A. *Definition*

Culture can be broadly defined as behaviors that are typical of a particular group. More specifically, Pinderhughes (1989) defines culture ". . . as the sum total of ways of living developed by a group of human beings to meet biological and psychosocial needs," and she asserts that the group's values, norms, beliefs, attitudes, folkways, behavior styles, and traditions are those elements necessary for its survival as a group (p. 6). Friedman (1988) warns, however, of the need to be aware that not all members of a culture agree to the same extent about the validity of the values and customs of their background. In noting that it is important to understand not only a person's loyalty to tradition but also how he responds to the position he has taken, he states: "Every religious tradition and cultural background has its own neurotic usefulness" (p. 123). Sometimes people use tradition as an excuse for not doing what they want to avoid or for not accepting change. He claims that drastic moves such as complete family cutoffs and disinheritances are about unresolved family of origin issues rather than about cultural or religious values, regardless of the family's protestations to the contrary.

B. *Therapeutic Principles and Culture*

1. CULTURAL DIVERSITY BETWEEN FAMILIES

Examining multicultural issues in family therapy requires that therapists not only be aware of differences between themselves and the families they serve but also be familiar with other dimensions of multiculturalism. This is frequently explored through very global cultural comparisons, for example, between Irish, Italians, Greeks, Blacks, Indians, and Koreans, to name a few. In fact, a very fine study of such comparisons has been done by McGoldrick, Pearce and Giordano (1982). They cover almost two dozen ethnic groups and include such information as historical perspectives, levels of acculturation, family patterns, rituals, roles, values, and treatment issues.

One difficulty encountered in such studies and comparisons, however, is the danger that accusations of stereotyping will occur. Many families within the same culture differ to some extent in the degree to which they hold onto values and traditions of that culture. A change in life-style and/or acculturation, for example, can cause dramatic shifts. Also, most cultures divide into differing subgroups and social class structures. Therefore, it is essential that the therapist consider not only the cultural heritage of the family being evaluated but also its socioeconomic status, level of acculturation, and traditional versus nontraditional attitudes. Recently, writing about Black families, Boyd-Franklin (1989) acknowledged that the material could be misused in a stereotypical way, but urged clinicians to treat it ". . . as presenting a set of hypotheses that can be accepted or rejected by each therapist with each new Black family in treatment . . . providing . . . a new beginning point for each new therapeutic encounter" (p. 258).

Another dimension against which multicultural issues can be explored is to look at fundamental concepts within the psychological field and how one's cultural background influences how one interprets those concepts.

Roland (1988) contrasts cultural differences in psychoanalysis as it is taught and practiced in Western society and in Japan and India. An interesting difference that he writes about is the concept of ego boundaries, both inner and outer. In Western societies, one is expected to maintain outer boundaries that are rigid enough to prevent merging. When describing families with schizophrenia, for example, early family therapists wrote of an "undifferentiated family ego mass" (Bowen, 1966) to emphasize their fusion and symbiosis. Those who were most undifferentiated, either through an inability to attain self-awareness due to a blurring of their feelings and their intellect (inner ego boundaries) or to a blurring between their own feelings and those of other family members (outer ego boundaries), proved to be those who functioned most poorly. However, in Indian and Japanese cultures, there is greater permeability of outer boundaries and more merging. A Western family is more likely to accept the concept of locked bedroom doors than either the Japanese or the Indian family. The therapist working with these families needs to be aware of such differences.

On the other hand, Roland (1988) points out that the Japanese and the Indians develop a more private inner self than do Westerners. The Indians, though very slow to trust, are very much in touch with their innermost conflicts and feelings and will eventually share them with their therapists once they trust them. The Japanese are likely to be less aware and also less direct.

Important variations in life-cycle issues also exist across cultures. While independence and a search for identity are stressed during the adolescence of Western teenagers, interdependence and dependence are the norm for teenagers in Japanese and Indian families.

Another significant distinction between these three cultures exists in the relationship between therapist and patient or family. The Western therapeutic relationship tends to be one of equality "ideals" even when there is, in fact, a hierarchy. This is not so in Japanese and in Indian therapeutic relationships, where the structure is experienced as being hierarchical, with a superior and a subordinate, leading to quite different transferential and countertransferential implications.

These examples of cultural differences relate to important concepts in psychoanalytic therapy—ego boundaries, transference, countertransference, resistance, and psychosocial development—and the therapist must be cautious in her approach to a family and her assumptions that these concepts have a certain universality. Further examples could be given for any family therapy theory.

Some of the tools that clinicians find useful and regularly rely on can have negative effects within the therapeutic relationship when the therapist is unaware of possible cultural implications. The genogram is one such tool. The genogram is a visual map of the family. (See pp. 56–60 for a detailed description of how it is constructed.) McGoldrick and Gerson (1985) describe the genogram, which is usually constructed in the first session, as an important method not only for helping the family to gain a new perspective of itself but also to facilitate the therapist's "joining" with the family. However, in some cultures eliciting the kinds of material required to fill out even the basic information about the nuclear family would be viewed as intrusive. Reticence or withholding of information could then easily be labeled as resistance by the therapist and conveyed to the family as lack of cooperation. Such negative connotations might well be avoided if that kind of information is elicited after the joining has already occurred.

2. CULTURAL DIVERSITY WITHIN FAMILIES

Problematical multicultural issues within families typically occur as a result of intermarriage. Intermarriage is often seen as a threat to cultural and religious groups. In the not too distant past, there were laws in several states in this country that prohibited interracial marriages. Rather than be considered a beneficial occurrence that allows the blending of positive attributes from both cultures, intermarriage is frequently feared as a threat to the group's survival. Marriage and founding a new family are deemed a continuity of a family's history and sense of beingness, which is disrupted through intermarriage.

McGoldrick (1982) points to the added complications inherent in intermarriage families and notes that adjustment difficulties are most significant when cultural differences between the spouses are greatest. While knowledge of cultural differences can help a spouse understand the other's behavior, it is important that knowledge not be used to absolve responsibility for either inappropriate or ineffectual behavior through excuses that imply that the behavior cannot be modified because it is culturally rooted.

Out of the intermarriages, of course, come children. And rearing conflicts that normally arise are frequently exacerbated by either the dual religion, the dual culture, or the biracial nature of the marriage. The intermarriage of children from intermarriages is even more complex culturally.

Barringer (1989) reports that the number of children born to multiracial couples has increased from an annual rate of 30,000 births in 1968 to 100,000 recorded in 1987. With over a million such children under the age of 20, they and their families represent a small but unique minority that appears to be steadily increasing. Barringer (1989) cited Federal statistics that as of 1987 showed a breakdown of mixed-race children as follows: 39 percent Black and White, 36 percent Asian and White, 18 percent American Indian and White, and seven percent Asian and Black or American Indian and Black parentage.

Gibbs and Wang (1989) point out that American society places a great deal of importance on labels, thus, a person's ethnicity and cultural background usually impact strongly on how others respond to him. That can lead to conflict and ambivalence for children of mixed races, not only about themselves but also about other family members.

Being required to racially identify themselves can be confusing for children of mixed races. On school forms do they check both the Black and the White or the White and the Asian boxes (although the instructions usually read "check only one box")? Or must they describe themselves as "Other," with an explanation? Children of both Black and White parentage are often traditionally considered Black because of their physical appearance. Such assumptions discard a large part of their cultural heritage, which can lead to resentment on their part. Additionally, those discriminated against often accept the prejudiced attitudes and negative attributes directed toward them. The Clark and Clark (1947) classic studies showed Black children preferred white dolls. Those studies have been replicated over the years with similar results. Despite the great strides in the passing of legal legislation against racial discrimination that evolved out of the civil rights struggles of the 1960s and the heightened Black pride alluded to in the slogan "Black is beautiful," many Blacks have not acquired a positive racial identify. Biracial children are not immune from also accepting some of the prejudicial attitudes toward their Black heritage and thus toward themselves.

Wright (1988) has illustrated some of the complexities faced by biracial children in the development of their identity. He cited the case of an eight-year-old girl whose mother was White and her father Black. Racial issues were not discussed in the home, but were rather acted out in parental disagreements over seemingly insignificant issues, such as the daughter's hairstyle. The mother admittedly did not consider her daughter to be Black, although that was how she was identified by the community in which they lived and by her fellow students—both Black and White—who rejected her. Clearly, an essential intervention with this family would be the acknowledgment of racial issues within the family that require resolution through change and/or acceptance, along with the need to help the daughter integrate her dual heritage and to learn the value of both of her cultures.

Coner-Edwards and Edwards (1988) refer to "identity confusion" in the context of the psychological consequences for Blacks who achieve middleclass status. They write of the conflict experienced by the achieving Black who is enjoying aspects of the dominant culture while feeling guilty about the Blacks (often family members) who have been left behind and whose opinions and love still matter a great deal. Hamburger (1964) refers to this phenomenon as experiencing "psychic bends," moving from one cultural context to another, but currently in between both—not willing to abandon the familiar but also not yet adept at the new. Pinderhughes (1989) writes of "biculturality" to describe how the Black middle-class family struggles to hold onto two worlds while maintaining their cultural identity and heritage. Watkins and Rountree (1984) noted that first generation Black professionals attempting to negotiate both the white corporate culture and their community often form an "in-between class" comprised of people who fail to achieve a sense of belonging in either world.

Many members of the Black middle class are insecure with their status, feel isolated, and overcompensate for such anxieties through a variety of ways. A major coping mechanism is self-denial by either not accepting their success as earned or not being able to fully enjoy it for fear it will soon disappear. Coner-Edwards and Edwards (1988) define the struggles for the Black middle class as being both internal (anxieties, insecurities, and selfdeprivation) and external (society's biases and prejudices), but stress that the progression into the middle class should also be viewed as an opportunity for greater growth.

Other problems arise for those who are not members of the dominant culture. They can suffer from social alienation which can lead to conflicts with and/or withdrawal from society. Feelings of rejection or victimization by the dominant culture are not unusual. Many minorities, lacking confidence about their ability to participate in the larger system, fail to even try. They might attempt to deny the dominant culture, associating as much as possible only with families of the same culture, often to encounter familial conflicts as younger children begin to acculturate. The other side of that problem can be evidenced through poor self-esteem and lack of respect and pride in their own identify. Lacking an understanding of the usefulness of their own customs and traditions, they shun the old culture and avoid other families that share it. Not all individuals want to be identified with their root culture or with the ethnic and racial group with which most people would identify them.

It is essential that the therapist explore these issues with the family to help them resolve possible conflicts that have arisen for them as a result of their in-between status. Jalali (1982) believes "biculturation" to be the ideal way for families, especially recent immigrants, to adapt to the anxieties and conflicts occasioned by being faced with a different culture. To take the best of both cultures without dropping all the old or familiar ways prevents a disruption in the family's sense of identify.

3. AMBIVALENCE REGARDING TREATMENT

In many cultural groups, analysis and therapy are often disparaged as a waste of time, a luxury, evidence of self indulgence, a sure sign of weakness, and lack of faith in either religion or in other family members. Those who seek therapy are more likely to feel embarrassment and guilt than pride in their decision to enter a treatment geared toward resolving family conflicts. They are often secretive and fearful of having their mental competence or stability questioned. For example, Edwards (1988) lists several fears that he believes middle class Blacks have about being in analysis, ranging from finding out or disclosing negative things about oneself to losing control either of one's feelings or of oneself to another. These are all issues the therapist must be aware of and appropriately address where needed.

II. STRUCTURED TECHNIQUES

The focus of the techniques outlined in this section is the use of cultural traditions to bring about positive therapeutic change. They are designed to enable families to understand how their idiosyncratic interpretation of their culture affects their functioning, and to assist them in seeing their cultural differences as a strength rather than as a liability. It is important to enhance the family members' sense of belonging not only within the family but also within their own and the dominant cultures.

A family that feels insecure and/or unsupported because of recent immigration status, language difficulties, loss of extended family, educational and economic deprivation, or discrimination is all too likely to isolate itself out of fear, anger, and frustration. Because various family members inevitably must have contact with the dominant culture—through attendance at school, work, or religious and social institutions—acculturation begins for some, if not all, family members. When the transitions do not occur for all family members at the same rate, conflicts can arise. Often it is those conflicts which propel families into therapy. Once they are identified, families can be helped in making cultural transitions and in ultimately overcoming their feelings of alienation.

A. We Shall Overcome

1. RATIONALE

The song "We Shall Overcome" is an old spiritual well known as a rallying theme first embraced in the 1960s by the Reverend Martin Luther King, Jr., and the Civil Rights Movement. Soon thereafter, it became symbolic of any struggle in which those involved felt they were dealing with injustices and difficult obstacles. This symbol embraces two very important themes for the African-American family: its history of having survived slavery and the importance it places on religion. The technique as described below for African-American families can be adapted to any cultural group that has struggled hard to survive and succeed against injustice and adversity.

2. PROCEDURE

This technique can be introduced to an African-American family, for example, by pointing out the strength of African-Americans who have survived years of slavery, Jim Crow laws, and institutionalized racism and discrimination. The family is then encouraged to talk about problems it has conquered, such as attaining employment where no jobs seemed available, attaining higher education when it seemed out of reach, or even day-to-day problems it has resolved. With the African-American family's tradition of strong religious beliefs, the therapist can underscore such faith by citing scriptures as is often done in the Black community. Two frequently quoted scriptures are "the Lord will provide" and "the Lord helps those who help themselves." Whichever basic philosophy the family embraces can be reinforced and then counterbalanced by the other statement with a "yes, but" response such as: "Yes, it is true he does provide, but . . ."

The therapist then proceeds to teach the family to use problem-solving techniques by discussing the nature of the problem and openly encouraging evaluation and selection of alternative solutions in a noninhibiting way, such as brainstorming. Following this, the family plans and implements the solution and evaluates the results (Epstein, Schlesinger & Dryden, 1988). Jacobson and Margolin (1979) propose a clear "problem-solving manual" that therapists can use with couples to resolve conflicts and discord. Included are such details as how long a problem should be discussed, how it should be defined, how to be specific and brief, and the importance of the complainer admitting his role in the problem about which he is complaining.

3. CASE EXAMPLE

Mrs. G. was a recently separated 36-year-old African-American mother of two daughters. The 10-year-old daughter was from Mrs. G.'s previous marriage and the 2-year-old from her current marriage. Her second husband had left the household six months earlier. Mrs. G.'s presenting problem was depression and an inability to "get moving."

Mrs. G. described feeling helpless. Her husband was not providing sufficient financial support and she was struggling with the bills. However, she had not gone either to family court or to a lawyer for advice. She was not working, but had past work experience and was very talented. In fact, earlier in her marriage she had considered working at home and marketing her own crafts. Several times during the session she repeated: "I don't know what to do."

When asked about support systems, she said that most of her family lived in distant states and that they were not close either geographically or emotionally. They were not available for support. She added that she spent a great deal of time on her knees praying for a solution. At that point, there was some discussion about the support that Mrs. G. derived from her religious convictions. Along the way, the therapist remarked that "the Lord not only provides a way but he helps those who help themselves." Mrs. G. was then encouraged to think of instances where she had been able to help herself while in difficult circumstances. She recalled that there were other times in her life when things looked bleak, the dissolution of her first marriage being one such instance, but that she had survived.

Mrs. G. was helped to sort out her most pressing problems; with the therapist's assistance she began to problem-solve around her financial woes. She first went to family court for a formal arrangement around child support. Later, she engaged in brainstorming regarding how she might earn money through her craft skills. She exhibited some hesitation about promoting her crafts, which appeared to be some reluctance on her part to seem immodest. The therapist reminded her of the biblical story admonishing a person to not hide his talent. Throughout the sessions, her personal survival and heritage of survival were stressed as were the inspirational aspects of her religious beliefs and faith.

4. USES

This technique can be used with many other ethnic and cultural groups, such as Jews and the legacy of the Holocaust, Poles and centuries of exploitation, or the Irish, who have suffered extreme poverty, famine, and war, to name just a few. It can also be used in less extreme situations such as to overcome a disagreement within a family that has shown a willingness to overcome conflicts in the past or to problem-solve how a family might spend a vacation together when each member wants something different from the other.

B. Linking

1. RATIONALE

Landau (1982) warns that it is important for a family experiencing conflicts due to cultural transition and acculturation to be allowed to choose its own direction and to set its own pace. She maintains that extended families generally avoid the inclusion of outside helpers and oppose the concept that the family requires treatment. One way she suggests getting through that rigid structure is for the therapist to engage primarily only one family member in the therapy, who then, through training and coaching from the family therapist, learns to function as therapist for his own family.

2. PROCEDURE

The first step is for the therapist to conduct an initial family assessment. At that time, both she and the family select the family member who is to become the link therapist. The reason for selecting a link therapist is explained to the family as a means of dealing with all the many directions and opinions in the family regarding how it should behave. The family's input into the selection process is important because the link therapist must be seen as effective and as having power in the family. Often, in more traditional families that means the selection of a male family member. It is important that this person be neither the most acculturated nor the most traditionally entrenched family member. Rather, he, too, should be conflicted and in the process of transitioning. As he resolves his own conflict, he helps the family resolve its conflict.

The link therapist agrees to attend four to six weekly or biweekly sessions with the therapist and to hold weekly sessions within the family home. A six-month follow-up session with the therapist and the entire family is also arranged in the beginning of the process. The coaching and supervision of the link therapist helps him decide how the transitional conflict within his family is to be resolved and gives him the confidence that he is competent to help create that change.

3. CASE EXAMPLE

Landau (1982) presents a case of an extended family that had immigrated five years earlier from Italy. The family, all of whom attended the initial family meeting, consisted of Mr. and Mrs. Casalviere; Mrs. Casalviere's parents, Mr. and Mrs. Girone; Mr. Casalviere's adult bachelor brother, Aldo; and Mr. and Mrs. Casalviere's three children, ages 14, 10 and 8. The Casalviere family had been referred for therapy because of the misbehavior in school of Fabrizio, their 10-year-old son.

In discussing the problem, Mr. Girone insisted there was none, Mr. Casalviere deemed it to be his son's behavior, and Mrs. Casalviere strongly alluded to an abandonment of their traditional Italian culture (language, religion, respect for elders, and familial closeness) as the source of the problem. The therapist, who believed that the more traditional members of the family would not allow therapy to succeed, selected Aldo as the link therapist. He was chosen because he was not only acceptable to both sides but also because he was currently exploring his own cultural transition.

Aldo met with the family therapist five times over a seven-week period. During those meetings, he formulated certain solutions: that the entire family should be bilingual; that Mr. Casalviere, who spent a lot of time outside the home with his friends, should include his wife in some of those activities; that the children should become more involved with their peers in school activities; and that Mr. and Mrs. Girone should become involved in community activities. During this time period, he also held weekly meetings with the family to discuss these ideas.

A second family consultation was scheduled for three months after the first. At that session, there appeared to be important changes. Mr. Girone was more relaxed, Mrs. Casalviere was more involved, and Fabrizio's behavior at school had improved. Aldo felt further treatment was unnecessary, but agreed to contact the therapist if the need arose. The school was contacted six months later and reported that there were no further problems with the children.

4. USES

Link therapy can be useful not only for families experiencing cultural transitions but also for any family where there is great resistance on the part of some members to being involved in the treatment. It can also be used in families that are geographically separated. In such instances, the link therapist, after receiving training and supervision from the therapist, might visit the side or faction of the family in another state or country. In cases where emotional cutoffs have occurred in families, one family member who is emotionally connected to all involved in the cutoff and who has not "taken sides" might be accepted by the family to provide a link and a means of resolving what seemed like irreconcilable differences.

C. Dual Sculpting

1. RATIONALE

Family sculpting is a nonverbal technique in which one family member, acting as a sculptor, arranges all the members, including himself, into a living sculpture which gives a portrait of that family's interrelationships. Several therapists (L'Abate, Ganahl, & Hansen, 1986; Sherman & Fredman, 1986; Papp, 1976; Duhl, Kantor, & Duhl, 1973) have noted how the physical proximity, facial expressions, and postures, as depicted in the sculpture, make forceful and concrete statements about a family's conflicts and coalitions.

Dual sculpting is a variation introduced by Landau (1982) in her work with families in transition. When one uses a sculptor from each of the two cultural factions—either between or within families—the conflicted sides, once depicted, can then be assisted to join together.

Families experiencing discomfort or conflict because members are acculturating at a different pace do not always recognize that as a source of their difficulties. The parents know, for example, that Dimitri has taken on an American-sounding nickname and does not always obey his father's wishes, and that Helena, at 16, continually complains about not being able to date and seems to prefer being with her friends to helping out at home. These attitudes are culturally unacceptable to the parents. The children are, in turn, sometimes resentful of the "old-fashioned" ways of their parents when compared to some of the parents of their friends at school.

2. PROCEDURE

The therapist should have as many family members available as possible, but at least four since two families or sides of the family are being represented. If the procedure takes place in a clinic or training institute, trainees can be asked to represent missing family members (Landau, 1982), but if it occurs in a private office, furniture or other objects might have to substitute (Sherman & Fredman, 1986).

The therapist might introduce the sculpting process by stating: "There appear to be two different sets of feelings or ideas about how the family is or should be. Let's try something a little different to see how it feels for each of you to be a part of this family. Since pictures are often worth a thousand words, I'd like you to form two living sculptures with yourselves as statues." In a family with intermarriage conflicts, two sculptors will be selected, each one to represent one of the two ethnic or religious sides. When acculturation issues are problematical, one sculptor should represent the more traditional side of the family while the other represents the more acculturated members. L'Abate, Ganahl and Hansen (1986) suggest it is better to have volunteer sculptors, if possible, to avoid spending a lot of time in the decision-making rather than in the sculpting process.

Next, the sculptors are told that they should arrange the part of the family that they are working with into a group of statues. They can place people into any position they wish and should also determine their facial expressions, the arrangement of their hands, and their stance. It should be emphasized that the sculpting is done with as little verbalization as possible—only to give directions but not to give explanations. The sculptors add each person to the sculpture one by one, while the therapist asks concrete questions throughout the process in order to get details, but not to influence content or the development of a theme. The therapist can add comments, such as, "Remember, you can add expressions, gestures, and change positions," or "Show father how you want him to hold his arms."

The first sculptor sculpts his view of the family as it exists in reality. Once that sculpture is completed, he is asked to fantasize and change it to conform to how he would like it to be. Landau (1982) suggests that when real rather than stand-in family members are participating, the family can "gently" discuss their reactions to the two sculptures. However, it might be more effective to merely ask for clarification but not interpretation from the sculptor, such as an explanation of the expression on someone's face or where someone is reaching. This helps to clarify the process for all involved before going on to the second sculptor. It also avoids diluting or influencing his responses. After the second sculptor has completed his "true to life" and fantasy sculptures and they have been clarified, both sculptors recreate their original true or realistic sculptures and change places with each other to experience how it feels. They discuss how they feel in the other sculptor's creation and then they change it to make it more comfortable for themselves. Next, they step back into their own sculpture that has been changed by the other and discuss their reactions to that change.

The last step in the dual sculpting calls for the two sculptors to negotiate how they might join the two original sculptures. During this process, the family, having seen both their conflicted realities and fantasized ideals as depicted by the two sculptors, are usually able to gain some insight into the problem and make some accommodations or compromises.

Finally, all of the participants are debriefed and the experience processed. While the processing usually cannot be done in one session, it should be started in the sculpting session. Participants' reactions and interpretations are thoroughly explored before the therapist adds her own. As L'Abate, Ganahl and Hansen (1986) explain: "This creates the proper implication that it is the family's job to do the work and sets the stage for later collaboration with them . . ."(p. 184). After questioning the sculptors about their creations, other family members may be asked questions, such as how it felt to be in that position, whether there was a place he or she would have rather occupied, or how it felt being on the periphery of the circle. After everyone has been debriefed and has made statements, the therapist can make some observations to stimulate further thought and discussion. A well orchestrated and explored sculpting session provides information for the therapist and family that can be reflected upon and referred to throughout the treatment.

3. CASE EXAMPLE

Mrs. B., a 36-year-old Algerian woman, sought therapy. She complained of feeling depressed. She felt her husband lacked both commitment to their marriage and sufficient concern for her as a wife and companion. She was seriously contemplating divorce, but was hesitant for several important reasons. First, Mr. and Mrs. B. had two children, a son and a daughter, ages 12 and 10, respectively. She feared the children would suffer both emotionally and financially without their father. In addition, she planned to return to Algeria to live, and divorce for women is still not acceptable there. Furthermore, she anticipated that her family would disapprove despite the fact that her mother was aware that Mrs. B. was unhappy in the marriage.

Mrs. B. and her husband had experienced quite different childhoods growing up in Algeria. Mr. B. came from a very large traditional family in which the boys were dealt with quite permissively. Mrs. B.'s father died in the Algerian war when she was quite young. After his death her mother became a full-time, independent career person, which was not common at that time. Mrs. B. and her younger brother had household chores and responsibilities.

Having spent several years in this country. Mrs. B. had become even less traditional in her thinking about her own and her husband's role within their marriage. Although he initially refused to come into therapy, Mr. B. eventually relented when it became clear that Mrs. B. was fully pre-pared to file for divorce should he not make any efforts to work on their relationship. The children, who were obviously affected by the conflict at home and by the different parental expectations of their behavior, were brought in as well.

The technique of dual sculpting was used to compare and contrast the more traditional family expectations, as represented by Mr. B.'s family of origin, and the less traditional, more acculturated ideas of Mrs. B. and her family of origin. Careful examination of all the feelings evoked allowed the couple to better understand each other's frame of reference and the need for some compromise.

4. USES

This technique can be used with any family in which conflict arises. The dual sculptures represent the two sides of the conflict. It actively involves all the family with each other and with the therapist and can be a means of engaging resistant families. Because sculpting is essentially nonverbal, it is also helpful in working with families where there are language barriers, either because the family and the therapist do not speak the same language, or with those families who use verbalizations as a defense (overelaborations, intellectualizations, rationalizations) or as a weapon (blaming, accusing, criticizing).

III. TIPS AND TACTICS

1. Family Pride Day

Special days, beyond recognized holidays, are frequently set aside in our society to bring attention to and/or express appreciation for certain groups, especially those not usually recognized. For example, there is Gay Pride Day, Black Solidarity Day, Mother's Day, and Grandparents' Day, just to name a few. The family that is dealing with cultural issues, whether as a result of acculturation or of interracial marriage, could be instructed to hold their own Family Pride Day in which the parents and children research and share all that they know about their cultural heritages. If the family has traditional dress, they should wear it on that day. Dinner should include some of their ethnic dishes. If the conflicts stem from acculturation, the younger family members can gain a greater appreciation of the customs their parents hold dear. In the case of biracial conflicts, such a sharing with all family members fosters enhanced positive identity development, especially for children who might be confused with split loyalties and denied parts of their heritage.

2. Bibliotherapy

Often people fail to appreciate that which they do not understand and they certainly cannot feel positive toward those things they do not even know exist. This is true whether one is dealing with various art forms or attempting to relate to another culture. Even today, African history and African-American contributions to this country get little attention in most school curricula. Assigning biographies of Blacks who have made important contributions and of significant African nations would go a long way toward promoting positive self-images, not only for the children in families but for their parents as well. Here again, families should be encouraged to share their newly discovered knowledge with each other. This tactic would be useful for families in transition as well.

3. Value Assessment

Often family members misperceive those things that are most important to each other. This can be problematic when acculturation is occurring. Parents often feel their children are disregarding all the values, customs, and beliefs they feel are important. This tactic is adapted from Floyd's (1982) Value Assessment Comparison technique used to increase families' awareness of their individual and common values.

The procedure is to assign the family homework. Each member is to think about those things most important to him or her and then independently draw up a rank-ordered list of those values. Next, each family member draws up a list for every other family member, rank ordering what he or she perceives to be their values. Thus, the mother in a family of four would have four lists: one for herself, one for her husband, and one for each of the two children. The family is instructed not to share or discuss the lists prior to the next session. At that session, with the therapist's help, the family explores similarities, differences, accuracy, or misperceptions around each member's values and clarifies family assumptions. An example of disparity would be the wife who lists "work" and "friends" as most important for her husband while he ranks "family" and "religion" as most important for himself. A family dealing with acculturation, for example, may be surprised to find that, although their adolescent son is becoming "Americanized," he still believes many, if not all, of the family's values to be important.

4. Seeing Through Another's Eyes

When families are experiencing cultural conflicts, especially regarding acculturation, the more traditional members can be asked to try to understand what the others might be going through. For example, a mother who fears her adolescent daughter is embracing another culture might be asked to role-play her daughter wanting to fit into a high school setting with different customs from those of her family. This could make the mother more sensitive to her daughter's viewpoint.

5. From Weakness to Strength

For those families that disparage therapy as a sign of weakness, believing they should be able to resolve their own problems, the therapist can explain how the family's seeking therapy actually shows how strong and independent-minded they are as a family. It should be pointed out to them that it takes real courage to be able to admit to themselves and to a stranger that they can benefit from some guidance in formulating solutions to their problems.

6. Therapist, Not Judge

Families from some cultures often feel they are going to be harshly judged by the therapist. It is important for the therapist to let such families know that she is not there to either pass judgment or assign blame. They need to know that only a higher authority than man can pass judgment, and that blame never helps.

7. Look on the Bright Side

Often families experiencing conflict along cultural lines are engaged in a tug of war over which culture is "better." The therapist can help them focus instead on those differences which can offer something positive to the family.

REFERENCES

Barringer, F. (1989, September 24). Mixed-race generation emerges but is not sure where it fits. *The New York Times*, p. 1.

Bowen, M. (1966) The use of family therapy in clinical practice. *Comprehensive Psychiatry*, 7, 345–374.

Boyd-Franklin, N. (1989). *Black families in therapy: A multisystems approach*. NY: Guilford Press.

Clark, K.B. and Clark, M. P. (1947). Racial identification and preference in Negro children. In T. M. Newcomb and E. L. Hartley (Eds.). *Readings in social psychology*. NY: Holt.

Comas-Diaz, L. and Griffith, E. E. H. (Eds.). (1988). *Clinical guidelines in cross-cultural mental health*. NY: Wiley.

Coner-Edwards, A. F. and Edwards, H. E. (1988). Relationship issues and treatment dilemmas for Black middle-class couples. In A. F. Coner-Edwards and J. Spurlock (Eds.). *Black families in crisis: The middle class*. NY: Brunner/Mazel.

Duhl, F. S., Kantor, D. and Duhl, B. S. (1973). Learning space and action in family therapy: A primer of sculpting. In D. Bloch (Ed.). *Techniques of family psychotherapy: A primer*. NY: Grune & Strattor.

Edwards, H. E. (1988). Dynamic psychotherapy when both patient and therapist are Black. In A. F. Coner-Edwards and J. Spurlock (Eds.). *Black families in crisis: The middle class*. NY: Brunner/Mazel.

Epstein, N., Schlesinger, S. E. and Dryden, W. (Eds.). (1988). *Cognitive-behavioral therapy with families*. NY: Brunner/Mazel.

Floyd, H. H. (1982). Values assessment comparison (VAC): A family therapy technique. *Family Therapy, 9* (3), 280–288.

Friedman, E. H. (1988). Systems and ceremonies: A family view of rites of passage. In B. Carter and M. McGoldrick (Eds.). *The changing family life cycle: A framework for family therapy,* 2nd Ed. NY: Gardner Press.

Gibbs, J. T. and Wang, L. (1989). *Children of color.* NY: Jossey-Bass.

Hamburger, M. (1964). Personal Communication.

Jacobson, N. S. and Margolin, G. (1979). *Marital therapy: Strategies based on social learning and behavior exchange principles.* NY: Brunner/Mazel.

Jalali, B. (1982). Iranian families. In M. McGoldrick, J. K. Pearce and J. Giordano (Eds.). *Ethnicity and family therapy.* NY: Guilford Press.

L'Abate, L., Ganahl, G. and Hansen, J.C. (1986). *Methods of family therapy.* Englewood Cliffs, NJ: Prentice-Hall.

Landau, J. (1982). Therapy with families in cultural transition. In M. McGoldrick, J. K. Pearce and J. Giordano (Eds.). *Ethnicity and family therapy.* NY: Guilford Press.

McGoldrick, M. (1982). Ethnicity and family therapy: An overview. In M. McGoldrick, J. K. Pearce and J. Giordano (Eds.). *Ethnicity and family therapy.* NY: Guilford Press.

McGoldrick, M. and Gerson, R. (1985). *Genograms in family assessment.* NY: W. W. Norton.

McGoldrick, M., Pearce, J. K. and Giordano, J. (Eds.). (1982) *Ethnicity and family therapy.* NY: Guilford Press.

Papp, P. (1976). Family choreography. In P. J. Guerin (Ed.). *Family therapy: Theory and practice.* NY: Gardner Press.

Pinderhughes, E. (1989). *Understanding race, ethnicity, and power: The key to efficacy in clinical practice.* NY: Free Press.

Roland, A. (1988). *In search of self in India and Japan: Toward a cross-cultural psychology.* NJ: Princeton University Press.

Sherman, R. and Fredman, N. (1986). *Handbook of structural techniques in marriage and family therapy.* NY: Brunner/Mazel.

Watkins, B. A. and Rountree, Y. B. (1984, April 28). *Bridging two worlds: The Black "in-between" class.* Presented at the Annual Convention of the New York State Psychological Association, New York.

Wright, H. H. (1988). Therapeutic interventions with troubled children. In A. F. Coner-Edwards and J. Spurlock (Eds.). *Black families in crisis: The middle class.* NY: Brunner/Mazel.

11

AVOIDING AND REPAIRING HURTS AND GRIEVANCES

Romeo: Courage, man; the hurt cannot be much.
Mercutio: No, 'tis not so deep as a well, nor so
wide as a church door; but 'tis enough, 'twill serve.
(Shakespeare. Romeo and Juliet: Act III, scene 1.)

I. INTRODUCTION

Discussion and Definitions

The family is essentially a coagulum of relationships in search of a state of well-being. Positive relationships develop out of a state of well-being. Positive relationships develop out of reciprocal ". . . trust, acceptance, respect, warmth, communication, and understanding" (Trotzer & Trotzer, 1986). Individual members' needs, values, and abilities continuously interact to define and create subjective ideations of the collective family goals. Members' daily interactions tend to move along those highways and byways perceived to lead to the fulfillment of their ambitions.

En route, minor wounds are inevitable. If these are attended to properly, before additional damage is done, permanent scars are avoided. Consider, for example, the television commercial in which a bubbly teenage girl comes bounding into the kitchen where her parents are sitting, waiting to begin a family breakfast. Her father takes one look at her and makes a quip about using jumper cables to tease her hair into style. His daughter stops in her tracks and retreats from the room in tears. As his wife glares across the table at him, he attempts to explain that it was meant to be funny, not insulting.

Later, still sobbing in her room, the teenager notices an envelope being slipped under the door. She reaches down, picks it up, opens it, takes out a card and breaks out into a warm grin. Immediately, she opens the door to find a smiling father awaiting her response to his apology. They embrace (Hallmark Hall of Fame, 1990). A wound was treated in time to prevent scarring.

Family-inflicted hurts left to heal on their own can result in the formation of grievances. The word "hurt," in Webster's Third New International Dictionary of the English Language Unabridged (1981), is derived from the Old French "hurter," meaning "to collide with," possibly connected with the idea that it denotes the "mark of a blow." "Grievance" is defined, in the aforementioned source, as "a cause of uneasiness or distress felt to afford rightful reason for reproach, complaint, or resistance."

Changes within the family unit, no matter how small, can produce conflict and distress. The resolution of disparate points of view sets the stage for the possibility of inflicting hurt and the formation of grievances. When members are faced with change, their behaviors tend to modify the dynamics which determine the future course of the family.

For example, Mr. H. opened the first therapy session for his family by complaining about mayonnaise. It seems that when he and his wife were married, she insisted upon using her brand of mayonnaise, which differed from the brand he preferred. This rigidity was attributed to her parents' refusal, upon her return home from college, to change to the brand she had developed a taste for while she was away at school. In setting up her own kitchen, Mrs. H. was determined to have her way with the brand of mayonnaise her family used. Mr. H. chose not argue the point. Instead, he insisted upon his brand of toothpaste.

Now, 12 years later, their son requests a change to the brand Mr. H. had preferred. At the next meal, the son's request is honored. Mr. H. felt hurt that his wife was so quick to honor the same request from their son that he had made 12 years ago, without success. This interaction seemed to open this family's Pandora's Box. A variety of hurts and grievances were subsequently brought to the fore by both parties, leading to arguments and a significant change in family dynamics, that resulted in their deciding to seek professional help.

In family H., differences were rarely ameliorated. They were accepted like dealt cards in an unending poker game—one for you, one for me; I'll take two; three for you. The game didn't change and each player won enough to stay in the game, but the dealers were randomly rotated. Some bluffs were called, others weren't. Occasionally, accusations of unfairness were made and from time to time there was a break in the playing. Teasing and smug remarks were made, depending upon who was in the chips at any given time. Hurts congealed into grievances which had to be avenged. The possibility of a crossgenerational alliance, however, was too much for either adult to deal with, so they attempted to call in reinforcements—a therapist.

Hurts and grievances generally develop as responses to individual differences within the family unit. Some hurts inevitably result from the lack of resources available to accommodate the needs of all parties or the inability of family members to reach a compromise solution to their difficulties. Examples of such situations abound. Three-year-old Khary cried hysterically for his mother's attention while she was bathing his one-year-old sister. Later, when his sister was asleep, he refused to play with his mother.

A husband could feel neglected by his wife who takes on the responsibilities of primary caretaker of the children. He begins to distance himself from his wife by decreasing the amount of time spent at home, becoming overly critical, withholding intimate exchanges. Behavioral patterns of this nature could result in extramarital affairs.

An elderly parent can no longer care for himself adequately, but would rather not spend the end of his life in a nursing home. His children feel that they cannot accommodate him in their homes, but would pay for a private nursing home. They are reminded by their father how he was always there for them when they were children, working a second job so that they could have nice clothes and go to rock concerts which he disliked. Hurts can be unintentionally inflicted when one's expectations are in conflict with others'.

In another family with elderly parents, a son volunteers to purchase a larger home to be able to look after them; his sister telephones from across the country every six months or so to find out how her parents are doing; she offers no other support to her brother who now finds himself having to restrict his life-style due to the demands made upon his time and finances. He is hurt that his sister doesn't make an offer to contribute to their parents' upkeep.

Sometimes, it is difficult or impossible to adjudicate a conflict. Dad promised to take the family on a two-week vacation overseas. A problem arises at work. He decides to handle it himself rather than risk a mishandling of the situation. The vacation has to be canceled. His family is hurt.

Dysfunctional conflict resolution patterns can also communicate inappropriate use of power. Indoctrination such as, "You will do this because I am an adult and I know what is best for you" and "I make the money and I will decide on how it is to be spent," rigidly applied to all family members is bound to generate scars.

Hurts can be delivered in an offhanded, flippant way without consideration of the effect a particular statement or action could have. "I married her because she could cook," said in mixed company might generate a spousal response from a hearty laugh followed by a statement similar in kind, or a flush of embarrassment, a smile in public and a stinging response or argument in the car on the way home.

Patterns evolve. Subsystems, boundaries, alliances, coalitions, and resistances facilitate or hinder the movement of the family unit and the individual members systemically through a variety of stages. The goal is to accomplish the life-tasks necessary to establish and maintain a life-style of choice. Unresolved grievances that transform into grudges will have a strong negative impact on family relationships and the ability to deal with the challenges of life.

For most people, isolated incidents of hurtful behavior may be forgotten or forgiven. Hurtful patterns, however, are far more pernicious. These destroy the ability to trust that a relationship is a benevolent one. Negative or inconsiderate behaviors bring into question the value placed upon the relationship. They weaken the ability to believe in, to confide in, to feel safe with, to rely upon, to feel secure, to predict or plan for the future. The following techniques and tactics can facilitate a return of trust and belief to the systemic interactive patterns within the family.

II. STRUCTURED TECHNIQUES

A. *Empowering Client Dominion Over the Symptom*

This technique is adapted here from "Putting the Client in Control of the Symptom" in Sherman and Fredman (1986). This paradoxical technique is commonly used by strategic therapists (Andolfi, Angelo, Menghi, Nicolo-Corigliano, 1983).

1. RATIONALE

Typically, families come to therapy when they have exhausted their remedies and feel that they can no longer deal with their situation without help.

Preoccupied with the systemic interactions surrounding their hurts and grudges, they frequently present an attitude of hopeless powerlessness when something different is suggested. They wish change to be implemented without their having to integrate anything new or divergent into their patterns of interaction.

In many cases, help directly offered is turned down, ignored, or rationalized away for any of an infinite number of subjective reasons. Therapy is frequently expected to be spelled r–e–l–i–e–f–by–therapist.

Instead of taking on this responsibility, the therapist can choose to place it back in the family's lap. The family needs to be empowered to deal with their situation despite their past failures to do so. The therapist suggests that the specific symptom, such as insulting, being disrespectful, complaining, or putting others down, be continued. This paradoxical technique satisfies two of the clients' expectations. It is prescribed by the therapist and it does not impose anything foreign upon the family. The family's symptomatic behavior is used to move the members toward gaining control over the symptom.

If the family carries out the recommendation as directed, there is a resumption of control. Should the clients reject the recommendation, they will remove the behavior from their interactions with each other, demonstrating ability to exercise control over their actions. In both possible scenarios, the client's choice is functional.

2. PROCEDURE

The therapist first needs to decrease the effect the symptom can have upon the system. To confine the symptom, a prescribed time, place, intensity, and method need to be established with the family. This can be accomplished through thoughtful circumscription of the time of day, intensity, and duration in the explanation of the intervention. The therapist paradoxically orders or cautions the family *not* to give up the behavior in its entirety, but merely to try to confine it to the prescribed time, place, intensity, and method agreed upon.

Ascertaining information about the appropriate setting for the family activity is helpful in accommodating the intervention to the family's lifestyle. This can be done by questioning the family members about the symptom. When does most of the putting down in this family take place? How much time is usually spent on putting others down? In which room does it usually take place? Do the parties stand or sit or pace? Far apart or close together? Is the television on or off? Are there any other activities that take place at the same time? What happens if the telephone rings or someone comes to the door? Are any special clothes worn? Who usually initiates the interactions? Who is best at it? Do they both or all do it at the same time and/or place or at different times and/or places?

From this information, the therapist devises an intervention. A particular room might be described as the "put-down room" or a specific time of day designated as "put down time." These labels can serve to facilitate the effectiveness of the intervention, especially if at least one family member seems to respond favorably to them.

If a family member wishes to put down another member, perhaps the whole family must be convened in the appropriate room. It could be that whatever other activities are going on in the room must cease so that the put-down could be delivered. Maybe the family members should save all of their put-downs for the half-hour period of time following dinner or before the youngest member's bedtime. When there aren't enough put-downs to fill the amount of time decided upon, the family could be required to vacate the room for the rest of the evening.

It is important to ask each member to communicate what the activity is prior to the end of the session. Everyone must be clear as to what is expected of each. The therapist should then end the session by obtaining agreement from each member to abide by the conditions specified until the next session.

3. CASE EXAMPLE

A stepfamily of four is having difficulties bringing their complaints under control. They are in their sixth session and seem to have an unlimited number of complaints about each other. They even complain about having to listen to the same complaints too often. The therapy has become stalled. Fifteen minutes into the session, the therapist rises from her chair and addresses the family.

Therapist: It appears that this family has a genuine need to complain. It is healthy, purposeful behavior. It is admirable that each of you thinks highly enough of each other to communicate your concerns. It is also encouraging to me that your self-images are strong enough to allow you to voice your dissatisfactions.

However, I understand also your concerns about the family's inability to get beyond the complaining stage to the resolution of some of these matters. A few questions: When does most of the complaining take place?

Father's Daughter: Usually at meals. (*Others nod in agreement.*) But we complain when something has to be done, too.

Father: It's impossible to get through a meal together without someone complaining. Myself included. If it's not about chores, it's about work, school, the heat, or the spinach.

Therapist: It seems that everyone would like to find a way to deal with the complaints?

Mother: My son and I would, too.

Therapist: How might we find time for complaints so that the family can relax at mealtimes?

Mother's son: In this family, it's not possible. Even when I didn't say anything at the table, someone always did. When else?

Therapist: You may need to write your complaints on a sheet of paper or just try to remember them until your "FCT."

Son: What's a "FCT"?

Therapist: Family Complaint Time. You seem to have many complaints which interfere with your daily activities. We need a more efficient system to deal with the dissatisfactions. Let's devote 45 minutes to the FCT. It is to end exactly on time. The time is to be divided equally among the persons wishing to make complaints. He or she must stop at the end of the allotted time. Each night another family member will chair the FCT to make sure it starts and stops on time and is not interrupted. This is not a problem-solving time. This is only to get complaints off your chest and to criticize others. Don't try to change anything because it will not work and will spoil the meetings. If people start solving problems, they cannot be so hurt and angry. If you have any complaints at any other time of day, write them on a sheet of paper and bring them up during the FCT. You are not, under any circumstances, to complain at any other time during the day. Agreed? (*Looks directly at each family member.*)

Father: Sounds good to me, except, when I have a complaint, I like to get it off my chest either right away or as soon as I see the other person. I don't know if I can wait until after dinner.

Therapist: I think everyone agrees with you that it is important to communicate dissatisfactions and hurts. What is being suggested here is a means of efficiently doing so. You have complained about not being able to enjoy a meal and, I suspect, each other's company, because when the family is together, a good deal of the time is spent complaining. The FCT. allocates family time daily to do just what you feel is important in a manner which allows everyone to be present to hear what is on your mind and to let you know what is on their mind as well. This will also free up some time to discuss other things as a family. Can you turn down such an audience and opportunity?

Father: You do have a point. Okay.

Son: I don't know. That's prime homework and television time.

Therapist: I think we understand that we will have to fit this time into the family schedule. In order for you to participate, you may have to do your homework a little earlier or later and tape the television program you're missing. Is that possible?

Son: Yeah, but I don't know.

Therapist: Can anyone suggest a better time for the family to get together for FCT.? (*Silence*) Can we count on your cooperation?

Son: Yeah, I'll do it.

Mother: Fine, but I may have some trouble timing my cooking.

Therapist: You may, but you can complain at FCT.

Mother: (*Smiling*) Okay, but the rest of you have to wait until the following FCT. to complain about supper. (*Others smile.*)

Daughter: (*Smiling*) I'll try, but on the weekend I sometimes have an early date.

Therapist: A young lady as charming and pretty as you probably will not lose too many dates if you tell your young man to pick you up a little later. Mother, could supper be a half hour earlier on Saturday?

Mother: I think that can be arranged.

Therapist: Are we all in agreement? (*All respond in the affirmative.*) Now, let's talk a little about what topics of discussion might be raised at the dinner table without complaining.

Prior to the end of the session the therapist reminded the family about their agreement. Each member was asked to restate the rules and procedures.

At the next session, the family reported that after the first attempt things went very well. The first time they had forgotten to time each other and Father took more than his fair share of the time. However, they reported that they did not exceed the time limit of 45 minutes and that by the end of the week they had finished with their complaints in about 20 minutes.

All agreed that the exercise was beneficial. They felt more relaxed at supper and during the day. It was felt that knowing that something was annoying to another family member affected others' behavior toward that individual.

Discussion regarding the use of the time for resolving issues came up, but it was decided to use the weekends for that purpose. The family agreed to continue the practice, which became a family ritual, for a maximum of 20 minutes after supper during the week. At school exam time, the ritual was practiced every other night.

4. USES

This technique is useful at any stage of therapy. A working hypothesis is not essential for prescribing the intervention. The symptom is being brought under control and not being replaced, thereby maintaining a degree of constancy within the system. The therapist's intervention can eliminate or reduce the occurrences of hurtful behaviors and the holding of grievances. It may also help to integrate these interactions into the system in a manner which can be beneficial to the family.

Used more frequently with rigid families, the technique provides for order at the same time it liberates the members from the oppression of having to constantly attend to the symptomatic behavior(s). Reframing the complaining behavior in a positive light encouraged family unity. Following the plan or resisting it, the clients will benefit.

B. Identifying Alternatives

1. RATIONALE

The technique as described here is adapted from Nelson (1976), Nelson & Friest (1980) and Sherman and Fredman (1986). We choose from among a variety of ways to initiate interaction and respond to others. Nelson places these choices upon a continuum ranging from major okay (acknowledging family support publicly in one's efforts to reach a goal) to major overdraft (physical abuse). An okay choice has a positive effect upon the system, whereas an overdraft is negative. A minor okay choice might be to say good morning; a minor overdraft choice could be to forget to take out the garbage. The decision not to decide or act is as important a choice as any other. It maintains the status quo.

Five categories of choice are identified by Nelson: "caring, ruling, enjoying, sorrowing, and thinking," which forms the acronym CREST. As these motivate behavior, they also represent types of intention. Specific choices, under different circumstances, could fall into different categories. In some families, a punch in the shoulder could communicate a congratulatory message; in another family, it is a signal to commence a physical confrontation. The overdraft response, "I hate you," may mask a caring intention. Intentions can also overlap, such as in the choice to engage in intercourse, sexual or otherwise.

In every family, both okay and overdraft choices are in evidence. To maintain good relationships within a family, enough okay choices need to be made by family members to compensate for the overdraft choices made.

Overdraft choices frequently cause inconvenience and hurt, tending to lead to grievances. Sherman and Fredman (1986) identify the "Well, that's the way I do things" statement as an excuse to maintain the status quo. Over a period of time, hurtful patterns can become established if overdraft behaviors increase in number and frequency. Negative expectations tend to give rise to grievances and getting even or getting-back behaviors. The parties, seeking to justify their positions to avoid hurt, may manipulate a discussion to the point at which even positive intentions are felt to be marooned in a sea of frustration.

The therapist can break this cycle by leading family members to understand that alternative choices are available and that they are capable of identifying them. By making okay choices, they can improve their relationships.

2. PROCEDURE

The procedure is described by Nelson (1976) and Sherman and Fredman (1986).

The therapist opens the session with a few statements about each person's ability to influence the outcomes of their interactions with others through choice. To demonstrate, the therapist might request that they all pound their chests and follow with a brief discussion about their thoughts prior to deciding whether or not to follow the instructions.

An explanation of okay and overdraft choices would be next. Work can then begin using family difficulties identified in prior sessions to help the family work through the process of increasing the number of positive choices.

The therapist can explain the CREST categories so as to increase the members' depth of understanding regarding the impact a choice may have on another person.

3. CASE EXAMPLE

The following case was cited by Sherman and Fredman (1986, pp. 173–175).

Therapist: Would you tell me what happened yesterday that had made you feel the way you do?

Wife: He walked into the house and got washed up and sat down to read the newspaper.

Husband: I don't know why that should bother her. I always walk in, wash up, and sit down and read the newspaper.

Therapist: You have been doing this since you got married?

Husband: I guess so, I never thought about it. And I really don't know what's wrong with my doing that. Most of the guys I know read the paper when they get home.

Wife: It's not the reading of the paper that's bothering me. It's just that the same thing happens day after day.

Therapist: You would like something to be different.

Wife: Yes.

Therapist: What changes would you like?

Wife: He used to say something when he came in. Now, it's as if I'm not even alive until he finishes the damn paper!

Therapist: After he reads the paper, you begin to talk to each other. Are you saying that you would like him to talk to you before he reads the paper?

Wife: I guess so.

Therapist: Would you be able to talk to her before you read the paper? Is this a choice that you would be able to make?

Husband: Not really. After working all day, I really like to sit by myself and read the paper. I'm not ready to talk until after I'm finished reading. I know that she's around, I just don't like getting into any big discussions for a while.

Therapist: There seems to be different needs that each of you have at that particular time of day. Your choice is that your husband talk to you and his choice is to read.

Wife: I don't need to have a whole conversation. I'd just like to know that he knows that I'm alive.

Therapist: How would you like him to do this? Perhaps you can go outside and enter the room and show him what you would like? Are you both willing to try this?

Wife: Yes.

Husband: Yes.

Therapist: Well you go outside and enter the room and make a choice that would be OK for you.

(*Wife leaves the room and reenters.*)

Wife: Hello honey. I'm home. Is everything all right?

Husband: What am I supposed to say?

Therapist: Just say whatever comes to your mind that you now feel would be her response. Then let's carry it a little further with each of you taking the other's part.

Husband: OK—that's funny—I guess I'm beginning to see that I can make an OK choice. I'd like to try to come in and say something. I'd like to work it out that way.

Therapist: Fine, Mr. H., you may go outside and come back in as if it's 7 P.M.

(*Husband goes outside and reenters the room.*)

Husband: Hello, honey. I'm home. (*Walks over and gives her a hug.*) Is everything all right?

Wife: That felt good!

Husband: I'm glad. I'm going to wash up and read the paper.

Wife: We have fish for supper.

Husband: That's OK. (*To therapist*) Is that OK?

Therapist: Why don't you ask her?

Husband: Is that what you meant?

Wife: Yes. I think that the evening would start off much better. I don't even think that I'd get bored with a hug every day. (*They both laugh.*)

The couple went on to work through their difficulties through learning to make positive choices. The therapist strengthened her relationship with both the husband and wife as evidenced by the husband's participation and the wife's success. The therapist, by moving to clarify the type of choice that could be made, joined the couple in pursuit of a positive choice acceptable to their needs.

4. USES

Sherman and Fredman (1986) point out that this technique can be effective at any stage of therapy. The role-play may or may not be included. Practice of overdraft choices is also helpful. Through the practice of both types of choices, the couple learns to communicate what is agreeable and disagreeable to each spouse.

The technique can also facilitate the defusing of a power play. One's ability to distinguish need and desire from lack of caring or approval enables family members to identify hidden agendas in their communication. An appropriate response to the underlying intention can then be made. This creates the opportunity for open and honest discussion of alternatives to reach underlying goals—an okay choice.

C. Perfect Family Fantasy Fulfillment Technique

1. RATIONALE

Conditions under which hurts and grievances become established excuses for family members' negative interactive behaviors are varied. Frequently, the reasons for maintaining such patterns are forgotten or withheld by the family. The Perfect Family Fantasy Fulfillment technique (Liberman et al., 1980) provides the therapist with a procedure through which the deleterious components of the family system can be addressed in a nonthreatening, positive manner. It moves the clients to a different vantage point from which to view and address their difficulties. The individual members' reality is shifted into a fantasy association from which a hurt or grievance will be redressed.

The therapist is seeking an answer to the question, "What would it take to relieve your hurt or enable you to give up your grievance?" Once the relief is identified by each person, the family is guided in making positive exchanges to satisfy the self-pleasing desires of the individual family members. In the process, cyclical patterns of hurt leading to grievance and resulting in another hurt are broken. Roles, boundaries, and expectations are reorganized.

The therapist moves the family's reality into a fantasy context from which the individuals' desires and family needs are reconciled, using available family resources. Reciprocal behaviors necessary for functional interactions are adopted by the family members to satisfy their own needs.

2. PROCEDURE

The therapist begins by asking members to identify several areas of difficulty commonly found in families. These may include child rearing, finances, allocation of time, household chores, recreation, work, understanding, and communication. A list could be provided for the family by the therapist. When one is working with adults only, intimacy and sexual issues might be added. The list should be written on a blackboard or sheet of posterboard mounted on an easel to aid in focusing the family's attention.

Each member is then told to imagine that he or she has resources to fulfill any personal need, whether realistic and reasonable or fantastic and unreasonable, which would make the family perfect in each of the listed categories. Conversation is banned. Members are encouraged to be as selfish as they wish and to write as many needs as they can come up with in each area. (These will provide the therapist with the new branches from which positive patterns of interaction within the family system can be cultivated.)

Upon completion of the list, the therapist requests each family member to choose to be read aloud the one desire which would result in the most improvement of the family. After all are read, the family might decide which request is to be considered first or the wishes can be satisfied in the order in which they were read.

The satisfaction of each desire must be considered. The therapist becomes actively involved in guiding the family to decide how each member's request can most fully be satisfied. Some of the more exotic or impossible requests may need interpretation so that an alternative activity capable of fulfilling the underlying need can be undertaken. Compromises may have to be negotiated. Perhaps one request will necessitate participation in a number of steps over a period of time instead of the one leap envisioned in the fantasy. For example, one might visit several culturally different restaurants or a variety of foreign movies instead of embarking upon a trip around the world. The reality into which the fulfillment of one's fantasy is fitted must provide satisfaction of the desire, resulting in the elicitation of positive feelings.

Following the formulation and agreement on one or two plans of action concerning one or two of the desires, the family would be encouraged to begin to put their plans into operation. With some families, however, it might be better to wait until all members' fantasies are expressed before suggesting implementation.

The plans decided upon will depend upon the availability of resources. Money may have to be saved. Arrangements or reservations might have to be made. The time of year might not be conducive to carrying out the agreed-upon plan of action. Schedules may have to be altered. One plan of action may be all that can be handled at once.

In subsequent sessions, the therapist needs to be attentive to the family's goal-focused behavior. A log of their experiences kept between meetings can serve to keep the members on track and enable the therapist to provide timely assistance, if needed. Positive experiences can be reinforced by the therapist reiterating the report and requesting additional information about every aspect of an episode. Questions about the procedure could be followed by inquiries into feelings and thoughts which accompanied the experience. Praise, congratulations, and perhaps some back-slapping or handshaking tend to add a nice touch when progress is made or a fantasy is fulfilled.

Should a plan fail to be implemented as expected or if any of the arrangements fall through, it is important to avoid criticism. In the real world, we do not always get what we want. The therapist needs to compliment individuals for trying and for imagining such a plan. This will facilitate future efforts, which need to be initiated immediately.

Such additional efforts might include helping in the identification of alternatives which are more likely to meet with success. Perhaps a less delicate problem could be tackled. More honest and specific descriptions of what members want and are willing to provide for each other may be needed. A more modest proposal might be called for.

Families in which there are more than three members might be encouraged to act upon a maximum of two desires per week. This would ensure enough time for positive reinforcement of success or for corrective measures to be discussed if the exercise was not satisfactory or was not completed.

3. CASE EXAMPLE

The H. family was a chaotic family. Everyone was at each others' throats over who should do what, when, how, and why. Ms. H. was feeling overwhelmed with the housekeeping and parenting of the girls. The two teenage girls felt that their parents were too restrictive in their dealings with them and overreactive to each other. Mr. H., although he enjoyed his work, felt that all he ever did was work. In his role as father, he particularly felt left out and abandoned. He was angry that no one appreciated him and how hard he worked for them. As a result, he would severely criticize all other family members about tasks and performance.

All expressed feelings of being put upon by the other members of the family to do things in addition to what they considered to be their responsibilities. The family looked forward to coming to therapy together, despite the arguing that took place.

After reading all four fantasies, the family decided to attempt Mr. H.'s first. He fantasized a magic carpet ride deep into a forest, away from it all, with just the family. They would have time to talk, get to catch up on what was going on in their lives, and discuss future directions. Mr. H. felt that he personally needed an outdoor activity which would completely remove his thoughts and attention from the everyday stresses of his daily routine. He listed this activity as a solution to a family problem in the area of understanding.

During a session of brainstorming, the family decided to investigate the possibility of spending a week camping in a National Park or Forest. Ms. H. volunteered to write letters of inquiry regarding reservations and additional information about the parks or forests as long as someone would relieve her of some of the cleaning around the house. The girls decided to take care of the laundry and dishes. They also volunteered to obtain information from the school and local library about the locations of parks and forests and information about camping equipment. Mr. H. agreed to set aside two hours a week to meet with everyone to discuss the progress, make decisions, and take care of the financial matters.

It was also decided that plans for other members' desires should be discussed in session and acted upon. The family became intrigued with a backpacking venture across an island in Lake Superior.

Two weeks of vacation were marked on the calendar for the trip. Inquiries were made, followed by the necessary reservations; needed equipment was identified; expenses were calculated. The family car (to be spotlessly cleaned inside and out) and a ferry, the only transportation to and from the island, became the family's magic carpets. ("two magic carpets for you, Mr. H. How do you feel about that?" remarked the therapist at one point.)

During the planning period, much of the bickering between members gradually subsided. By the end of the two months, it was agreed that even if they did not actually go, they had an improved family. They then implemented their plan.

The stories they told about howling wolves and shadows at night and their trekking and wildlife observations during the day were quite intriguing. The troubles they had with the equipment at first, their aching feet and backs after a couple of days, and a few serious discussions they had en route, on the island, and on the return home seemed to instill a renewed sense of family. The family then moved on to planning and fulfilling the other members' fantasies.

The fantasy work becomes the instrument that blocks and heals the hurt as all family members pitch in and make the fantasy a reality. The attacking and blaming behaviors which characterized much of family life when everyone was at home had significantly decreased by the time the family returned from their trip. Whatever it was that had previously kept them from inter-acting harmoniously continued to dissolve as they worked on the other members' desires.

In another family, a wife's cruise became a day spent touring on the "Queen Mary," a tourist attraction in Long Beach, California (Liberman et al., 1980). A family in which a child whose fantasy was to run away to join the circus and make other people happy because his parents and older sibling did not spend enough time with him went to the circus at Madison Square Garden and the Nassau Coliseum. In addition, the youngster was to be taken to at least one circus per year as long as he continued to want to go. In the course of fulfilling the fantasy, the other family members agreed to increase the amount of time spent with their youngest member between circuses as well.

4. USES

This technique is useful with a wide variety of families whether the basis for the hurtful pattern of transactions is easily discussed or deliberately with-held, unknown, or forgotten. Catering to individual members' needs within the context of improving family life makes the procedure effective with many resistant clients. The reason(s) for holding a grievance may be per-ceived as silly, immature, or at odds with the individual's desired self-perception when related to anyone outside the immediate family. The Perfect Family Fantasy Fulfillment technique uncovers hurts and grievances and frames them in a positive workable structure.

The technique may not be effective in families in which members are unable to freely express their fantasies. In one family, a youngster wanted to be the devil. His parents forbade even discussing the request and threatened to terminate therapy if the therapist pursued it in any way.

III. TIPS AND TACTICS

1. Encourage the Use of Complimentary Language

The good is often taken for granted in dysfunctional families. Comments such as "I expect my children to do the right thing" or "What is so special about my husband buying me a watch when the other one couldn't be repaired" or "My wife chose to stay home and raise the children" are fre-quently suggested as excuses for the lack of praise.

2. Avoid Exaggeration When Upset

Magnification of facts or events to support a point of view tends to lead the parties away from the issue. State as clearly and succinctly as possible what is requested or necessary.

3. Introduce a Time-Out Procedure

In session, when discussions begin to get off track or a little too emotional, introduce a time-out procedure. One family member could be coached to say, "Darling, this discussion is beginning to get too emotional/ out of hand. Let's table it until tomorrow night so we can continue in a calmer frame of mind. How about 6:30? We both will also have had an opportunity to think over what has been said so far." It is important to set a new date for the resumption of talks and to obtain agreement on the day and time for the next round of discussion.

4. Visualize a Plan in Action

The therapist might facilitate a family member's verbal description of how to avoid verbally abusing another member and follow up the description with the client visualizing himself in the situation, interacting with other family members to accomplish the goal. This can be accomplished one segment at a time or as a unit. Following repeated visualizations, the plan can be put into operation. It is important that the family member feel confident of the success of the plan prior to implementing it.

5. Identify How Each Brings Out the Worst in Others

Beavers (1985) suggests that the therapist have each family member identify his or her own role in bringing out the worst in other members. The behaviors contributing to the unwanted actions in the other family members can then be eliminated. This can be accomplished by increasing the frequency of behaviors which result in a positive response or through the identification of new ways to elicit what is desired.

6. Help Family Members Make Their Needs Known to Other Members

If a wife wants an attentive husband, she needs to make that known to her mate in a positive rather than a put-down manner. She should also be encouraged to describe positively what would constitute being attentive. Without that knowledge, a husband could find his attentive behaviors unrecognized by his wife (Beavers, 1985).

7. Have a Member Interact With the Empty Chair

Bauer (1981) suggests the empty chair projective tactic as a variation of the technique described by Perls, Hefferline and Goodman (1951). The therapist would see each family member separately or work with cotherapists who would conduct their sessions in other rooms. The individual would enter into a dialogue with another family member who is not present. Positive and negative thoughts and feelings can be expressed or the client could be restricted to either positive or negative communication. The session could be audio or video taped and shared with the absent member in a subsequent session, or observed by the absent member through a one-way mirror. It is common for the therapist to help a client begin by asking questions. However, it is best if it is made clear that the family member is expected to speak his mind without external help or focus.

Ms. A., despite her husband's assurances that he would refrain from verbally harassing her over her criticism of him in session, found it extremely difficult to do so. Her position was that she felt uncomfortable saying negative things about him in front of him and the children. After much discussion, the family members and the therapist were able to convince her to direct her comments to the chair her husband usually occupied in session.

The family left the room and she was able to talk about an unhappy interaction in which she felt unfairly treated by her husband and the children. The discussion was taped. Upon completion, Ms. A. asked to leave the room while her family returned to listen to what she had said. The therapist discussed the incident with the family and then called Ms. A. into the room. After a few sessions, Ms. A. was able to interact more freely in such discussions.

8. Reinforce Positive Interactions Within the Family System

Jacobson and Margolin (1979) point out that once the therapist stops assigning or inquiring about positive interactions, they tend to decrease in frequency prior to becoming integrated into a family's pattern of interaction. Three suggestions to prevent this from occurring are included below. The experiences would be followed up with discussion in the next session(s).

a. The therapist can instruct the family members to choose one day of the week between sessions to acknowledge other members' pleasing behaviors.
b. Have the spouses record the pleasing interactions they receive and then read their lists at the end of the day. This could be carried out on a daily basis or the list could be compiled over the course of a week and read once a week.
c. Family members could be instructed to leave each other one note of appreciation daily between sessions. The experience would then be discussed in subsequent sessions.

9. Discuss Differences in Male-Female Values

Zuk (1981, p. 241) has identified observed differences in male and female values. The masculine tendency is to ascribe more importance to "discontinuity values," described as "order, authority, reason, systemic functioning, compartmentalization of life, efficiency, schedules, and *respect*." Feminine tendencies are towards "continuity values"—expressiveness, warmth, nurturance, disclosure of emotions, exceptions to rules, egalitarianism, viewing life as a whole, and, *love*".

Engaging a family in discussions of the relevance of these observations to their family patterns generally opens up the system to scrutiny. "Do these gender-specific values hold true in this family? How so? Can you describe specific behaviors exhibited by family members which support these observations? weaken their validity? Why do you think these values become so deeply ingrained in us?" Then, inquiries as to why or how the values are acquired can initiate the discussion. "How does this happen? Are these differences in values the source of the hurt that you are experiencing? What kinds of changes would you like to see, if any? " Later, discussion as to methods of harmonious integration of what seems to be discordant on the surface may lead to functional changes. The process normalizes their differences as gender issues within the culture and diffuses them as personal assaults. The responses of the children are usually quite interesting and challenging.

10. Discuss Family Members' Expectations of Other Family Members

"What do you expect from your wife? husband? mother? father? sister? brother? child(ren)? Which are the important ones? Are other family members aware of your expectations?" (*Ask the respective family members if they were aware of these expectations.*) "How are expectations communicated in this family? How are your expectations of family members met? (*Request the clients to be specific.*) How can you help family members to live up to those expectations you feel they have not been able to satisfy? Is it necessary that they live up to all of your expectations? Where did you learn to expect these things?"

11. Teach Appropriate Expressions of Anger

Anger is an emotion we all need to express from time to time. It is usually a spontaneous response to a remark or an event. The emotion itself is natural and healthy. The behavior that expresses anger, however, is frequently of the dysfunctional kind, resulting in hurt and the formation of grievances.

Mace and Mace (1986) suggest that the therapist help clients deal with their anger by removing the cause. The family members would enter into a contract agreeing to use the following method to deal with their anger:

a. *Acknowledgment*: As soon as a family member is aware of his/her anger, that emotional state will be communicated. The communication is to be accepted as fact, without blame or accusations.

b. *Recantation*: The acknowledgment is followed by a statement reassuring the other member(s) that they will not be attacked. "Although I'm angry with you, I will not attack you." This signals that defensive maneuvers will not be necessary, thereby avoiding conflict.

c. *Entreaty*: The angry party requests the help of the other(s) in the dispersement of the angry feeling. Once a coalition is formed, there is a significant decrease in the possibility of dysfunctional negative behavior occurring.

d. *Resolution*: Both parties begin to deal with the situation as soon as possible. Either the anger was unwarranted and due to a misunderstanding or it was appropriate as a result of being provoked. The conclusion is an apology, which helps to reduce the hurt and anger.

Initially, the family may need to practice this tactic in session, guided by the therapist. Additional help is generally needed with the resolution phase. In aiding the family in the acceptance and resolution of anger, the therapist provides the family with a means to remove a significant obstacle in their path toward a functional family system.

12. Get the Parents Together

Hayes (1979) strongly recommends that, especially in families with children, parents plan time to be together, as a couple, on a daily basis. The therapist could help them to find some time in their schedules and, perhaps, initially aid the couple in identifying discussion topics or activities, if this is difficult for them. This time need not be for an extended period during the day, nor must it be for the same amount of time at the same time every day. What is important is that the adult subsystem remain a viable part of the family life.

Therapy needs to help maintain the couple relationship within the family. Kirschner and Kirschner (1986) suggest that the couple go out together—to have a meal (perhaps breakfast, if it could be arranged) to see a movie, or go to the gym. It is also suggested that they be encouraged to spend time to catch up on each other's thoughts, concerns, intimate exchanges. If need be, the therapist might help them to explore the areas of dressing attractively for each other, the exchange of gifts, and romantic behavior.

13. Build Mutual Trust

Trust is often the victim of hurt.

It is, therefore, important that the therapist strengthen the feeling of trust among family members. In session, Jacobson and Margolin (1979) suggest the therapist monitor the positive by: a) requesting clients to list the pleasing things done by other members, b) continuously separating members' intentions from actions, c) identifying positive exchanges within sessions, and d) inquiring as to the positive transactions which may have occurred between sessions.

Beavers (1985) suggests that it is important for family members to view themselves as fighting for the same objectives. He suggests that: a) the therapeutic setting encourage the expression of mixed feelings and confusions, b) all behavior be viewed as helpful and complex, c) parodying be discouraged, d) the good guy/bad guy perspective be discouraged, e) the realization that living together involves influencing, complementing, and colluding with others be encouraged, and f) the notion that family members' needs tend toward similarity and complementarity when they are not the same be reinforced.

REFERENCES

Andolf, M., Angelo, C., Menghi, P., and Nicolo-Corigliano, A. (1983). *Behind the family mask: Therapeutic change in rigid family systems.* New York: Brunner/Mazel.

Bauer, R. (1981). Gestalt therapy strategies to reduce projection in families. In A. Gurman (Ed.), *Questions and answers in the practice of family therapy* (pp. 417–420). New York: Brunner/Mazel.

Beavers, R. W. (1985). *Successful marriage: A systems approach to couples therapy.* New York: W. W. Norton & Company.

Cameron-Bandler, L. (1978). *They lived happily ever after: A book about achieving happy endings in coupling.* Cupertino, CA: Meta Publications.

Hallmark Cards (April 29, 1990). Hallmark Hall of Fame: *Caroline.* Commercial Advertisement, CBS: Channel 2.

Hayes, M. P. (1979). Strengthening marriage in the middle years. In N. Stinnet, B. Chesser, and J. De Frain (Eds.), *Building family strengths: Blueprints for action* (pp. 387–398). Nebraska: University of Nebraska Press.

Jacobson, N. S., and Margolin, G. (1979). *Marital therapy: Strategies based on social learning and behavior exchange principles.* New York: Brunner/Mazel.

Kirschner, D. A. and Kirschner, S. (1986). *Comprehensive family therapy: An integration of systemic and psychodynamic treatment models.* New York: Brunner/Mazel.

Liberman, R. P., Wheeler, E. G., de Visser, L. A. J. M., Kuehnel, J. and Kuehnel, T. (1980). *Handbook of marital therapy: A positive approach to helping troubled relationships.* New York: Plenum Press.

Mace, D. and Mace, V. (1986). *How to have a happy marriage: A step by step guide to an enriched relationship.* Nashville, TN: Abingdon Press.

Nelson, R. C. (1976). Choice awareness: An unlimited horizon. *Personnel and Guidance Journal, 54,* 462–467.

Nelson, R. C. and Friest, W. P. (1980). Marriage enrichment through choice awareness. *Journal of Marital and Family Therapy, 6*(4), 399–407.

Perls, F. S., Hefferline, R. F., and Goodman, P. (1951). *Gestalt therapy.* New York: Julian Press.

Sherman, R. and Fredman, N. (1986). *Handbook of structured techniques in marriage and family therapy.* New York: Brunner/Mazel.

Trotzer, J. P., and Trotzer, T. B. (1986). *Marriage and family: Better ready than not.* Muncie, IN. Accelerated Development.

Webster's third new international dictionary of the English language, unabridged (1981). P. B. Gove (Ed.). Springfield, MA: G&C Merriam Company.

Zuk, G. (1981). *Family therapy: A triadic based approach* (rev. ed.). New York: Human Sciences Press.

Additional Resources

Crosby, J. F. (1989). *When one wants out and the other doesn't: Doing therapy with polarized couples.* New York: Brunner/Mazel.

Imber-Black, E., Roberts, J. & Whiting, R. (1988). *Rituals in families and family therapy.* New York: W. W. Norton & Company.

Isaacs, M. B., Montalvo, B. & Abelsohn, D. (1986). *The difficult divorce: Therapy for children and families.* New York: Basic Books.

Moultrup, D. J. (1990). *Husbands, wives and lovers.* New York: Guilford Publications.

Visher, E. B. & Visher, J. S. (1988). *Old loyalties, new ties: Therapeutic strategies with stepfamilies.* New York: Brunner/Mazel.

White, G. L. & Mullen, P. E. (1989). *Jealousy: Theory, research and clinical strategies.* New York: Guilford Publications.

12

DEFUSING AND REDIRECTING THE POWER PLAY

I. INTRODUCTION: CONFLICT AND POWER

Symptoms in couple and family therapy are often most dramatically evident in conflicts among the members. Conflicts typically lead to power plays in which the members try to overcome the others rather than negotiating the differences to achieve a cooperative and constructive agreement. If the pattern persists, it is clear that neither is strong enough to win the conflict and the opposing sides are evenly balanced. If there were a winner, the conflict would end. However, as an example, the attacker is frustrated by the passive-aggressive one who withholds. Neither gets what he wants. Why, then, do they persist?

Each theory provides its own answers to that question. In general, the various systems theories advocate that the dysfunctional pattern serves some useful purpose in the system. A few examples are: (1) the child's misbehavior gets the parents to focus their attention upon him, thereby detouring a more serious fight between the parents that might break up the family; (2) the conflict helps to mobilize a depressed member; or (3) the conflict is the only way the distancing members know how to maintain connection. The purpose may also be to teach one another the "right" or "better" way to be or to do, such as honing important skills or becoming more aggressive, relaxed, or responsible.

Individuals create the system and behave with intentionality and purposiveness (Sherman & Dinkmeyer, 1987). We work to convince others to meet the needs and expectations consistent with our perceptions of self (Dreikurs, 1964). For example, a person who believes he is not good enough will engage others to stroke him with appreciation, to criticize him as not good enough, or to take a one-down position on him.

A major motivating force in human behavior is the striving for personal significance and belongingness (Dreikurs, 1953: Lombardi, 1975). Toward that end, we create myths, expectations, goals, and patterns of interactive behavior to achieve the goals. We also hope to influence others to conform to our wishes. Thus, operationally, the beliefs and goals form the foundation for the purposes of our behavior patterns. Power is the line of movement or actions taken toward fulfilling those purposes (Sherman, 1983).

We hold a great many beliefs, some of which are antagonistic to one another. A few are more pressing than the others and we tend to organize our behavior around them both individually and systemically. We make them our *priority* in terms of attention, goals, and resources. We use our power and energies most directly in the service of these priorities (Satir & Baldwin, 1983; Kfir, 1981; Bitter, 1987). In the competition among beliefs and in our willingness to devote power, energy, and resources lies the concept of the hierarchy of values. Regardless of what we say about our beliefs, the actual patterns of behavior that we follow provide the best indication of our hierarchy of values. So, observing what we do (how we use power) is more crucial than what we say we want or believe (Adler, 1966).

By observing the repetitive direction of the behavior and the consequences of the behavior to self and within the system (that is, what behavior is elicited in return), we can assess the priority value of the behavior, its likely goal, and what reinforces its continuation.

The systemic pattern is created when two or more persons cooperate in a reciprocal interaction. The repeating power play exists and continues only as long as the participants continue to cooperate, each performing his or her part according to the rules of the game they have established.

In addition to the desire to get what one wants, the power play can arise from many other sources. (1) The tone of voice is itself often an invitation to a fight, irrespective of content, when the voice is perceived as an attack because of hardness, irony, shrillness, or yelling. (2) Similarly, body language may signal hostility even when the spoken words do not. Sometimes, merely alerting the person to the hostile half of the double message can be helpful in clarifying the communication (See "Checking Intentionality," p.261). (3) Complaining is often perceived as a negative put-down requiring a vigorous defense. Learning instead to set forth positive proposals sets a more acceptable tone to the forthcoming discussion (See the "Negotiation Guide," pp. 258–261). (4) Lengthy explaining may well be experienced as a put-off as well as a put-down. It is useful to coach clients on how to put a period at the end of a sentence. (5) Lying, distorting or withholding information is frequently an invitation to a fight. (6) Projecting what I think you think and then acting as if that is what you think is another kind of invitation to a fight. (7) Attributing evil intentions to the other person will lead to frequent negative interpretations of what others say or do. (8) Being innocent or superreasonable is a good way to lay bait upon the waters for fish to swallow. An example is the child who "forgets" and leaves his books on the stairs each day to be discovered, or the very reasonable person who is always right and says, "If only you would do it my way, which everyone would agree is the right way," implying that the other is wrong, stupid, and stubborn. (9) Displacing anger and hurt from some other source upon family members because it is safe is another common source of conflict.

It is vital for effective functioning that both the individual and the family feel empowered and optimistic and recognize the strengths that they have (See Chapter 2: The Art of Encouragement). Even those who feel weak use a great deal of power, such as the impact of the depressed person's behavior upon those around him. For broader perspectives on power, consult May (1972) and Boulding (1989).

To defuse and redirect the power play to more constructive lines of movement is the task of therapy. This can be done in numerous ways through (1) direct methods based on expected member compliance, (2) disengagement methods to stop the fighting, and (3) indirect methods to help the clients overcome their rigid adherence to the game either by changing the rules of the game or by changing the game. A more extensive discussion of the power play and models to defuse it may be found in Sherman (1983) and Heitler (1990).

II. STRUCTURED TECHNIQUES

A. The Truce

1. RATIONALE

When a couple or parent and child are in a bitter dispute that is constantly repeated and escalating in intensity, it is useful to call a truce. Clearly, if the fight continues, no one is winning. Whatever each is doing is not working in overcoming or totally controlling the others. The purpose of the truce, developed by Sherman (1983), is to temporarily stop the fighting around the symptom. Since each person cannot control others, each is asked to control his/her own behavior. When the truce is in effect, it reduces the hurt, tension, and anger, producing a more favorable climate in which to work to bring about better solutions. Implementing the truce is also encouraging because it shows the participants that they can stop the fighting if they choose to. It permits the therapist to point out that the participants have some control over the situation and that the fighting is not inevitable. They do have some power.

2. PROCEDURE

The therapist acknowledges that each person has a point in the dispute coming from his/her point of view. She describes the failure of their efforts to win and how effectively they cooperate in order to maintain the conflict. She suggests the possibility that they can control their own behavior even if they can't control someone else's. To the oft-made complaint that the other one does something that "makes me" do or feel something, she answers, "No one can really make you do anything except by brute force. And you are in charge of your own thinking and feeling."

The therapist then invites the people to implement a truce between them. "Between now and the next session, you are to try to avoid in every way possible doing or saying things that typically lead to this fight. If the other person does do or say such a thing, you are not to be suckered into the hassle. There will be peace in the house from now until our next meeting. This will not solve or cure anything, but it will calm things down and give us a better climate to work in to find solutions to your conflict. Are you willing to cooperate to make peace rather than war?" After some discussion, a firm commitment is obtained that they will neither set up the other nor bite on any invitations to fight set by the other. The therapist then adds: "Of course, you might do the opposite of fighting. You each know some things that would please the other. You might do a few of those things as a gesture of goodwill and as a peace offering, not expecting anything in return."

If the therapist is not able quickly to build upon the truce, the honeymoon period is not likely to last very long.

3. CASE EXAMPLE

Mr. and Mrs. L., a remarried couple, were in heated conflict over differences in child-rearing practices, among other things. He called her a bully and a dictator and she said that he makes decisions without consulting her. They were at an impasse without resolving the conflicts on how to deal with the children (his and hers) or feel good about each other.

The therapist agreed and validated that the husband was experiencing his wife as intruding upon his space and independence and that the wife perceived her husband as discounting her and insulting her.

The therapist prescribed the truce as described above in the procedures section. Mrs. L. complained that that would be fine for her husband. He simply wouldn't tell her anything, so he would get her off his back, but what benefit would she get? The therapist asked what benefit was she getting from the fighting other than venting her feelings? She replied that she was only getting more and more aggravated. The therapist indicated that she would at least get herself and her husband less aggravated. The therapist also reiterated that this was not intended as a solution, but only as a way of reducing the tension so that they could begin to seek more effective ways of dealing with the conflict. The therapist also indicated that since they both knew what would please the other they might try some peace offerings during the truce. At that point both agreed to implement the truce.

The couple returned 10 days later. They appeared more relaxed physically and did not open up the session by assaulting each other. They reported that they had indeed carried out the truce most of the time and had gotten into only two big fights during the 10 days. Both felt quite relieved. Mr. L. had done two things particularly to please his wife and she appreciated that. But he had made no moves to inform her anymore than before. The therapist then began to work on the sources of their different expectations.

4. USES

This technique is used to help as an introductory part of the process of conflict resolution. It disengages the couple from continued aggravating behavior and creates an improved climate for further therapeutic work. It is effective between parents and adolescents, between couples, and between parents and adult children.

B. The Family Negotiating Guide

1. RATIONALE

Couples or parents and children in conflict need to learn a handy, simple set of skills to negotiate their differences and to resolve future differences and conflicts. The Family Negotiating Guide developed by Robert Sherman in his practice is designed to provide for that purpose. It is based upon commonly known and widely used conflict resolution methods that rely on mutual respect and cooperation. The object is for all participants to feel empowered and counted in the decision-making process. Couples and families do consist of individual members who have legitimate differences in needs, beliefs, preferences, and expectations. People who care for each other need to recognize and accept that fact as normal. When you care about and are interested in others, you also realize that you cannot demand to get your way all the time, that life is a give-and-take proposition. Respect for self and for others is the basis for a caring negotiation. The process is built largely on the ancient Greek philosophy of beginning with a thesis, presenting an antithesis, and finally arriving at a synthesis.

2. PROCEDURE

After defining the conflict, the therapist asks if those involved would like to learn some useful techniques for handling their differences. Upon agreement, she explains that differences are normal and inevitable, providing us with a broader view of life. They also provide us with important opportunities for growth and add excitement to our lives. She affirms that each person's point of view in the presenting conflict makes sense based on his/her perception of need or correctness. She restates those points of view in terms of the perceptions of each. "You already know that neither of you is going to be boss over the other and you both care about each other. You want to feel good and you want the other person to feel good too. I'm going to be a teacher for a few minutes and I will teach you four ways of resolving a conflict. Then you will apply the model to one of the differences that you have to work out. You choose one of the four as the best way to settle each conflict."

The therapist continues describing each of the four methods.

"1. *Give in all the way.* This is a person whom you care about. Sometimes one needs to receive the entire thing that one wants in order to enjoy the richness of life. Try to say "Yes" as often as you can to this other person. And when you give in, you do it graciously and see to it that the other person is fully satisfied and does not have to pay back because of your future resentment and hostility in having given in. Since the other person is doing the same thing for you, you will each fully get your way a reasonable share of the time. In general, it should not be thought of as a 50–50 even split, this one for me, the next for you. Unless a fixed deal has been made for a particular occurrence, it is a more spontaneous process in which you both have faith that the other will also do for you some reasonable amount of the time.

"2. *Compromise or make a deal*. It may seem inappropriate for either of you to give in sometimes. On those occasions, you create a compromise by making a deal. Typically, in a conflict someone is making demands or heavy complaints and the other is resisting. Try to avoid demands and complaints. They are usually ineffective. The steps to follow are:

"a. Decide what you want rather than what you don't want.

"b. Say what you want in a positive and brief way. ('It would make me feel good if you would do the supper dishes each night,' rather than 'You never do anything around here.').

"c. This statement is to be considered a proposal rather than a demand; demands often elicit resistance.

"d. The second person might come back with a counterproposal. ('I can't do the supper dishes every night because . . . but I'm willing to do them twice a week.')

"e. The first person comes back with a countercounter-proposal. ('I most particularly would appreciate your doing them on Monday, Tuesday, and Thursday because. . . .')

"f. The process continues until an agreement is reached."

"3. *Move the discussion to a higher level*. If no agreement or compromise is emerging, can you agree to put the issue on a higher plane? For example, no agreement seems possible in getting the family together for a Friday night dinner or any other night. The higher-level desire is to find times to get together. If not Friday night, then maybe a Sunday afternoon softball game, or whatever. The idea is to recognize that apples and oranges are different, yet they both fit together as fruit. Can you find a level at which your opposing positions fit together?"

"4. *Let 'fate' decide*. A quick way to settle a dispute is to use some method of choosing, such as the toss of a coin, the display of odd/even fingers, or drawing the highest card in a deck of cards. Whoever wins gets his or her way this time. The loser agrees to cooperate.

"Now let us try it out. Pick one issue in dispute. Select one of the conflict resolution models. Try to solve the problem."

The therapist assists when necessary, either in refining the instructions or in coaching the pair to come to a resolution. They can then at home or in subsequent sessions use the guide as a model to deal with other conflicts. Some practice sessions are necessary to instill the process as a natural and effective means of solving differences.

3. CASE EXAMPLE

Mr. and Mrs. H., a remarried couple, could not agree on how to deal with Mr. H.'s noncustodial children living with their mother and very resentful of father for having left the family. Mrs. H. insisted her husband be more firm with the children in terms of their manners and exploitation of her husband, since they came mostly to demand money for their wants. Mr. H. insisted that he would deal with his children his own way.

After clarifying the issues involved, the therapist taught the couple the four methods for conflict resolution. They could not accept giving in all the way. They became frustrated after a few stabs at making a compromise. Mrs. H. did not trust that her husband would carry out the agreements being discussed. They finally elected to try working at a higher level. They decided that the higher level was the best interests of the children. This took it out of the mine/yours jealousy, the special interests of the parents, and the meaning of the conflict in their marriage. At that level, they were able to identify the needs of each child and how they would provide for those needs. They then moved to the method of compromise to work out a deal wherein the wife would be more friendly toward his children and show her interest in them, while the husband would be less accommodating to their demands.

Of course there are many other issues here for therapeutic involvement, such as the father's sense of guilt and the wife's wish to protect her own children and the rules of "her family." The Negotiation Guide provides them with concrete tools for solving problems as they arise, without taking positions as rivals or enemies.

4. USES

Even in a democratic society based largely on the idea of social contracts, we provide little information or training to people on how they can effectively handle social disputes and negotiate acceptable agreements utilizing democratic principles and mutual respect. The Negotiation Guide is one technique that can help fill this gap by educating couples and families in such methods. It is possible that it could be adapted for use in the classroom and for intergroup disputes.

III. TIPS AND TACTICS

A. Direct Methods

1. *Checking intentionality.* The therapist can help the clients to examine their modes of communication and the intentions of their communication. Encourage the clients to check it out. "Is this what you mean . . .?" or, "I'm feeling or doing thus and so in reaction to what you just said or did. Is that the reaction you were seeking from me?"

2. *Reframing differences*

a. The concept of differences can be elevated to an exciting and challenging positive rather than an unloving or wrong negative. "Isn't it lucky that you can look at this from different perspectives and broaden your views."

b. The specific difference can be framed more positively as legitimate for each contestant. "So, based on your background, Sam, you felt the need for more space and alone time. And Muriel you enjoy a great deal of closeness and intimacy, more than Sam is used to."

c. The repeating pattern can be reframed to assert that each is trying to be helpful to the other. "Sam, is it possible that Muriel is trying to show you that there is no risk in closeness and that you might really enjoy it if you let go more? And Muriel, is it possible that Sam is trying to show you that you don't have to be so dependent on his constant contact for you to be all right and enjoy doing more things on your own?"

3. *Substituting new roles.* Clients can be helped to examine both the roles they undertake in the power plays and the self-enhancing roles they seek that lead to and reinforce the conflict. They can further examine the consequences of the power plays to determine if the results are worth it or if some change is in order. For example, Susan watches her children's behavior very carefully and is very critical of most of what they do. She assumes the role of "judge" or "inspector general." Her purpose is to control the children's behavior so that they will effectively implement her fantasies for them in order to enhance her role as the "good mother." The consequence is that her daughter becomes a "rebel" to protect her self as a separate person. She often fails in fulfilling mother's expectations, which stimulates mother to be critical, which further stimulates daughter's rebellious behavior in a continuing power play. Can

mother become a "cheerleader" instead of an "inspector general" and can daughter become a "winner" instead of being a "rebel?"

4. *Teach negotiation skills.* Clients can be taught concrete negotiating and conflict resolution attitudes and skills. For example, complaints and demands can be redirected to a process of making proposals and counter-proposals (see the Family Negotiating Guide pp. 258–261). Couple and family meetings can be taught and prescribed as methods for making plans and dealing with differences (See pp. 175–179).

5. *Catching the other being "good."* Help clients to practice focusing their attention on catching each other being right or good. "You are each to observe carefully the behavior of the other and compliment the person each time he/she does something that pleases you in some way."

6. *Writing letters.* Sometimes the oral face-to-face engagement is too toxic. Neither gets a chance to finish expressing him/herself before the other has interrupted to attack, defend, or withdraw. There also may be a lack of deliberate consideration in the heat of an argument. Further, some people express themselves better in writing than orally or receive the information more effectively in writing than orally. For those reasons, it is useful to have the disputants write letters to each other in which they propose what they want and explain what is hurtful. Finally, when they each think before they act, there is often a more controlled response and a major amelioration of the conflict.

B. Disengagement Methods

1. *Stop cooperating in the fight.* If one of the opponents can agree to stop cooperating in the fight, the game will collapse. The therapist and compliant member devise together a series of responses that constitute refusal to play the game. Some such responses might be: (a) "Thank you. I'll think about that and we'll discuss it after dinner." (b) "I'm sorry you are so upset." (c) "If you don't stop abusing me, I'll leave and we'll discuss this later when we can talk about it more calmly."

2. *Prescribe a truce.* The therapist can prescribe a truce and instruct the opponents for a fixed period that they are neither allowed to trigger the conflict nor to take the bait of the other to start the fight (see the Truce, pp. 255–257).

3. *Shift attention to families of origin.* The issue can be detoxified by shifting attention from the combat to exploring the roots of the issues in the families of origin (Bowen, 1978; Framo, 1982; Boszormenyi-Nagy & Krasner, 1986). The therapist can more briefly adapt some of those ideas by asking such questions

as: (a) "Where did this expectation come from?" "Where did you learn that?" (b) "What does this remind you of in the family in which you grew up?" (c) "In terms of your background, what makes this so important?" (d) "To whom would you be disloyal if you didn't do this?"

4. *Help the other.* Ask each opponent to see what he or she can do to help the other one. Since they will both be doing that, each will get more of what he or she needs.

5. *Alternating the combatants as cotherapist.* Since each participant has a problem with the situation, the therapist invites them alternately to serve as her co-helper to work with one at a time and assist that person to overcome his/her problem. They are engaged cooperatively with the therapist to help rather than to fight.

6. *Invoke the therapist's law.* In cases of severe verbal abuse or actual violence, the therapist can announce with great conviction her (therapist's name) irrevocable, unbreachable law. "Since all members of this family are worthy and valuable people, I cannot permit any of them to be hurt. There cannot and will not be ever again any violence or abuse in this family regardless of how provoked you may feel. You will have to learn other ways of handling those situations. I will report any cases of violence to the proper authorities and I am legally bound to do so. You are all deserving of respect and kindness."

C. Indirect Methods

The therapeutic intention in the following methods is to change the rules of the game or to change the game itself. The prescriptions must be spelled out positively and very carefully to the client.

1. *Increase the price of the behavior.* If the cost of the fight is raised significantly, the fight may become less attractive. This is adapted from Haley's idea of ordeal therapy (1984). An ordeal has to be constructed so that it reflects the inappropriate pattern and will act to block that pattern because to continue it is too onerous to all the participants. "Each time you criticize the way someone else performs a task, the next three times that task is to be performed you must stand there and watch and talk the person through it every step of the way. Let's outline the steps." The hope is that they will recoil after some dose of the prescription; the criticizer will become less prone to criticize; and the performer will be more responsible to get the other off his back. However, the members usually have to be teased into accepting the prescription. They are already dissatisfied with the situation. It is presented as a definite solution to the problem. The therapist knows

it is likely to work. If they really want to solve the problem, then this is a way to do it.

2. *Demand more of what is not wanted.* Identify one person who will cooperate with the therapist. Have that person ask for more of what the other person is doing that precipitates or continues the fight. For example, instead of resisting mother-in-law's advice or gifts, thank her and enthusiastically ask her for a great deal more in the way of gifts, services, or advice so that she finds it difficult to give so much and pulls back. The receiver becomes more positive, courteous, and accepting. The giver becomes more prudent in her giving. The pattern of demand and resistance is broken. This is an example of a compliance/defiance paradox (Papp, 1983).

3. *Play helpless.* In dealing with an overadequate/inadequate pair in conflict, the therapist can seek the cooperation of the overadequate one to play more helpless and inadequate. Typically, he/she is chasing the inadequate one, who withholds. Changing the rules of the game here would be to get a role reversal. The therapist suggests that maybe it's time for the responsible person to have lapses in memory and fail to do what the other wants with profuse apologies when confronted about it. Favored or important tasks are "forgotten" or performed very poorly. The inadequate one then has to do them over or take charge of them in some way. The responsible person learns to do less and is less critical. The inadequate person learns to mobilize more, do more, and take charge of more things. The decrease in activity by the responsible member is never done for spite or as a punishment hurled in the other's face. It's a new game. This technique is another example of a compliance/defiance paradox (Papp, 1983).

4. *Forbidding what is wanted.* This is a method of stealing the oppositional child's "No" position. The child who is defiant is refusing to comply for spite or revenge, or to gain attention or to deflect attention from some other serious matter in the family. The therapist prescribes that the child is not allowed to do the desired activity. He is needed by the family to continue to sacrifice himself for the good of the family and it is very loving of him to do so. Or else the therapist coaches the parent to make a new rule forbidding the desired behavior because the child is not ready or mature enough for it, the family is not ready for it, or the child is really not good enough to achieve those things. By using this reverse psychology, the parents reduce their pressure upon the child. The child, in order to maintain his defiant stance, can only do the desirable thing that the parents are now forbidding. The child may finally feel heard and understood, which reduces his need to be defiant. A similar technique called "The Winner's Bet With Adolescents," developed by Peckman, is reported in Sherman and Fredman

(1986). In essence, the therapist bets the adolescent that he can't do what is demanded of him.

5. *Visualize a better way.* We can ask the contestants to step back from reality to enter a world of fantasy and imagination. In the world of imagination they can create a new scene in their own minds in which they behave differently, a new scenario in which they explore better ways of getting what they want and succeeding without engaging in the same old power play. After thinking up imaginary scenarios, they are asked now to enact the situation in a more successful way thus arriving at a mutually favorable solution.

REFERENCES

Adler, A. (1966). The psychology of power. *Journal of Individual Psychology.* 22:166–172.

Bitter, J.R. (1987). Communication and meaning: Satir in Adlerian context. In R. Sherman and D. Dinkmeyer. *Systems of family therapy. An Adlerian integration.* New York: Brunner/Mazel.

Boszormenyi-Nagy, I. and Krasner, B. R. (1986). *Between give and take. A clinical guide to contextual therapy.* New York: Brunner/Mazel.

Boulding, K. E. (1989). *Three faces of power.* Newbury Park, CA: Sage.

Bowen, M. (1978). *Family therapy in clinical practice.* New York: Jason Aronson.

Dreikurs, R. (1953). *Fundamentals of Adlerian psychology.* Chicago: Alfred Adler Institute.

Dreikurs, R. (1964). *The challenge of marriage.* New York: Hawthorne.

Framo, J. (1982). *Explorations in marital and family therapy.* New York: Springer.

Haley, J. (1984). *Ordeal therapy.* San Francisco: Jossey-Bass.

Heitler, S. M. (1990). *From conflict to resolution. Strategies for diagnosis and treatment of distressed individuals, couples and families.* New York: Norton.

Kfir, N. (1981). Impasse priority therapy. In Corsini, R. J. (Ed.). *Handbook of innovative psychotherapy* (pp. 401–415). New York: Wiley.

Lombardi, D. (1975). *Search for significance.* Chicago: Nelson Hall.

May, R. (1972). *Power and innocence.* New York: Norton.

Papp, P. (1983). *The process of change.* New York: Guilford.

Satir, V. and Baldwin, M. (1983). *Satir: Step by step.* Palo Alto, CA: Science and Behavior Books.

Sherman, R. (1983). Power in the family: Alderian Perspectives. *American Journal of Family Therapy.* 11:3, 43–53.

Sherman, R. and Dinkmeyer, D. (1987). *Systems of family therapy: An Adlerian integration.* New York: Brunner/Mazel.

Sherman, R. and Fredman, N. (1986). *Handbook of structured techniques in marriage and family therapy.* New York: Brunner/Mazel.

ADDITIONAL RESOURCES

Ascher, L. M. Editor. (1989). *Therapeutic paradox.* New York: Guilford.

Barkley, R. A. (1987).. *Defiant children. A clinician manual for parent training.* New York: Guilford.

Fisher, R. and Brown, S. (1989). *Getting together. Building relationships as we negotiate.* New York: Penguin. (business negotiations)

Fisher, R. and Ury, W. (1983). *Getting to yes. Negotiating agreements without giving in.* New York: Penguin.

Golann, S. (1988). On second-order family therapy. *Family Process.* 27:51–63.

Guerin, P. J. Jr., Fay, L. F., Burden, S. L. and Kuatto, J. G. (1987). *The evaluation and treatment of marital conflict: A four stage approach.* New York: Basic Books.

Horne, A. M. and Sayger, T. V. (1990). *Treating conduct and oppositional defiant disorders in children.* New York: Pergamon.

Kirschner, S. and Kirschner, D. A. (1989). Love and other difficulties: Goals in couple therapy. *Family Therapy Today.* 4:3, 1–4.

Lankton, C. H. and Lankton, S. R. (1989). *Tales of enchantment. Goal-oriented metaphors for adults and children in therapy.* New York: Brunner/Mazel.

Rosellini, G. and Worden, M. (1990). *Barriers to intimacy for people torn by addiction.* Center City, MN: Hazelden.

Prata, G. (1990). *A systemic harpoon into family games. Preventive interventions in therapy.* New York: Brunner/Mazel.

Sieburg, E. (1985). *Family communication. An integrated systems approach.* New York: Gardner.

Weeks, G. R. Editor. (1989). *Treating couples. The intersystem model of the Marriage Council of Philadelphia.* New York: Brunner/Mazel.

13

HOGGING CENTER STAGE
The Chronically
Ill Family Member

I. INTRODUCTION

The family with a chronically ill member faces tremendous problems. Whether the illness stems from psychological or from physiological causes, the ill member is generally in the limelight and the stress experienced by all the family members can be overwhelming. This chapter will look at the problems facing such families and offer some solutions for getting that mentally or physically ill family member off center stage.

A. *Mental Illness*

Since deinstitutionalization began in the late 1960s, the number of psychiatric patients living in the community has increased dramatically. The original hope for the deinstitutionalized patient was that a less restrictive environment, away from state hospitals and into the community, would be highly beneficial and curative. He or she would attain a greater sense of normality, assisted by the new miracle drugs and supported by the newly established community mental health centers. That hope has not been realized and, indeed, many suggest that deinstitutionalization has done far more harm than good (Bachrach, 1982; Lamb, 1982; Sheets, Prevost, & Reihman, 1982; Talbott, 1981). Many of those discharged patients have become the drifters and homeless in our society as many state hospitals have either closed or decreased their number of beds. Furthermore, the community mental health centers opened for the purpose of treating those newly released patients have been filled by neighborhood residents suffering from everyday stress and anxiety. "The old stereotype of the drunk on skid row is being replaced by the reality of the schizophrenic on skid row: from Thunderbird to Thorazine" (Walsh, 1985, p. 134).

Most deinstitutionalized patients do not return home. Those who have a home where they are supported by family are, indeed, fortunate in many ways. However, both they and their families typically struggle through a daily sea of discontent, misunderstanding, anger, frustration, and extreme disappointment.

The psychiatric patient is disappointed as he feels his family not only lacks sympathy for his plight but also blames him for the illness. The patient's family is disappointed because everything has gone sour. Life has not turned out according to "the script." Often, at a time when they had anticipated that their children would be fully emancipated and that they themselves could enjoy the independence that an empty nest implies, they are providing caretaking for an adult child.

Families with a seriously disturbed member often feel they are prisoners in their own home and that all their energies are being expended on the ill member. Some families not only sacrifice vacations and weekend trips, but also give up interest in going to the movies, attending to hobbies, or even visiting with friends and family. Sometimes this is because they feel constrained to watch over the ill member. However, sometimes, in the words of Walsh (1985), they are "hidden in the world's largest closet" to avoid the blame that they experience being heaped upon them by the world for having produced mentally ill offspring.

This center stage occupied by the mentally ill within their family— whether obtained by demand or simply conferred—is a disaster for all concerned. The level of resentment, depression and other symptoms within the family can only increase as time goes by. Therefore, it is imperative that these families be helped to deal more effectively with the illness in their midst—that they try to normalize the family interactions.

Generally, the majority of the chronically mentally ill, as referred to in this text, are those persons who suffer from either the schizophrenic disorders or from severe affective disorders, such as manic depression.

Schizophrenia is a brain disorder that affects approximately one out of every hundred people throughout the world and that is more and more thought to be biologically based. Researchers have discovered abnormalities in the neurotransmitters of the brain. There tends to be a genetic predisposition based on the incidence of schizophrenia in families where the illness has previously occurred versus the incidence of the illness in the population at large. A person suffering from this disease experiences great disturbances in perception and sensations. While a small percentage of those afflicted are thought to recover, most do not and the disease process tends to be chronic. Many persons, but certainly not all, who have schizophrenia can control most of the symptoms with psychotropic medication, but relapses can occur, especially when the mentally ill person experiences stress.

Affective disorders are marked primarily by extreme disturbances in mood and in judgment. In these disorders, there is greater familial loading, especially for depression. While the course of these disorders is also usually a chronic one, they are generally more responsive to both medication and to spontaneous remission. A critical distinction between the affective and the schizophrenic disorders is that those who have affective disorders usually return to a higher level of functioning once the symptoms remit. One of the tragic features of schizophrenia is that typically the person is unable to return to the premorbid level of functioning he enjoyed prior to the appearance of symptoms. Schizophrenia is a debilitating disease which frequently becomes progressively worse with each exacerbation of symptomology.

Another very important distinction between schizophrenic and affective disorders is the response by the family to the ill member. Janowsky, Leff and Epstein (1970) point out that while the manic-depressive patient is undergoing a manic phase, he is often perceived by family members as willfully, purposely, and maliciously making them miserable. They believe the manic could control the behavior if only he wished to do so. This misperception on the part of the family seems to occur because the person in a manic stage can often show periods of being logical, coherent, and reasonable. However, this period of seeming calm is then shattered by the manic's inability to follow through and by his angry and hostile blaming and projecting.

On the other hand, when the affect is one of depression, the ill family member is usually self-blaming, guilt-ridden, and sometimes grateful for the family's forbearance. The family is much more likely to see this sad, inactive, and occasionally helpless person as ill, just as one who hears voices, is delusional and thought disordered, and is unable to become self-motivated can be so considered.

B. Medical Illness

It is suggested (Masterson, 1985) that families with a medically ill child or adolescent generally seek psychotherapy only when the ill member's disease fails to respond as expected, given the medical treatment provided and without psychological reasons to explain the lack of progress.

Family therapists have long seen a strong circular cause and effect between chronic illness—whether medical or psychiatric—and family dysfunction. Much of the work has focused on young children with psychosomatic disorders, such as intractable asthma, infantile diabetes, and eating disorders and the mother-child dyad, or the effect of the parental dyad on the child. When parental disagreements get played out through the child's illness, the child can receive contradictory messages about medical management or comes to realize he can exert some control over the parents' conflict depending on how well the illness is or is not being controlled.

In presenting the rationale for family treatment in families with severe psychosomatic disorders, Karasu (1979) writes of a "mutual symbiosis" between mother and child which, when changed, may reverse the disorder. This premise is one often offered, that is, that the psychosomatic child has a special role and function in the family that is supported by the other family members. Thus, only when the family system changes can the child's role and the role of his illness be changed.

Whether the chronically ill family member takes center stage with a vengeance, as can occur in the case of the manic patient, or the ill one is pushed onto the stage, as frequently appears to be the case with the psychosomatic child, the family faces similar struggles in its attempt to cope with such highly intense interactions.

C. Problems in the Family System

1. ANGER AND BLAME

There can be major problems in families with a chronically ill member. Where there is mental illness, generally there are also poor communication skills. Negative affect marked by blaming, hostility, and hypercriticalness abounds. Much of the blame and criticism arises out of a lack of understanding on the part of the family members. They are seldom informed by the health profession of all the ramifications of the illness—of the limitations faced by the ill member or the limitations of their profession to either cure or alleviate the symptoms. The family is angry because the patient is not trying hard enough and the doctor's medication is not good enough. The patient is angry because he feels somehow blamed for things beyond his control and forced to take medications he does not think he needs. Patients, especially those with paranoid ideation, often complain that they are being "punished" or "persecuted" through the prescribing of medication.

Another source of anger and blaming derives from fears that arise within the family when a member is chronically ill. There are fears of a genetic component to the illness—whether siblings or children will be affected. A spouse will frequently blame the other spouse or the spouse's side of the family for the problem, especially where mental illness is involved. This blaming is often not openly communicated, but is rather hinted at, as in the case of a family treated by one of the authors. The mother in that family became increasingly angry as the son, aged 21, was diagnosed as having schizophrenia. After much exploration, it became clear that she blamed her husband for the son's illness because the husband had suffered from epilepsy as a child. She was convinced his epilepsy had translated into schizophrenia for their son.

2. FINANCIAL DIFFICULTIES

The financial burden experienced by the family is yet another reason for hostility and blame. The cost of caring for a family member who is chronically ill can be devastating. When hospitalization is required, the family frequently begins treatment for its ill member at private facilities or offices, attempting to get "only the best" help for him. Usually the hospitalization coverage expires fairly quickly. In the case of mental illness, four months is the norm. Throughout this period, uncovered medical expenses mount. The family is often required to make serious adjustments in its living arrangements. As the chronicity continues, it is not unheard of for families to experience a decrease in their standard of living or even to lose a family home in order to secure continued care for their loved one.

Despair over their financial plight can be directed toward many quarters: anger toward the system and the authorities for draining them of their finances; anger toward each other in acts of displacement; and anger toward the ill member for being the cause of their misfortune. The anger toward the ill member, in turn, usually engenders feelings of guilt, which then fuel the flames of anger even higher.

3. EXTREME AFFECT

Affect tends to be at one end of an extreme—either highly emotional or impoverished. Such families frequently show poor problem-solving skills. Cancro (1987) writes of the destructive effect on a mentally ill patient when his family either withdraws because of disappointment and lack of understanding or becomes overinvolved and exerts undue pressure. Goldberg, Schooler, Hogarty, and Roger (1977) also point out that unrealistic expectations on the part of the family can lead to relapses. There are some important studies which measure the effect that a family's emotional expressiveness has on its ability to cope with schizophrenia and the rate of relapse in such families (Brown, Birley & Wing, 1972; Vaughn & Leff, 1976). Families with high "expressed emotion," defined as critical and overinvolved comments, are more likely to experience a higher relapse rate, especially if their ill member spends more than 35 hours a week with the family. Thus, overstimulation and criticism intensify the stress experienced by the patient and facilitate relapse. Such families need to understand that blaming does not help.

4. FAMILY STRUCTURE

Other areas of concern in the family system where there is chronic illness include structural problems. Role deficiencies can exist when parents have inadequate parenting skills or have abdicated their roles in some way. Role reversals exist when parentified children are expected to nurture their own parents and run the household or act as parents to their siblings. These are examples of impaired generational boundaries which often cause confusion and dismay within the home. Chaos, which is often born of continued crises, thrives on blurred boundaries. Issues of disengagement or enmeshment as related to family structure are discussed in Chapter 5.

Where the chronic illness is a physical one, whether in a psychosomatic child or in an adult suffering from such maladies as kidney or coronary artery diseases, multiple sclerosis, or some traumatic injury, the family life can become so organized around the illness that normal developmental needs of both the individual family members and of the family group as a whole go unmet. Here again, family structural problems arise with often dramatic changes in both the roles and the rules within such illness-centered families. Fathers who heretofore functioned as a strong family caretaker may have to be literally fed by their young offspring while mothers go out to become the breadwinners. Or, once the husband has suffered a severe stroke, the rules change in the family and his once assertive wife can no longer disagree with anything he says for fear of upsetting him.

Daily routines are almost always altered. Management of the illness can require so much time in some families that activities not related to the illness, but important to the well-being of family members, can be greatly curtailed or even eliminated. Such sacrifices can leave one feeling deprived, taken for granted, misused, unappreciated, and angry—even when voluntarily and silently made.

5. VIOLENCE

Parents can feel utterly overwhelmed by the added tensions, stress, and unexpected responsibilities that accompany such illnesses. Although most persons suffering from schizophrenia or some other chronic mental illness are not violent, physical abuse is a possibility. The fear of such violence, whether actual or not, and thus the sense of "walking on eggs" that can result from such fears can deplete the emotional resources of any family. In the case of a chronic physical illness, the ill family member might be pampered, fussed over, and infantilized to the detriment of the entire family. Of course, the opposite can occur for both the mentally and the physically ill. There are unfortunately many instances of abusiveness toward the ill member.

6. LACK OF HOPE

There is often a lack of hope in these families, with little sense of family goals, and a style of coping which focuses mainly on day-to-day crises rather than on the future. Their experiences have often shown them that planning for an event next month or even the next day can be abruptly disrupted by the exacerbation of symptomatology of the ill member. Sometimes, rather than face anticipated disappointment, they simply fail to plan or to entertain expectations.

With such a multitude of problems confronting these families, what seems most relevant is the notion of defusing the emotional reactivity and decreasing the tension and stress. Issues of boundaries have been discussed earlier. Role deficiencies, reversals, enmeshment, and disengagement have also been touched on in previous chapters. The techniques that follow have been chosen to inform, to calm, and to show how some situations can be improved without a radical transformation of the entire family.

II. STRUCTURED TECHNIQUES

A. *Psychoeducation: Ignorance Is Not Bliss*

1. RATIONALE

Generally people are better able to manage that which they understand. Illness, especially of a chronic nature, is no exception. However, it has only been over the past 15 years that the importance of the family's understanding of such illness has been recognized, especially in the case of mental illness. Families were expected to follow the doctor's orders without necessarily understanding why and how they would be helpful. In psychiatric facilities, diagnoses were seldom shared with families, who often had to muddle through a maze of misinformation, little information, or no information.

Fortunately, something of a small revolution has taken place in the health fields over the past 10 years—something called psychoeducation (Anderson, Hogarty & Reiss, 1980). To be most effective, this technique deals with three very important elements: family understanding, family support, and family limit-setting.

2. PROCEDURE

Understanding. Families are told very clearly the name and nature of the illness from which their member suffers. They are also educated regarding what to expect regarding symptomatology, including which symptoms respond to which interventions. Understanding in schizophrenia, for example, that excessive sleeping and withdrawal is a frequent symptom of the illness rather than evidence of either malingering or an attempt to purposely upset everyone can be helpful to both the patient and to his family, who are in turn less likely to become angry with him. They are told about those responses which make family life more manageable and pleasant, and warned of those responses which tend to increase stress and encourage chaos.

Psychoeducation begins with a thorough explanation of the illness. In the case of schizophrenia, for example, the therapist explains to the family, including the patient, that he is suffering from an illness called schizophrenia where it is difficult for him to distinguish between what is real and what is not. They should be told briefly that no one knows the exact cause of the disease, but that current scientific investigations strongly suggest problems in brain functioning—most notably the neurotransmitters—and that these chemical dysfunctions leave the person especially vulnerable to stresses. The patient may even experience difficulties handling everyday events and situations in the family that might seem quite ordinary. While not everyone has all the symptoms associated with schizophrenia, the main ones, such as, thought disorders, delusions, ideas of reference, hallucinations, withdrawal, and decreased affect, should be defined, described, and discussed.

Families are also told what the illness is not. Regarding schizophrenia, for example, it is not a "multiple personality," an idea popularized in books and movies. It is also not synonymous with violence, although some who suffer from it occasionally have violent outbursts.

It also helps families to know that schizophrenia is a major mental illness and that it is found in all countries; that it usually begins in early adult life, but can begin as early as childhood; and that symptoms are generally continuous or recurrent for approximately 85 percent of those who develop it (Falloon, McGill & Boyd, 1980).

The next step would be to discuss medication with the family and the fact that, because schizophrenia is a biological disorder, there are medications which appear to improve the imbalance and the symptoms and thereby the patient's level of functioning. There should be a discussion not only about any medication the patient is taking, including possible side effects, but also about any "new theories" they might have heard about, such as megavitamin treatment, which have not proved helpful.

Schizophrenia tends to occur more frequently within families than within the general public; that information should be shared and discussed with the family. They usually have fears and fantasies about the genetic implications so it helps to clarify and confront that issue. While the chance of someone having schizophrenia in the general population is one out of every 100 people, the chance of having it if a brother, sister, or parent has it is one out of 10. With a twin, the chances are even greater.

Issues such as what causes an illness, its genetic implications, the pros and cons of medication, the search for magic cures, and confusion over how to ease the stress and pain are so prevalent in these families that motivating them to participate in a psychoeducational program is seldom difficult. Offering them an opportunity to learn more about the underpinnings of their family member's illness as a way of gaining more control over it is a powerful incentive.

Providing support. In a hospital setting the structure for psychoeducational programs is quite formal and includes input and participation from a clinical team usually consisting of a psychiatrist, a psychologist, a social worker, nursing staff, and a vocational or recreational therapist. Sessions are usually held with several or multiple families simultaneously (Anderson & McFarlane, 1985). Even a private practitioner working with several families with a chronically ill member might consider bringing those families together as a group. However, that discussion is beyond the scope of this chapter.

Instead, the focus here will be on working with a single such family. The introduction of psychoeducation to the family usually works best near the beginning phase of therapy with the family.

After some history about the family and the course of the illness and its effect on the family have been gathered, focus quickly settles on the present concerns and stressors. The therapist at that point can empathize with the family, stating that she can understand how confusing all the factors are to them, and then offer to teach them some facts and practical information that should make things clearer. Another way to lead into the technique would be during the early discussion of goals for the family. The therapist could ask each of the family members to list all the things they believe about the illness—whether fact or fiction or fantasy—and what things they wish could be changed or improved. Then she offers to explore all those issues in a learning experience to discover what changes might reasonably be possible and how to effect them.

The therapist might suggest that four weekly sessions be spent on psychoeducation in order to give each family member ample time to ask questions, share observations, and think through the information both within and between sessions. Each of the four sessions should have a main topic—for example, a definition of the illness, medication and side effects, etc. If the therapist can present a videotape, it can be helpful, but certainly not necessary. Both the language the therapist uses and the depth of the explanations should be simple. A detailed discussion to a nonmedical person about all the aspects of the dopamine theories of schizophrenia and how the chemical neurotransmitters function would be boring as well as not helpful. Stating that there appears to be a chemical imbalance in the brain which frequently responds well to certain neuroleptics or psychotropic medication and that the old theory of a schizophrenogenic mother who causes schizophrenia is no longer believed to be valid is usually more to the point in helping the family sort through possible causes.

At each session, the therapist could give a 15 minute explanation of the topic and then encourage the family to respond—much like teaching a class. Some brief reading material, such as an article, might be assigned. At the end of the four weeks, it would be helpful to review the family's original concerns to determine if and how well they have been addressed.

While some therapists do not see their role as teacher in a structured sense, this technique can be invaluable in helping families quickly feel more in control while at the same time illuminating many of their concerns, conflicts, and family dynamics both for themselves and for the therapist.

To effect the second element of psychoeducation, it is necessary to help the family understand that while they cannot cause schizophrenia, stressful events and tense environments worsen symptoms and often start a relapse. Blaming, criticizing, and nagging—high expressions of emotion, as discussed above—do not help. A supportive and encouraging family does.

There are a number of things a family can do to demonstrate their support. Shollar (1988) encouraged families to "adopt a policy of benign indifference" where the family can leave the patient to himself without rejecting him; the patient can thus attain needed distance and relief from family expectations, such as participation in family activities. Since we often believe that keeping busy is a virtue, it is hard to understand that for someone with an illness rest and isolation can be experienced as healing.

Setting limits. The third goal of psychoeducation should be to set limits for the ill family member. This is not at odds with a certain attitude of indifference cited above. This refers to setting some basic rules that will enable family members to live in a more cooperative manner since everyone will have a clear idea of what is expected of him or her, not only at home but also in terms of what is allowable outside of the home. Limits should be set up only for important issues; they should be clear, simple and concrete; they should be well thought out rather than a response to a crisis where some situation has gotten out of hand; they should be geared toward behavior rather than toward chronological age; they should be doable; and they must be exercised consistently. When everyone knows what the others' needs are, what can and cannot be expected, and what will or will not be tolerated, guess work, tension, and stress are reduced in the family.

3. CASE EXAMPLE

George, a 20-year-old male, had recently been readmitted for his third psychiatric hospitalization in 18 months with a diagnosis of schizophrenia. He was experiencing auditory hallucinations, believing the voices came from his feet, and he was delusional. George was the only child of Margaret, a single mother. George's father had not been involved with the family since George was an infant. George and Margaret lived with her parents, Mr. and

Mrs. Z. All four family members were asked to participate in weekly psychotherapy sessions.

The presenting problem posed by the family was that George was uncooperative, as evidenced by his refusal to take psychotropic medication, resulting in the need for repeated rehospitalization. They described him as "lazy," as he refused to help with household chores and slept off and on during the day. They further accused him of purposely harassing them by his bizarre statements and irrational requests. Their solution was to have George retained in the hospital until he could be placed in a residence for the emotionally ill.

By the second session it became clear that the family, including George, had no understanding of George's illness. In fact, Mrs. Z. asked: "What do you call what's wrong with him?" This was clearly a family that needed to be educated about their family member's illness, beginning with his diagnosis. The family stated that no one had ever mentioned "schizophrenia" to them.

There followed a discussion about what is currently known about the etiology of schizophrenia—for example, that it is not clear what causes it, but that there are a few theories which are predominantly biochemically based; that there are no known common environmental factors that appear in those who develop it; that stress appears to play an important role in causing and exacerbating the symptoms; and that at present there is no cure but there are things that improve the mental state of one who has it (Hatfield, undated). Symptoms and medications were also discussed.

All this information was shared and discussed with the family in a supportive atmosphere. When members began to blame or criticize in a nonhelpful way, they were reminded that blame and unconstructive criticism do not help. They were helped to work through feelings of guilt, helplessness, hopelessness, and anger. Several times throughout the session, Margaret would get angry because she felt unsupported and stalked out of the session, or George would sulk because he felt rejected, or Mrs. Z. would become tearful because she felt helpless. All members had to be supported and were shown how to support each other.

Finally, the family was taught to set limits for George. In order to gain certain privileges and the family's trust that he would act with responsibility, there was a progression of behaviors he had to follow. For example, he had to take his medication (which became slightly easier for him as he at least knew why he was being given it, although he never believed it to be necessary). His response to that was usually, "If it will make you happy, I'll take it, but I don't need it." Then he had to attend certain ward activities. Next, he was expected to participate in certain off-the-ward activities. Finally, he was required to attend vocational rehabilitation. By that time, his parents had agreed to take him home for well proscribed visits.

4. USES

While psychoeducation has been discussed here mainly in the context of mental illness, it is no less effective in working with families where chronic physical illness exists. An explanation of the etiology, symptoms, and course of the disease, as well as of the efficacy and side effects of medications, is crucial to any positive management of the disease and of the affect in the family around the illness. A series of structured educational family sessions similar to that already outlined would be invaluable.

Psychoeducation can also be used with families to help them understand almost any issue that arises within the context of therapy, albeit in a less extensive way than illustrated here. For example, in working with a family in which one member suffers from panic attacks, it is helpful to explain to the entire family the symptoms and how they are experienced. Often, when a family has a name and an explanation for something—whether they fully understand or not—it provides them with some sense of control over the situation.

B. Reduction of Intensity: Take Five

1. RATIONALE

The technique of "time-out" is familiar to therapists who train parents in behavioral methods of dealing with their children (Gordon & Davidson, 1981). This technique is used to decelerate behavior by removing opportunities for reinforcement of the behavior through isolation, removal of the stimulant, or ignoring the child. Anderson, Hogarty and Reiss (1980) make a point that is well taken: One considers the behavior rather than the chronological age of the ill family member. Thus, if an adult family member is experiencing something akin to a temper tantrum or escalation toward acting out, such a technique geared to squelch problematical behavior in acting-out children should be appropriate.

2. PROCEDURE

Forehand (1977) and others have concluded that the simplest way to an effective time-out is for the family member to leave the room. Another important factor is the time duration of the time-out, which seems to be optimal between four and five minutes (Hobbs, Forehand, & Murray, 1978; Kendall, Nay, & Jeffers, 1976). A third aspect of time-out that has proved important is that release from time-out be contingent upon some behavior, usually a brief period of quietness prior to ending the time-out (Hobbs & Forehand, 1975).

Therefore, in families in which a chronically ill member was behaving inappropriately or in a threatening manner, the family, rather than allow the behavior to escalate, would announce to the person that he needed time out and would either withdraw from the room or ask the ill member to leave the room for five minutes. If he were able to do so and calm down, interaction could then resume. The potentially acting-out person would soon see that his behavior was not being tolerated and should soon avoid engaging in it.

3. CASE EXAMPLE

Harry was a 21-year-old male seen in family therapy with his parents, Mr. and Mrs. Y., and his 25-year-old married sister, Doris, following his second brief hospitalization for a manic episode.

Harry behaved somewhat immaturely for his age, pouting or stomping his foot, for example, when his father refused to give him money. He and his mother teased each other, until one of them lost his or her temper.

Frequently, at the beginning of the treatment, the family sessions were disrupted by Harry's yelling, pouting, or provocative behavior. Efforts to help his parents effect limits for him were unsuccessful at that point. Mr. Y. would throw up his hands and declare helplessness. Mrs. Y. would call him "stupid" and "hardheaded." His sister would start a litany about how he should be kicked out of the house and the session would begin to deteriorate.

The therapist then decided that she and the family should give Harry time out and recognize that when he was feeling a lot of stress and anxiety, either his own or that of another family member, his way to avoid dealing with the issues at hand was to change the session focus. At that point in the therapy, he was not able to control the behavior sufficiently. The disruptive behavior could be seen as a signal to the therapist and family not only that intense feelings were being experienced but also that Harry needed time to calm down.

In subsequent sessions when Harry began to act out, he was immediately asked to step outside the office for a five-minute time-out. If he attempted to re-enter the office, even if apparently calm, after only three minutes had elapsed, for example, he was told he still had two minutes left and really needed that time as well. When he returned to the sessions, he was not brought up to date on what had transpired, but rather was urged to try to remain in the room in the future so as not to miss any of the discussion. After five or six such incidents, Harry's disruptive behavior decreased significantly.

4. USES

As has been mentioned, time-out has often been used as a behavioral technique in training parents how to cope with their children. However, it is also helpful as a technique when working with abusive families. In fact, this technique is useful in any stressful situation where family members need help in stepping away from volatile or escalating situations.

C. Shaping

1. RATIONALE

Jacobson and Margolin (1979) write about shaping as a modifier of behavior that is used in marriage. They define it as, "The process of reinforcing successive approximations to the ultimately desired response . . ." (p. 11). Shaping as a therapeutic technique is also familiar to those who work in the area of behavioral parent training (Bernal, Williams, Miller, & Reagor, 1972; Johnson & Brown, 1969).

When openly criticized or expected to make drastic behavioral changes, people often respond in a negative way, either refusing outright to make the effort or failing to try and asserting that the impossible is being requested.

2. PROCEDURE

One way to avoid negative reactions to a request for change is to ask the person to make only a very slight change and then reinforce that change by giving positive feedback. Having been successful and having received pleasant feedback without feeling terribly put upon, the person might go one step further the next time. Another way to encourage change through shaping is not to ask for change but rather to track positive behavior, taking inventory of the good times. The therapist can note the period of time the patient has remained asymptomatic in a therapy session and then compliment him: "Gee, for the last 20 minutes you did okay." It is important that the therapist not ask for more, as that might be experienced as increased pressure and stress for the patient. However, at the next session the therapist would again comment in a positive way on the patient's ability to control the behavior being discouraged. Once the desired behavior began to occur on a somewhat regular basis, the reinforcement would be forthcoming only when the period of time increased, for example to 25 and then to 30 minutes. It is important for the therapist to be consistent in order to effect constant successive steps toward the desired behavior.

3. CASE EXAMPLE

Ann, the mother of two children ages four and 14, initially entered therapy alone, her husband Arthur insisting he had no interest in being involved. Ann's presenting problem was that of feeling depressed—tearful, tired, overeating, and disturbed sleep pattern. She had recently experienced a tragic family loss which accounted for some of her sadness, but it soon became clear that she was quite dissatisfied with some aspects of her marriage and was even contemplating a separation. A major issue for her was that although both she and her husband worked full time, he refused to take on any household responsibilities, insisting that was "woman's work."

At the therapist's urging, Ann was successful in getting Arthur to join the sessions. At first he stated that he thought his wife was making a big deal out of nothing. Once Ann produced a list of all her chores and Arthur could concede that indeed she had a lot to do, he was asked if he would be willing to take on just one chore and, if so, which one. He chose to be responsible for going to the cleaners every two weeks. Certainly, this was far less than Ann wanted. However, she responded favorably when Arthur took care of that task, telling him how he had saved her from making the trip and how she appreciated his help. A few days after his second trip to the cleaners, Arthur, spontaneously and without discussion, collected the dinner dishes and washed them. This was another small step, but one which left both Ann and Arthur pleased—she because she felt he had listened and was willing to try, he because he realized how appreciative she was and liked the compliments and positive regard he received when he pleased her.

4. USES

This technique can also be effective in working with phobic behavior, especially agoraphobia. It is very effective in behavioral training for parents of children with various behavioral problems.

III. TIPS AND TACTICS

1. Reframing

Fisch, Weakland, and Segal (1982) refer to the importance of parents providing limit-setting for their child with schizophrenia. They note that parents might resist the idea that they set limits because they consider that as being too harsh, but they might respond favorably to the notion that they can help their child's life become better organized by providing structure. They explain how the therapist must "sell" the task through redefining it in a way that concurs with the client's viewpoint. In this instance, the parents see setting limits as being "mean," but providing structure is seen as being supportive.

2. Keeping Your Head While All About You . . .

When a family member becomes very loud and bombastic, the therapist can immediately appear to be very calm and still, leaning back in her chair with a relaxed expression. She should lower her voice, speaking softly and slowly. Other family members can be helped to respond in the same way. Suddenly, the screamer is alone; with no one to join in and fuel the fire, he will generally calm down. Furthermore, he must quiet down in order to hear the soft-toned responses of the others in the room. Positive results usually occur in less than five minutes. Although even two minutes can seem like a long time when someone is screaming, this tactic can also be quite effective in decreasing the frequency of such incidents.

3. Scheduling Sleep and Withdrawal Periods

Families often become angry with the ill member who becomes withdrawn and sleeps a lot—two frequent symptoms of schizophrenia. By making allowances for such behavior as part of the expected family schedule, the family defuses the situation, to the relief of all concerned. The therapist can help the family develop this sleep and/or withdrawal schedule by helping them become increasingly aware of the ill member's pattern of withdrawal. If the family knows when the person is likely to be most withdrawn, it can plan activities accordingly, without fear that the plans will be disrupted. In a family where one person is used to being the center of attraction, this form of limit-setting will not work overnight, but the family must remain consistent.

4. See Positive Meaning in Seemingly Negative Behavior

This tactic might be used with an asthmatic child who begins to experience wheezing symptoms during the family session. It is helpful for the therapist to put into words what the child cannot express verbally. A response might be: "I know you are very anxious that Mommy (or Daddy or your sister) not be unhappy (or angry or sad), and maybe this is a way for you to express your concern. Thank you for cautioning us to go slowly and carefully, but we need to talk about this now. Try not to worry too much. We are here to make things better." When the therapist can validate the child's misery and verbalize what he often somatizes, the child can feel understood and relieved.

5. Compromising the Ideal

Jacobson and Margolin (1979), in assisting couples resolve their marital difficulties, suggest a simple exercise to help them reach compromises with which they both can live. One partner is asked what she or he would want from the other under the most ideal circumstances. The other partner is then asked how close to the ideal he or she is willing to come. Barbara tells Bill, for example, that she would like him to give up watching televised football games every Sunday and that they spend the day together instead. Bill might counter that he is not willing to give up his T.V. games entirely, but that he will take Barbara out one Sunday a month. Both partners benefit from the agreement they have worked out together. The wife gets more attention from her husband and the husband gets to watch his games without sacrificing too much or having to hear his wife complain. They learn a new way to resolve their problems.

REFERENCES

Anderson, C. M., Hogarty, G. E., and Reiss, D. J. (1980). Family treatment of adult schizophrenic patients: A psycho-educational approach. *Schizophrenia Bulletin*, 6 (3), 490–505.

Anderson, C. M. with McFarlane, W. R. (1985). *Treatment manual: Psychoeducational single family therapy in schizophrenia*. Prepared for a family support demonstration project.

Bachrach, L. L. (1982). Young adult chronic patients: An analytical review of the literature. *Hospital and Community Psychiatry*, 33, 189–197.

Bernal, M. E., Williams, D. E., Miller, W. H. and Reagor, P. A. (1972). The use of videotape feedback and operant learning principles in training parents in management of deviant children. In R. D. Robin, H. Festerheim, J. D. Henderson and L. P. Ullmann (Eds). *Advances in behavior therapy*. NY: Academic Press.

Brown, G. W., Birley, T. L. T. and Wing, J. K. (1972). The influence of family life on the course of schizophrenic disorder: A replication. *British Journal of Psychiatry*, 121, 241–258.

Cancro, R. (1987). The schizophrenic disorders. In P. Buirski (Ed). *Frontiers of dynamic psychotherapy: Essays in honor of Arlene and Lewis R. Wolberg*. NY: Brunner/Mazel.

Falloon, I., Boyd, J. and McGill, C. (1984). *Family care of schizophrenia*. NY: Guilford Press.

Falloon, I., McGill, C. and Boyd, J. (1980). *What is schizophrenia?* Family Aftercare Program at University of Southern CA., Los Angeles, CA.

Fisch, R., Weakland, J. H. and Segal, L. (1982). *The tactics of change: Doing therapy briefly*. San Francisco, CA: Jossey-Bass.

Forehand, R. (1977). Child noncompliance to parental requests: Behavioral analysis and treatment. In M. Hersen, R. M. Eisler and P. M. Miller (Eds). *Progress in behavior modification*. NY: Academic Press.

Goldberg, S. C., Schooler, N. R., Hogarty, G. E., and Roper, M. (1977). Prediction of relapse in schizophrenic outpatients treated by drug and social therapy. *Archives of General Psychiatry*, 34, 171–184.

Gonzales, S., Steinglass, P. and Reiss, D. (1989). Putting the illness in its place: Discussion groups for families with chronic medical illnesses. *Family Process*, 28, 69–87.

Gordon, S. B. and Davidson, N. (1981). Behavioral parent training. In A. S. Gurman and D. P. Kniskern (Eds). *Handbook of family therapy*. NY: Brunner/Mazel.

Gralnick, A. (1983). Deinstitutionalization: Origins and signs of failure. *American Journal of Social Psychiatry*, 3(4), 8–12.

Hatfield, A. B. *Coping with mental illness in the family: A family guide*. Maryland Department of Health and Mental Hygiene, Mental Hygiene Admin.

Hobbs, S. A. and Forehand, R. (1975). Effects of differential release from time-out on children's deviant behavior. *Journal of Behavior Therapy and Experimental Psychiatry*, 6, 256–257.

Hobbs, S. A., Forehand, R. and Murray, R. G. (1978). Effects of various durations of timeout on the non-compliant behavior of children. *Behavior Therapy*, 9, 652–656.

Jacobson, N. S. and Margolin, G. (1979). *Marital therapy: Strategies based on social learning and behavior exchange principles*. NY: Brunner/Mazel.

Janowsky, D. S., Leff, M. and Epstein, R. S. (1970). Playing the manic game: Interpersonal maneuvers of the acutely manic patient. *Archives of General Psychiatry*, 22, 252–261.

Johnson, S. M. and Brown, B. A. (1969). Producing behavior change in parents of disturbed children. *Journal of Child Psychology and Psychiatry*. 10, 107–121.

Karasu, T. B. (1979). Psychotherapy of the medically ill. *American Journal of Psychiatry*, 136(1), 1–11.

Kendall, P. C., Nay, W. R., and Jeffers, J. (1976). Timeout duration and contrast effects: A systematic evaluation of a successive treatment design. *Behavior Therapy*, 7, 609–615.

Lamb, H. R. (1982). Young adult chronic patients: The new drifters. *Hospital and Community Psychiatry*. 33, 465–468.

McFarlane, W. R. (Ed). (1983). *Family therapy in schizophrenia*. NY: Guilford Press.

Masterson, J. (1985). Family assessment of the child with intractable asthma. *Journal of Developmental and Behavioral Pediatrics*, 6(5), 244–251.

Sheets, J. L., Prevost, J. A. and Reihman, J. (1982). Young adult chronic patients: Three hypothesized subgroups. *Hospital and Community Psychiatry*, 33, 197–203.

Shollar, A. (1988). *Living with mental illness*. Prepared for psychoeducation night. Bronx Psychiatric Center, A. Einstein College of Medicine, Bronx, NY.

Talbott, J. A. (1981). The emerging crisis in chronic care. *Hospital and Community Psychiatry*, 32, 447.

Vaughn, C. E. and Leff, J. (1976). The measurement of expressed emotion in the families of psychiatric patients. *British Journal of Social and Clinical Psychology*, 15, 157–165.

Walsh, M. (1985). *Schiz-o-phre-ni-a: Straight talk for family and friends*. NY: Warner Books.

14

HANDS OFF

Stopping the Physical and Sexual Abuse

I. INTRODUCTION

A. Scope

This chapter will focus on the process of stopping the abuses rather than on the actual ongoing treatment of the family in which abuse has occurred. While continued intervention is an absolute must for understanding the dynamics of the abuse and for ensuring that abusive behavior does not recur, the initial step of stopping the abuse so that treatment can occur is often quite difficult for all concerned. The main thrust here is on physical and sexual assault. The chapter will describe issues in abuse and present models and tactics for stopping the abuse. Of course, emotional abuse cannot be completely separated from any discussion of physical or sexual abuse; however, it will not be treated in this chapter.

B. Definitions

1. PHYSICAL ABUSE

A generally accepted definition of physical abuse is any nonaccidental act, such as kicking, biting, punching, hitting with an object, or threatening to use or using a weapon which will probably lead to an injury. Straus and Gelles (1988) define violence as "an act carried out with the intention, or perceived intention, of causing physical pain or injury to another person."

In the case of child abuse, abusers seldom intend to inflict severe pain. The abuser usually starts out to mildly punish, but is then unable to self-monitor his actions. This failure at modulation often occurs where alcohol or drug abuse are present or living conditions are very stressful, as in over-crowding and deprivation.

There is a continuum from physical punishment to abuse. Gelles (1980) makes a distinction between what he terms "normal violence" and "abusive violence." The normal violence includes slapping, spanking, and the throwing of objects. Straus, Gelles, and Steinmetz's (1980) research survey results estimated that each year minimally 58 percent of American children are spanked, and that 71 percent of all American children have been spanked or slapped at least once. Their definition of abusive violence was cited earlier.

The New York State Family Court Act, Section 1012(e) defines child abuse as:

An "abused child" is a child less than eighteen years of age whose parent or other person legally responsible for his care:

(1) inflicts or allows to be inflicted upon the child serious physical injury, or

(2) creates or allows to be created a substantial risk of physical injury, or

(3) commits or allows to be committed against the child a sexual offense as defined in the penal law.

2. SEXUAL ABUSE

Definitions of sexual abuse have ranged from exhibitionism to intercourse, but most definitions take into account that the abused person is being exploited solely for the satisfaction of the abuser without regard for the one being abused.

When the sexually abused person is an adult, the most prevalent form of such abuse is rape by a stranger, relative, acquaintance, date, or spouse. The emphasis in this chapter is on the sexual abuse of female children in the form of incest. This is not to imply that only female children are victims of incest, but research shows (Finkelhor, 1984; Russell, 1986) that the majority of incest victims are female.

Incest, too, has been variously defined. Asher (1988) defines incest as "sexual experiences between children and adults in parental roles" (p. 3).

However, other writers include sexual interactions between siblings, whether step- or blood-related, and with other relatives, such as cousins, uncles and in-laws.

Courtois (1988) distinguishes between abusive and nonabusive incest, the nonabusive incest being that which occurs as *"mutual* exploratory sex play" between relatives who are peers. In other words, incest should be considered abusive when one person can exert undue pressure on the other because of age, status, or unequal power.

C. Cultural Differences

What is considered physically abusive to children also varies to some extent in relationship to cultural norms. Physical punishment, such as the spanking or slapping of a child is acceptable in many cultures and appears to neither lead to nor be associated with abuse. On the other hand, in some cultures, spanking is unacceptable, as in Sweden where it is illegal (Straus & Gelles, 1988).

As Welts (1982) and Hines and Boyd-Franklin (1982) point out, the therapist is not expected to voice approval of or encourage the physical punishment. Rather she should understand it as culturally acceptable and work with the families to understand the possible intervention of social service agencies and the probable lack of understanding on the part of the child, given the society's current emphasis on nonphysical punishment as the ideal, while helping the families find other means of discipline.

D. Background

1. HISTORY

Wife beating and child abuse have occurred throughout history. In fact, until very recently such practices were not only legal but sanctioned. Straus and Gelles (1988) contend that as recently as 1867 a North Carolina appellate court upheld a law "that husbands had the right to physically 'chastise' an errant wife provided the stick was no bigger than his thumb." In addition, everyone is familiar with the biblical warning that to spare the rod is to spoil the child.

As a result of social changes such as the increased employment of women outside the home, the rights movements of the sixties, the women's movement of the seventies, including the establishment of shelters for battered women, and the public's growing awareness and concern about the brutality

so many women faced in the eighties, much more attention is being focused
on how to prevent the brutalization of women. Similarly, children's rights
have gradually become an important social issue. However, the reporting
of child abuse and neglect has been legally mandatory in all 50 States only
for the past thirty years.

Straus and Gelles (1988) point out that ". . . wife beating (and child
abuse) is a crime in every American State because assault and battery are
crimes in every state." Despite this, the prevalence of both spousal and child
abuse is very high.

2. PREVALENCE

Over the past decade, the reported incidents of sexual and physical abuse,
including those against children, spouses, and parents, have increased dramatically. Some suggest that the actual incidence of violent behavior is
increasing, while others believe that society has merely made it easier for
those who are abused to report it and hold those who are abusive account-
able for their actions. Nevertheless, it is widely suspected that only a fraction
of abuse cases come to light and that estimates given for the frequency of
sexual and physical abuse are thought to be grossly understated.

Russell (1988) conducted extensive research on the incidence and prevalence of sexual abuse of female children. In her study, she made a distinction between extrafamilial and intrafamilial child sexual abuse. The former
was defined as "one or more unwanted sexual experiences with persons
unrelated by blood or marriage, ranging from petting (touching of breasts
or genitals or attempts at such touching) to rape, before the victim turned
14 years, and completed or attempted forcible rape experiences from the
ages of 14 to 17 years (inclusive)" (p. 22). Her definition of intrafamilial
child sexual abuse was broader, as she believes it to be more traumatic, and
is as follows: "Any kind of exploitative sexual contact that occurred between
relatives, no matter how distant the relationship, before the victim turned
18 years old" (p. 22).

Russell (1988) also reported that 16 percent (or 152 of the 930 women
who took part in her study) reported being sexually abused by a relative
before the age of 18. Of those 152 women, 108 of them had been sexually
abused by a relative before age 14. When the 930 women were asked about
incidents of sexual abuse with either relatives or non-relatives, 28 percent
reported having had such an experience before age 14 and 38 percent had
had such an experience before age 18. If the definitions of sexual abuse
had been expanded to include other than direct physical contact, such as

exposure of genitals and unwanted non-genital touching such as kisses, over half the respondents would have been included.

Despite what appear to be high figures, it is likely that some respondents failed to disclose incidents of sexual abuse, whether from shame or guilt or because those experiences have been repressed. Given that Russell's (1988) study also showed that very few cases of abuse get reported to the authorities (two percent involving relatives and six percent where non-relatives are involved), there is an enormous need for therapists and other mental health workers to be alert to the signs of such abuse and to be able to effectively intervene to stop its occurrence.

Straus, Gelles, and Steinmetz (1980) conducted a national survey of family violence which included 2,143 interviews with families from 103 counties in different geographic areas of the United States. Of these families, 1,146 of them had children in the home between the ages of three and 17. The researchers found that the highest incidence of child abuse occurred in the Midwestern states. However, the reasons why that might be so are inconclusive. Whether it is more frequently reported or whether the rate is highest in that area is unclear.

The stereotypical belief is that both physical and sexual abuse occur more frequently in lower socioeconomic households; that is frequently translated to mean Black homes. However, Straus, Gelles, and Steinmetz (1980) reported that the amount of physical abuse against children was not significantly different between Black and White families. Their research did, however, indicate that physical abuse against children is more likely to occur in other minority homes, such as Asian and American Indian homes, than in either Black or White ones. They speculated that the traditional extended family system in the Black community may provide sufficient support to decrease the misdirection of violence toward those children.

In the case of incest, as with physical violence, the stereotypical idea is that incest mostly occurs in lower socioeconomic groups, especially among Blacks. Russell's extensive study (1986) found that the highest incidence occurred with Hispanics while the lowest rates occurred with Asians and Jews. Contrary to expectations, incest also occurred more frequently to girls from high- rather than low-income families. She cautioned, however, that more research is needed.

Given the documented high prevalence of physical and sexual abuse, it is helpful to look at what might be causing such serious problems.

3. CAUSES

Sexual abuse. As mentioned earlier, the socioeconomic standing of the family has long been considered a major factor in the incidence of both physical and sexual abuse. However, most research linking socioeconomic status with frequency of incest is inconclusive.

Looking at family systems theory, Courtois (1988) posits that incestuous families are likely to be somewhat isolated, both emotionally and physically, with rigid boundaries when it comes to the outside world. However, internally, the family is likely to be enmeshed, overdependent, and lacking either individual or generational boundaries. An additional factor which contributes to incestuous relationships is that there is also emotional deprivation in such families, which is then inappropriately compensated for through sexuality that becomes a substitute for nurturance and affection.

Kempe and Kempe (1984), in writing about incestuous families, divide them into two categories: the "chaotic family" and the "normal-appearing" family. The chaotic family is described along the lines most typically used in the literature—low socioeconomic status, substance abuse, unstable relationships, unemployment, etc. Blurring generational boundaries is only one of many symptoms in these families. On the other hand, the normal-appearing family seems to be stable and functioning well to all outsiders even though in actuality it is not. Here, too, emotional deprivation is a strong factor, with inappropriate sexuality used between parent and child or between siblings as a substitute for emotional nurturance.

Another causal theory of incest is intergenerational transmission (Cooper & Cormier, 1982; Goodwin, Cormier, & Owen, 1983). This pattern can be established when unresolved feelings about incest prevent the incest survivors from effectively preventing their own children from becoming incest victims. It can also occur in triangulated families where children are poorly protected and are used to meet the needs of the parents, including being a substitute sexual partner.

Physical abuse. Another long held notion is that children who have been physically abused grow up to be abusive in their own families. Straus, Gelles and Steinmetz (1980) believe that theory has been misused to support a kind of "family determinism" that has not been supported by research. They did find that children who were either victims of or witnesses to violence were more likely to use violence against their own children. However, all victims of such abusiveness do not become abusive.

Goleman (1989) reports findings from research, some of which comes out of the C. Henry Kempe Center for Prevention and Treatment of Child

Abuse and Neglect, in Colorado, indicating that many adults who were physically abused as children grow up without evidence of being either abusive or engaged in pathological behavior. Altemeier, et al. (1986) also found support for this conclusion in their study of pregnant women, most of whom had been abused as children. They found the strongest predictor for who as adults would become abusive toward their own children to be those adults—whether abused or not as children—who had nevertheless felt unwanted and unloved.

One other category of those who would most likely become abusive as adults were those who denied that what they had experienced as children was abusive, but rather felt it was deserved punishment, regardless of the harshness of the physical encounters.

E. Difficulties in Intervention

1. DIFFICULTIES FOR THE THERAPIST

Dealing with family abuse, whether the abuse is physical or emotional, is a very difficult task for many therapists. This is true not only when the abuse is merely suspected but also when it has been confirmed either by intervening agencies or by the family itself.

One reason for the therapist's difficulty stems from her training. Emerging from a theoretical orientation which often cautions her to neither tell clients what to do nor how to behave, but rather to guide, suggest, and explore, she is frequently uncomfortable with situations in which she must take full control, especially during an initial crisis intervention.

Another aspect which contributes to the difficulties encountered by the therapist in working with abusive families often lies in the poor response rate on the part of the person being abused who is reluctant to do what is necessary to help stop the abuse. For example, studies show that most battered wives who leave their abusive husbands do so only temporarily (Giles-Sims, 1983), and they generally fail to use their separation as a bargaining tactic to attempt to get the abuser to stop the behavior.

Hatcher (1981) believes that when beginning treatment with abusive families the therapist's two fundamental goals are to help the abusive family member delay his impulsive behavior and to help him and his family recognize the signs that precede such behavior. Once the impulsive behavior has been delayed, there is an opportunity for the abuser to consider more appropriate alternatives. Initially, however, control that is lacking within the family must be supplied by the therapist.

The therapist must be able to encourage a discussion of the abusive behavior while simultaneously containing any emotions that are aroused so as to avoid an explosion of violence either in her office during the session or in the family's home after the session takes place. The family must feel that the therapist's office is a safe place and that the therapist can exert control over their impulses even when they are uncertain of their own ability to do so.

It is not only the family that must feel safe in the therapist's office—the therapist, too, must feel safe in her own office. Fears that the wife batterer or sexual abuser might attack her out of anger can be very intimidating. Such fears exist for male therapists as well. Concerns on the part of the therapist can be realistic. A father who has already shown the capacity to be out of control and who now feels threatened with being reported to authorities or senses that his family will no longer tolerate his aberrant behavior or might reject him completely is capable of unpredictable behavior.

To maintain control in the midst of such anxieties over safety issues, the therapist must do two things. First, she must closely examine her own feelings about working with such families; second, she must be able to set behavioral limits within the therapeutic setting.

In the process of self-assessment Petretic-Jackson and Jackson (1990) point out the importance of not harboring certain feelings or prejudices toward sexual assault victims that might lead to "revictimization" of the patient through somehow blaming the victims, disbelieving either the experience or the victims' experience of the experience, or somehow labeling the victims in such a way that their experience is not taken as seriously as the situation warrants. This self-examination and a resolution of feelings evoked are especially essential if the clinician has, herself, been a victim of emotional, physical, or sexual abuse.

To set limits in an abusing family, the therapist should clearly state behavior that cannot take place, whether in or outside of the sessions. A simple statement that you and the family cannot effectively work on the abuse problem that brought them into treatment if the abuse continues can be helpful. Even more forceful is a statement that the abuse, particularly in cases in which children are involved, is against the law and as such must be reported to the authorities if it were to continue. Here, too, "I" statements can be quite effective: "I cannot work with you when you are yelling and threatening me. Such behavior makes it almost impossible for you to be heard because other feelings get in the way."

Finally, the therapist must be aware of her liability during the course of therapy. While there is no legal obligation to report physical abuse against a spouse as there is against a child, there is the "duty to warn" both the police and the spouse in the event the therapist believes the spouse's life is in grave danger. The seriousness of such concerns renders these types of cases quite difficult, indeed.

2. Difficulties for the Family

With the disclosure of child sexual abuse within the family, shock, disbelief, denial, divided loyalties, blaming, anger, and guilt are just a few of the emotional reactions that the family members experience as they anxiously and fearfully try to weather the storm of family disruption which is sure to follow.

Courtois (1988) notes that the abuser is usually defensive and hostile not only toward the child but also toward anyone who supports the child, whether other family members or the therapist. Avoidance of negative publicity, of the intervention of social service agencies, or of the police often seems to be of higher priority. There is a great deal of pressure for the child and his or her supporters to retract the allegation rather than for the family to come together to openly discuss and attempt to work through the problems in the family.

> . . . the burden of both the (repeated) sexual assault and of disclosure and proof usually falls on the child, the individual least capable of dealing with them due to physical and emotional immaturity and economic and emotional dependence. In all likelihood, the child who complains of incest faces disbelief, criticism, and hostility rather than concern, compassion, and protection. (Courtois, 1988, p. 32)

As noted earlier, incestuous families are often socially isolated with blurred boundaries and role confusion, along with other problems such as substance abuse. With the addition of family denial, secrets, and distorted realities also associated with such families, intervention becomes an awesome task.

3. Difficulties for the Abused

Sexual abuse prevention and training for children has been routinely available only in very recent years. Courtois (1988) suggests that in the past children who knew of no options, especially in the case of intrafamilial abuse, usually maintained the secret of incest—sometimes for life. When disclosure does occur, whether accidentally or on purpose, it elicits a lot of negative feelings in the child.

A common concern of the child is either fear of loss of love or fear of retaliation. Often, children are coerced into incestuous relationships through being made to feel special and then coerced into secrecy by believing that if they tell they will destroy the family through their disloyalty. As Courtois (1988) points out:

> When a child is incestuously abused, the reality strongly contradicts what she has been taught about the meaning of family. Family members are safe; strangers are dangerous and are to be feared. (p. 34)

Children also fail to disclose because of feelings of guilt and shame. They accept responsibility for the incest because they did not prevent it or feel that maybe they even caused it. Summit (1983) writes about a phenomenon he calls the "Sexual Abuse Accommodation Syndrome," which consists of five parts: secrecy; helplessness; entrapment and accommodation; delayed, unconvincing disclosure; and retraction. While the first two conditions must exist in order for the incest to occur, the other three describe the likely outcome.

Some of these same issues hold true for the physically abused. The wife who has been battered frequently blames herself for her predicament and certainly feels helpless to stop it. Coupled with this is her often realistic assessment that to leave her marriage is to doom her children to a lowered and less stable economic status. Thus, the wife often colludes with the abusive husband in the therapist's office, denying the seriousness of the abuse, hoping that miraculously her husband will spontaneously stop the battering as he has usually promised after each serious offense.

4. Difficulties for the Abuser

The accused family member rarely admits to the abuse, especially if it is a question of incest. Denial and defensiveness are the usual responses. Most often, the abuser, if given the opportunity, will try to get the victim to retract the disclosure rather than admit and attempt to work on the problem.

If the problem is physical abuse, such as wife battering, the husband often attempts to rationalize his behavior through blaming his wife for his behavior.

Often the abuser fears punishment were he to admit his abusiveness or, in the case of incest, the loss of his family and negative social sanctions, including jail.

It is necessary to help the physically abusive family member understand that his behavior is self-defeating. As Arias and O'Leary (1988) point out, in using physical aggression to gain something he wants, he more frequently ends up with a situation he does not want, that is, the abused person harboring enormous resentment and anger against him. Though he might fear loss of love were he to admit the destructiveness of his behavior, he certainly faces that loss were he to do nothing to change it.

5. Intractable Families

Having noted that abusers rarely admit to abuse, especially when incest is involved, it should also be noted that their voluntary entry into treatment also is rare. Abusers will go into treatment either through a court order or after an especially serious life-threatening incident that frightened even them.

It is, of course, necessary for the therapist to recognize those situations in which separation, not therapy, is more appropriate, at least as a short-term goal. There are families in which recognition of anger and its antecedents are not sufficient to diminish or stop the abusiveness. When dealing with a system where the abuser is unwilling to stop the abusiveness, the therapist should work with the abused person in an effort to help that person find protection and safety.

Given the abuser's frequent lack of willingness to cooperate with treatment, the therapist is more likely to find herself working with everyone in the family except the abuser. However, in those families where the abuser becomes involved, the techniques that follow are useful.

II. STRUCTURED TREATMENT MODELS

A. Strategic Rapid Intervention

1. RATIONALE

The "strategic rapid intervention in wife beating" (Fraser, 1988) is based on a systemic model of family or couple therapy. This model views the members of the system as continuously changing and being changed by each other as they react to variations in their environment. Systems are self-regulating, with their own rules and roles. Systems also develop patterns of interacting. These patterns are described by Fraser (1988) as being either "virtuous" or "vicious" cycles, depending on whether they are considered positive or negative patterns.

The strategic approach Fraser (1988) follows is akin to the approach used by Fisch, Weakland, and Segal (1982) at their Brief Therapy Center of the Mental Research Institute in Palo Alto. The goal of the strategy is to introduce a small change within the system that is nevertheless of sufficient impact that it will interrupt the vicious cycle and allow a virtuous one to be introduced.

Because families in which battering occurs are often characterized as at least partially closed off and isolated, focus is directed toward more openness. Specifically, Fraser (1988) states:

> The primary goals of strategic rapid intervention are to decrease isolation, equalize power differentials, disqualify violence as an accepted option, increase the woman's perception of self-respect and control, and increase the man's acceptance of responsibility for his actions while offering new options. (p. 166)

2. PROCEDURE

A thorough assessment of the existing pattern of violence within the family to determine the phase of the battering the couple is currently engaged in and to determine how best to intervene needs to be conducted first. Most family members appear to seek therapeutic intervention following a violent incident and during the "I'm sorry; let's make up" stage. Of course, if the therapist is called upon during an act of violence or discovers that battering is occurring during the therapy, she must act directly and immediately in a range of behaviors from helping the battered spouse and children find safety to calling in the police to arrest the batterer. Such crises, while seriously dangerous for all concerned, do provide significant opportunities for change.

In addition, the therapist needs to assess the degree of isolation the family experiences; to understand what each member wants to accomplish via therapy; to evaluate the financial and emotional strengths of each partner; to determine if there are other problems, such as alcohol or/and drug abuse, which require concomitant treatment; and to learn what the family roles and expectations are for its members, including the influence and value system of the families of origin.

One departure from systems theory as it is usually practiced is that couples are encouraged to be seen separately as well as together. These separate meetings, though often causing the couple anxiety, foster more open disclosure as well as possibly permitting an opening up of the system.

The immediate specific information to solicit from the woman includes why she is contacting the therapist; when last the violence occurred (including that very moment if she is making contact by telephone); and whether she and/or any children that might be involved need police or other authorities to be contacted in order to secure their safety. If the woman is currently being battered, she may want help to leave the setting or she may want help to enable her to remain. It cannot automatically be assumed she wants to escape. Women are frequently reluctant to admit they are in such situations and the therapist must move with empathy and persistence, while also aware that if the woman feels too pressured she might well cut off contact with the therapist.

Frequently, the therapist feels that the only "sensible" thing the woman can do is immediately leave the relationship. However, many battered women face a real dilemma between remaining in a noxious relationship or leaving it to face economic and sometimes social hardships. In addition, they fear that leaving can potentially enrage the man to a point where he can inflict serious injury or death. The woman needs to know the therapist understands these issues and her conflict around them.

Next, the therapist needs to determine the pattern of violence and the woman's attitude about it. For example, does she seem to blame herself and excuse it or has she condemned the violence and sought support for that purpose. Her attitude, especially after the first incident of violence, is a good prognostic indicator of whether the violence will escalate.

Fraser (1988) stresses that a most important goal in working with battered women

> is to *align* with and *empower* the woman. . . . The woman should be offered as many choices as possible, and her decisions should be respected. Only in this way can she be empowered, and the therapist maintains the ability to alter future interactions. (p. 171)

When assessing the male batterer, it is necessary to carefully determine what he is asking for. He may feel justified in his behavior, but fears losing the woman. Thus, he contacts the therapist in a manipulative move as opposed to being truly repulsed by and repentant of his behavior. Such an attitude speaks volumes about how conducive he is to change. If the man is currently being physically abusive, he should be considered dangerous not only to the woman but also to her helpers. Appropriate measures should be taken to either effect his arrest or file necessary complaint papers, depending upon local laws. The probability of deterring future violence should outweigh the risk of increasing violence during legal proceedings. Of course, while gathering all of this information, the therapist has begun the intervention.

There are other specific interventions that are important in decreasing the violence and in providing more balanced power and openness in the system. People generally want their situations but not themselves to change because of the anxiety personal change evokes. Fraser (1988) thus cautions the therapist to go slowly; make predictions about what might lie ahead, such as future escalation or regression to former behaviors; and ascribe different motives to both old and new behaviors so that they may be thought of negatively and positively, respectively. Of course, violence is never prescribed, but where there is an old behavior that is very likely to reoccur, such as the woman relenting and returning after a violent incident, that return home can be reframed as a necessary step to help her determine if the battering will again occur. This time, however, she should be encouraged to approach the situation differently. To follow such a prescription would alter the process and allow change.

Once the therapist discovers what each person in the relationship wants to change or maintain, he or she can be shown how the current behavior sabotages that goal. Also, different phases of the abuse cycle can be utilized to introduce change. For example, during the acute stage of battering, issues such as safety and sanctions against violence can be introduced. What Fraser (1988) terms the "loving respite phase"—that period in the cycle where apologies, promises, and denial run rampant and the system believes once more that all will be well and closes off again—provides an opportunity for the therapist to help institute change through providing new information and suggesting different actions. It is at this point that seeing the couple separately as well as together is especially useful. The acute nature of this phase provides the therapist with opportunities to enter what is generally a closed and secret system.

What follows is an example of how the strategic rapid intervention can be used in a family where wife beating occurs.

3. CASE EXAMPLE

Mr. and Mrs. A. have been married for 10 years. They have two children, a boy aged eight and a six-year-old daughter. Mrs. A. telephones to request an appointment. When questioned, she states that she has had the therapist's number for several months but had not called because she thought things would get better, but they have not. She begins to cry and says, "I can't take it anymore." With further questioning, she admits that her husband "hits" her.

Therapist: Is your husband home now?

Mrs. A.: No. He doesn't know I'm calling you.

Therapist: When last did he hit you?

Mrs. A.: Last night.

Therapist: How many times did he hit you? And with what?

Mrs. A.: He hit me with his fists. I don't know how many times. A lot.

Therapist: Do you have any bruises, swellings, or cuts?

Mrs. A.: Just a black eye and a few bruises.

Therapist: Has it ever been worse after your husband has beaten you?

Mrs. A.: Oh yes, but it had gotten better.

Therapist: When do you expect your husband to return home?

Mrs. A.: This evening after work.

Therapist: How do you expect him to behave when he comes in?

Mrs. A.: He'll probably bring me flowers. That's what usually happens when he hits me. He'll be contrite for a few days or a few weeks.

Therapist: Are the children safe?

Mrs. A.: Oh sure. He doesn't hit them.

Therapist: Do you feel you're in any danger now?

Mrs. A.: Not now. I just don't want to go through this anymore.

The therapist has quickly determined that the abused spouse does not appear to be in any immediate danger, that the children are relatively safe, and that the couple are entering the "loving respite phase" in a cycle of abuse. The therapist realizes that the wife is not expressing a desire to separate from Mr. A. and that this respite period is the best time for rapid intervention.

Therapist: I'm making an appointment for you and Mr. A. to come in tomorrow evening at 7 P.M.

Mrs. A.: Oh, my husband won't come, and he'll be furious that I called you.

Therapist: He might be angry that you called, but it sounds as if you expect him to be contrite and willing to please you right now. That is your bargaining tool.

When the couple come in the next evening, they will initially be seen separately. The therapist will want to assess the pattern of violence in the family by asking detailed questions about the very first incident of violence, what was going on in the family at the time, what was the violent act, how did each person respond to it, what did they do, say, feel—and what occurred next. The therapist will want to know whether anyone else knows about the act of violence and, if so, how they found out. For example, did neighbors call the police, did the wife seek support from a family member, or did the children witness the violence. Then the therapist will need to ask about the second act of violence, eliciting the same details in order to care-fully establish the pattern as well as determine how the couple feels about the violence, their roles in it, their responsibility or lack of responsibility for the behavior, where they can seek support, and what they have done in the past to try to ameliorate the situation.

After seeing the husband and wife separately, the therapist brings them together. If, as is usually the case, their attempts at resolution have not been helpful, it is crucial to point this out so that they might realize they need to try something new in order to begin to stop the vicious cycle of violence.

After determining that Mr. and Mrs. A. wanted to remain together, found the violence abhorrent, and were willing to work for change, the therapist pointed out that the pattern outlined in the session showed that the violence had worsened and, despite hiatuses, still continued. The therapist then made two small but significant interventions. She pointed out that they would probably "backslide" and return to their old pattern of violence and that the degree of violence in the future cycles would probably escalate despite the extreme danger that would pose.

Having been forewarned of the possibility of regressing, the couple would be more determined to avoid it. However, if further violence should occur, they could more openly and with less shame explore with the therapist the reasons it happened, while looking at other alternatives.

4. USES

Although this model was developed specifically to stop physical violence by men against their mates, it can also be used in any family in which abuse is perpetrated against another. Issues such as decreasing the abusing family's isolation, disqualifying the abuse, increasing the abused person's self-esteem, and helping the abuser accept responsibility for his or her actions are vitally important, whether the problem is wife battering, child abuse or incest.

B. Repent and Repair

1. RATIONALE

This is a strategy by Madanes (1990) that deals with many of the difficulties in intervening with families where sexual abuse has occurred. The issues of pressuring and blaming the victims, as well as the issues of family denial and secrets, are most effectively handled through this technique.

2. PROCEDURE

Madanes (1990) proposes a 16-step model which begins with full disclosure by all members of the family concerning what they know about the incestuous relationship. This includes exactly what happened, where, when, how often, etc. Pressure to talk is exerted on all members except the victim, who is encouraged but not required to talk. This open communication hopefully does two important things: It prevents denial and it exposes the secretiveness that would allow incest to continue. There is a presumption that others knew that an incestuous relationship was occurring. It is not clear how often that is the case, but certainly it does occur.

The family members are then helped to recognize all the ways in which the sexual abuse was harmful to each of them, especially spiritually. Next, the offender must get down on bended knees in front of the victim and repent. This repentance must occur in order for therapy to proceed and it must be repeated until everyone in the room is convinced of the repenter's sincerity. However, the victim should never be pressured to forgive the offender. After the offender has repented, the rest of the family, also on bended knees in front of the victim, express sorrow and repentance for having failed to protect the victim. According to Madanes (1990):

> It is important to have a humiliating apology as soon as possible, preferably by the end of the first or second session. This is therapeutic for the offender and very therapeutic for the victim. It establishes publicly, in front of the whole family, that the victim was a victim, that she does not have to apologize, that nobody is interested in what she

contributed to the situation, and that she does not even have to forgive. (p. 54)

The final eight steps of this model involve determining consequences if the behavior were to be repeated; allowing the victim the opportunity to privately explore her feelings with the therapist; finding a temporary "protector" for the victim until her mother is strong enough to function in that capacity; helping the family to devise a way in which the offender can make at least symbolic reparation to the victim; and then helping the offender through participation in other therapies, such as group, and through a kind of reincorporation into the family with love, an appropriate role, and self-forgiveness. Of course, if the offender was a parent, another step must be added through which the marital pair's sexual and other problems can be resolved.

3. CASE EXAMPLE

Madanes (1990) cites the case of a 12-year-old boy who sexually assaulted his eight-year-old brother and his five-year-old twin sisters. Therapy included his repenting and apologizing to his siblings in therapy sessions and at home on bended knees every day for a year. When after a year he again attempted to sexually attack one of his sisters, the therapist directed his family to tie bells to his ankles and wrists so that his whereabouts in the house would always be known. The bells deprived him of privacy just as he had so deprived others. He cried with humiliation, but he never sexually assaulted his siblings again.

4. USES

This technique can be modified depending upon individual circumstances, for example, the severity of the abuse, the constellation of the family, and the status of the case. While Madanes' emphasis was on incestuous relationships between older and younger siblings, parent and child incest can also be successfully addressed by this model.

Most cases that are referred for therapy do not go smoothly. Even in the face of evidence and accusations, the accused abusers may continue to deny the offense. In such cases, they can be asked to apologize on bended knees for having behaved in such a way as to cast suspicion of sexual abuse. Many of the same steps outlined above would be followed by the therapist and the family.

C. Preparing a Defense

1. RATIONALE

It is often said that to be forewarned is to be forearmed. After a pattern of abuse has been established and it is fairly clear that the abuse was not a one-time aberrant behavior, the abused person needs to be helped to understand, if possible, what the antecedents to the abusive behavior might be. For example, does it usually occur in the evenings, on the weekends, or near the first of the month when bills are due; is it after alcohol or drugs have been consumed; or is it more likely to happen when the children have been crying or the couple has argued? Any awareness of what appears to either precipitate or aggravate abusive behavior can be an invaluable signal alerting the abused to attempt to either escape or short circuit anticipated behavior.

2. PROCEDURE

The target of the behavior does not have time for fancy footwork, but must have on hand several steps and strategies which the therapist can help the abused develop, depending upon the nature of the abuse. In the case of children, for example, if at any time they feel in danger they should know how to call the police and what they should say. They should know how to remain as calm as possible so that they stay alert to their environment. This can be achieved by teaching them simple deep-breathing exercises. If there is more than one child in the family, they should be vigilant over each other's social interactions and aware of each other's physical proximity both at home and outside the home to the extent possible. They need to be taught how to handle themselves should they be approached. Often, a sexually abusive parent will attempt to remove a child from school during the day on some pretense or another. Finally, the children must know that they have the therapist's complete support and should be required to memorize her emergency telephone number, be it at home or at a 24-hour answering service.

3. CASE EXAMPLE

The case study which follows was related by a colleague (Duncan, 1990), and clearly illustrates how these preparations can be effective.

Judy and Jennifer were 12 and 13 years of age, respectively. Their mother had been physically abusive toward them and there was some question of their stepfather's behavior being sexually provocative. The girls were removed from their parents' custody by the courts and placed in the home of a maternal aunt. The Social Service agency involved recommended psychotherapy for the girls.

Fearful of their mother, the girls refused to be alone with her. Jennifer was more forceful and more capable of defending herself both verbally and physically than was Judy, who became paralyzed in the face of her mother's rage and displeasure. The court had decreed that any visits between the girls and their mother should be supervised by either the aunt or the agency.

One evening, both girls attended a school play in which Jennifer performed. After her performance, Jennifer walked to the back of the auditorium where she was stopped by her stepfather. He told her to quickly get her sister and come with him, as he had a cab waiting that would take them to her mother's home.

In therapy sessions, the therapist had warned the girls that if they were ever accosted by either their mother or their stepfather they were to call attention to the event immediately. One method used with them was role-playing how they should talk very loudly to draw attention to the situation.

Jennifer began to loudly announce that she did not want to go; that she was going to tell her aunt; and that she wanted someone to get the police. The stepfather promptly left the premises as the school guard arrived.

Later in sessions, the girls talked about this experience and their reactions to it. Judy, the more timid sibling, had heard and seen the exchange while sitting in the audience. She told the therapist that had her stepfather approached her she would have been too terrified to not go quietly. However, witnessing her sister's behavior gave her an opportunity to question her own response and to feel stronger. Additional role-playing of such situations then took place. Jennifer talked very confidently about feeling more in control of any future situation that might arise.

4. USES

This technique of preparing for anticipated abuse can be modified to help families prepare for any stressful situation. Role-playing and a discussion of all possible reactions can allay anxiety in such widely different situations as preparing a child for a hospital stay or helping a phobic family member to work with self-assertiveness issues.

III. TIPS AND TACTICS

1. Clarify the Range of Anger

The Anger Checklist (Margolin, Olkin, & Baum, cited in Jacobson & Margolin, 1979) is a somewhat effortless way to elicit detailed information from a couple about the kinds of angry exchanges that occur between them and to then help them eliminate those that are either physically or emotionally harmful. The checklist includes 79 items that include angry physiological responses, emotional feelings, actions, thoughts, and words. They make note not only of the mate's responses but also of their own in an effort to become increasingly aware of signs of anger so as to be better able to control the more destructive ones.

2. Make a Small Strategic Change

Fisch, Weakland, and Segal (1982) write about the enormous impact a small strategic change can have on how a problem is handled. They give the example of a couple who usually fight in one room of their house. The therapist can suggest that they not stop the fight, but that they move it into a different room. The couple is likely to accept the suggestion as it seems rather minor, but the action needed to consciously decide to move the fight into another room makes the fighting less spontaneous and somewhat less realistic.

3. Provide an Opportunity to Mourn

Courtois and Sprei (1988) write of the many losses experienced by the survivor of sexual abuse, including loss of childhood, innocence, trust, self-image, and good parenting. Helping the patient mourn these losses can be a healing experience. Also see Chapter 15, on Grief Work, for some helpful methods.

4. Normalize Post-Traumatic Stress Symptoms

Symptoms associated with post-traumatic stress disorder frequently occur during the initial period of therapy if the patient enters therapy during a crisis or during the patient's reworking the trauma. Flashbacks, sleep disturbances, hypervigilance, and other such symptoms can be alleviated by the therapist's explanation that such intrusive symptoms are normal and will become less intense over time.

5. Stress Inoculation Training

Additionally, stress inoculation training, referral to self-help groups, and relaxation techniques can be quite helpful. The relaxation techniques provide the individual with mastery over the stressful event and reduce tension, which is frequently the first sign of anger leading to physical aggression.

6. Sabotage the Aggression

Another tactic that the therapist can use with a physically aggressive spouse is to instruct that person to sit down when he perceives himself becoming tense or angry, as it is much more difficult to strike out when sitting back in a chair, just as it is difficult for disagreements to escalate out of control when the individuals are instructed not to speak above a whisper (Arias & O'Leary, 1988). Aggressive spouses can also be instructed to keep their hands behind their back when angry, to count before yelling, to close their eyes and picture the other spouse in pain, or to picture some previously agreed-upon image. Arias and O'Leary point out that interventions such as these might sound "extreme," but considering that the aggressor's behavior is extreme, whatever measures might work need to be employed.

7. The Written Contract

A contract is an agreement between two or more people to comply with certain terms and conditions. A contract or plan regarding how and to what ends treatment will take place is necessary in any family therapy. To make the terms of the contract explicit has a number of advantages. It not only aids in clarifying the issues, but it also helps in setting the limits of the process. The family, having actively participated in defining the goals and their priorities and then signing their names to the document outlining them, are more likely to take responsibility for carrying them out. At the very least it acts as a concrete, vivid reminder of the reasons for and purpose of the therapy. When the abuser has signed a contract agreeing to certain rules, it is difficult for him to not take responsibility for his behavior should he fail to comply. Willbach

(1989) states that until an abuser can agree to and follow an explicit contract to not be abusive, he should be seen only individually or in a group setting, but not in couple or family therapy.

8. Appeal to Position and Role in Family

The therapist can explore with the father, for example, how he sees his role in the family. If that role includes being a provider and protector, he can be questioned about how he can hurt and protect his family at the same time.

9. Engender Shame

The therapist can define violence as a response that comes out of weakness or a lack of knowledge of other alternatives. She can tell the abuser that the violence is an act of picking on someone who is physically weaker—that it is not heroism but rather bullying.

10. Use of Empathy

The abuser has probably received a great deal of hostility, angry responses, and negative affect by the time he reaches therapy. The therapist can join with the abuser and hope to influence him in that way. This is certainly not to condone the abuser's behavior, but rather the therapist can let the abuser know that she understands he must feel overwhelmed at times and experiences himself as being out of control. This acknowledgment can be quite a relief to the abuser. If the therapist believes it to be true, she can add that she believes he really wants to gain control over his behavior and is willing to learn. After all, he has come into treatment.

11. Empower the Abused

Frequently, an abused person will say, "I can't do anything about it." The therapist can help that person find something that he has been successful at in the past—for example, how he succeeded in a sales promotion at work or how he taught his child to negotiate some task. He can then be encouraged to use those same inner strengths to bring about this desired change.

REFERENCES

Altemeier, W. A., O'Connor, S., Sherrod, K. B., and Tucker, D. (1986). Outcome of abuse during childhood among pregnant low income women. *Child Abuse and Neglect*, 10, 319–330.

Arias, I. and O'Leary, K. D. (1988). Cognitive-behavioral treatment of physical aggression in marriage. In N. Epstein, S. E. Schlesinger and W. Dryden (Eds.). *Cognitive-behavioral therapy with families*. NY: Brunner/Mazel.

Asher, S. J. (1988). The effects of childhood sexual abuse: A review of the issues and evidence. In L. E. A. Walker (Ed.). *Handbook on sexual abuse of children: Assessment and treatment issues*. NY: Springer.

Cooper, I. and Cormier (1982). Inter-generational transmission of incest. *Canadian Journal of Psychiatry*, 278, 231–235.

Courtois, C. A. (1988). *Healing the incest wound: Adult survivors in therapy*. NY: W. W. Norton.

Courtois, C. A. and Sprei, J. E. (1988). Retrospective incest therapy for women. In L. E. A. Walker (Ed.). *Handbook on sexual abuse of children: Assessment and treatment issues*. NY: Springer.

Duncan, B. W. (1990). Personal communication.

Finkelhor, D. (1984). *Child sexual abuse: New theory and research*. NY: Free Press.

Fisch, R., Weakland, J. H. and Segal, L. (1982). *The tactics of change: Doing therapy briefly*. San Francisco, CA: Jossey-Bass.

Fraser, J. S. (1988). Strategic rapid intervention in wife beating. In E. W. Nunnally, C. S. Chilman and F. M. Cox (Eds.). *Troubled relationships: Families in trouble series* (Vol. 1). CA: Sage.

Gelles, R. J. (1980). A profile of violence toward children in the United States. In G. Gerbner, C. J. Ross and E. Zigler (Eds.). *Child abuse: An agenda for action*. NY: Oxford University Press.

Giles-Sims, J. (1983). *Wife battering: A systems theory approach*. NY: Guilford Press.

Goleman, D. (1989, January 24). Sad legacy of abuse: The search for remedies. *The New York Times*, pp. c1, c6.

Goodwin, J., Cormier, L. and Owen, J. (1983). Grandfather-granddaughter incest: A trigenerational view. *Child Abuse and Neglect*, 7, 163–170.

Hatcher, C. (1981). Managing the violent family. In A. S. Gurman (Ed.). *Questions and answers in family therapy*. NY: Brunner/Mazel.

Hines, P. M. and Boyd-Franklin, N. (1982). Black families. In M.

McGoldrick, J. K. Pearce and J. Giordano (Eds.). *Ethnicity and family therapy*. NY: Guilford Press.

Jacobson, N. S. and Margolin, G. (1979). *Marital therapy: Strategies based on social learning and behavior exchange principles*. NY: Brunner/Mazel.

Kempe, R. and Kempe, H. (1984). *The common secret*. NY: W. H. Freeman.

Madanes, C. (1990). *Sex, love and violence: Strategies for transformation*. NY: W. W. Norton.

New York State Social Services Law, Article 6, Title 6. Section 412, Definitions.

Petretic-Jackson, P. and Jackson, T. (1990). Assessment and crisis intervention with rape and incest victims: Strategies, techniques and case illustrations. In A. R. Roberts (Ed.). *Crisis intervention handbook: Assessment, treatment and research*. Belmont, CA: Wadsworth Publishing.

Pittman, F. S., III. (1984). Wet cocker spaniel therapy: An essay on technique in family therapy. *Family Process*, 23(1), 1–9.

Russell, D. E. H. (1986). *The secret trauma: Incest in the lives of girls and women*. NY: Basic Books.

Russell, D. E. H. (1988). The incidence and prevalence of intrafamilial and extrafamilial sexual abuse of female children. In L. E. A. Walker (Ed.). *Handbook on sexual abuse of children: Assessment and treatment issues*. NY: Springer Publishing.

Straus, M. A. and Gelles, R. J. (1988). Violence in American families: How much is there and why does it occur? In E. W. Nunnally, C. S. Chilman and F. M. Cox (Eds.). *Troubled relationships: Families in trouble series* (Vol. 3). CA: Sage.

Straus, M. A., Gelles, R. J. and Steinmetz, S. K. (1980). *Behind closed doors: Violence in the American family*. NY: Anchor/Doubleday.

Summit, R. (1983). The child abuse accommodation syndrome. *Child Abuse and Neglect*, 7, 177–193.

Welts, E. P. (1982). Greek families. In M. McGoldrick, J. K. Pearce and J. Giordano (Eds.). *Ethnicity and family therapy*. NY: Guilford Press.

Willbach, D. (1989). Ethics and family therapy: The case management of family violence. *Journal of Marital and Family Therapy*, 15(1), 43–52.

15

GRIEF WORK

I. INTRODUCTION: COPING WITH GRIEF

All through life we are faced with important losses and must cope with grief. It may be the young child's feared loss of the parent who he thinks may not return; the loss of cherished possessions, job, or life-style; the loss of a marriage through divorce; the separation of a child leaving home, particularly moving to a distant location; the death of a loved pet; the loss of important physical functions due to illness, accident, or aging; the death of a loved one; or one's own impending demise. Many unmarried people and elderly people may have non-romantic, long-term roommates whose demise is keenly felt and who are much missed. Most of these losses involve critical life-cycle transitions.

Losses inflict many changes on both the psyche and the system. Feelings and beliefs may revolve around shock, anger, frustration, fear, pity, sympathy, and even relief. Anger may be expressed against the self in the form of self-blame—"If only I had . . ."; against the other—"How could he do this?"; against the deity—"How could He let this happen?"; against other people or things (deficient care, interfering parents, alcohol), blaming them for the loss.

Beliefs about the nature of the world and one's place in it may be completely shaken. Frustration results from the lack of power to alter or control the events and the need to deal with the consequences of the loss. Fear is engendered by both confronting one's own vulnerability and mortality and the need to reorganize self, system, and sense of identity in the face of the loss. Compassion, pity, and sympathy are aroused in behalf of the person or entity lost. And relief may well be experienced on death following a very painful decline or illness that has been draining the emotions, strengths, and resources of the survivors. The above is true for both adults and children.

The separation from a loved one, or former loved one as in the case of divorce, usually results in a loss of accustomed services and support. The survivors may question their competence to undertake the demands and challenges now before them. A feeling of being overwhelmed frequently ensues, followed by increasing anxiety.

Death or separation may also involve a change of identity. Often, after the death of a spouse, there is a feeling of personal incompleteness—"A major part of me died too and I can never be a whole person again." The same thing may occur upon the death of a parent when there is a strong dependency on the relationship or a strong unfulfilled need for parental approval. In the case of a widow or divorced person—"Am I married or single? By what name am I to be known?" "How am I to be treated if I am not accompanied by a partner and am not part of a couple?"

The death of a child is abnormal in the life-stage sequence and arouses much pain and suffering for the parents and dislocations among the siblings. When a child dies or suffers a severe loss of function, there is a tendency for parents to try to assert blame either for the loss or with respect to the care of the child, thus imperiling the marital bond. One parent, usually the mother, may become severely depressed and partly dysfunctional, further upsetting the family. Worst for most survivors is death by suicide because this is a deliberate act. To compensate for the loss of a parent or child, adults may try to replace the lost one by immediately having another child or adopting one as part of their grief. Obviously, being expected to live for another may pose some problems for the new child in the family system.

The system has to reorganize in terms of roles, the division of labor, the distribution of power, and the patterns of communication and interactions with the extended family and other systems. One legacy of divorce or death of a spouse is a single-parent family. "Am I now supposed to be both mother and father?" "Whom can I depend upon to take over some of the positions of the departed one?" "How can I replace that love?" "Am I desirable to anyone else?" "Whom can I confide in?" "Will I be alone the rest of my life?" Even older adults may experience a feeling of being orphaned when a parent dies. Children may wonder how and where they will live; who will take care of them; will the other parent die too; will they die; do they now have to take care of the surviving parent.

The death or disappearance of a cherished pet should not be minimized. It can have an enormous impact on one or more members of a family and may trigger the same mourning process.

A more pernicious form of grieving that is often manifested in low self-esteem and bouts of depression is due to the experience by children of abuse, neglect, or other serious trauma at the hands of those who are expected to love and care for them. The grief is experienced as the betrayal of trust by others, the loss of respect for the self, a feeling of powerlessness or self-blame for not doing something about it, and the repression of anger toward those upon whom we depend.

The most prominent feature in grieving is a depressed mood. If this develops into a reactive depression (DSM III-R), then we will have a dysfunctional member and possibly a dysfunctional family. A common issue is where to draw the line between mourning and excessive grief and depression. It is the authors' impression that most cultures with which they are familiar expect the mourners to resume daily functioning within a week or two and for reasonable healing to take place within a year so that the mourners are once more seeking and receiving pleasure in being alive and are reasonably coping with the challenges of life. This chapter does not deal with the issues of persistent depression or grief due to personal trauma such as physical or sexual abuse.

Since loss and grieving are a permanent part of the human condition, every culture has invented rites of passage to help people transact such life experiences in a "normal" way. Since the vast majority of us identify with some cultural group, the rites of that group with which our clients identify can be implemented to help our clients deal with their loss.

Many writers have examined issues of death and dying. Among them are Frantz (1984), Sanders (1989), Worden (1989). Kubler-Ross (1969) has defined a stage theory for coping with death. There are also a number of books that cover the specific loss brought about by suicide (Dunne, McIntosh & Dunne-Maxim, 1987; Orbach, 1988; Peck, Farberow & Litman, 1985; Richman, 1986).

The tactics and techniques presented in this chapter are designed to cope with grief in general. Each should be adapted to the specific needs and circumstances of the mourners. In addition to feelings, identity, and family organization, the therapist may need to assist the mourners in identifying and carrying out many practical tasks ranging from changing bank accounts, obtaining welfare payments, and learning how to reconnect a blown circuit breaker to learning better time management, stress reduction techniques, or a new occupation.

II. STRUCTURED TECHNIQUE

Making the Self Whole Again

1. RATIONALE

Many people develop dependent relationships with a parent or spouse. They conceive of themselves as incomplete or inadequate persons who cannot manage in the world without the active presence and help of the chosen other. If the chosen one dies, the survivor is not only bereft, but feels utterly helpless to go on. The feelings of loneliness are intense. Typically, after a period of mourning, the person believes that this sense of incompleteness, loneliness, and helplessness can be ameliorated only if a substitute can be found to replace the lost one. The feeling of helplessness then fuels the conclusion that finding such a person is impossible, leading to further depression.

Making the Self Whole Again is an exercise developed by Robert Sherman to join with the client and to create a more potent sense of being. It employs a combination of techniques such as encouragement, imagery, suggestions, and strength bombardment. It is designed to help the client introject the value of the deceased and use that value as a continuing guide to performance, build ego, and initiate feelings of optimism. The use of imagery permits us to bypass the existing myths connected with dependency, introduce new positive beliefs, and accomplish the object relations tasks of introjecting valued objects while defining the self as a separate and complete whole. We usually think of imagery only in visual terms. But as Araoz (1982) informs us, people may concoct images related to any of the five senses.

2. PROCEDURE

1. Ask the client to share positive stories about the deceased in order to create a positive mood.

2. Help the client to relax his body by taking three long deep breaths and thinking of a very pleasant scene. Have him enjoy the scene for a moment.

3. Suggest to the client that he imagine the deceased in his mind's eye. "Where in your body do you experience your loved one?" (*Client response*) "Do you notice, then, that the person is always there with you? You can experience the person at any time you choose. Can you feel the value of that person inside you right now?" (*Client response*) "That value is with you always. It's part of you."

4. "Can you imagine yourself as you are now?" (*Response*) "Do you imagine yourself whole or in part? (*If whole, go on to the next instruction*) If part, inquire, "What part is missing?" (*Response*). Help the client in imagery to add the missing parts to make a whole being by suggesting the parts to be added to the image. "Is the image clear or fuzzy?" If fuzzy, suggest that he fine tune the image like correcting the picture on a television screen until it comes in clearly. "You observe that you are a whole and complete person in this image. Just stay with the image for a moment and recognize your wholeness. You really are a whole and complete person, a total entity in your own right." Repeat this suggestion in varying words several times while the person observes the image of himself. Have the client repeat several times that he is indeed a complete person.

5. "Please imagine yourself now as an infant lying in the crib." Use the same procedure as above until there is a clear image. "Could you please imagine yourself at this current stage of your life." Again, follow the above procedure until there is a clear image. "Now, could you imagine the big you in the same scene as the infant you lying in the crib?" (*Response*) Get a clear image. "Let the big you carefully observe that infant. Is the child a complete human being or is the child somewhat deficient?" The typical answer is that the child is complete. Sometimes, the client in some way communicates that the infant is sad or lonely. Work with the responses, making suggestions to help achieve a wholeness. Suggest to the client, "Wouldn't you like to hold and hug that child? How does it feel to hold him? How does the child feel to be held? Is this child lovable? Love him for a while. Enjoy loving and being loved by each other."

6. "Notice that both the big you and the little you are whole and complete. You were whole and complete when you were born and you are still whole and complete."

7. The therapist now wants to use the imagery to build a sense of personal competence. "Can you imagine now the time before (*name*) died?" To elicit strengths and positive performances, the therapist can ask questions such as the following: "Imagine some of the things that you are taking care of. Imagine some of the things you are doing. Imagine that you are contributing something in the family. Imagine that you are doing something for yourself." The therapist elicits images in which the client is responsible and active. "So you observe that you can and do accomplish many things." Compliment the client on any noteworthy activities or qualities of character that emerge from the imagery: "It appears that you are in charge of aesthetics in your family." "You really made (*name of the deceased one*) feel good by doing that."

If the client expresses negative activities, reframe them to positive meanings. For example, "I never initiated anything" is reframed to "You mean you allowed your partner to be the leader, which is what he wanted. That was very kind of you." Some coaxing or a few examples may be necessary to get the client started in this round of imagery because he is unaccustomed to thinking that he does anything that is worthwhile.

8. "Notice in these images that you play an important part. You are an important person in this family. Apparently you (*summarize a list of positives*). Is it possible that you and (*name of the deceased*) really helped and supported each other in different ways and you were just as important to him as he to you? So you are the kind of person who can hold up her end of things." Based on the concept of complementarity, most dependent relationships are co-dependent. This idea can be utilized to underline the strengths of the now dependent one.

9. Another line of imagery is to ask the client spouse of the person who died: "Can you imagine yourself when you were single? Are you whole or part? If part, what's missing?" Complete the whole figure. "Is the image clear or fuzzy?" Fine tune it until it is clear. "What are you doing?" Elicit scenes in which the person is actively engaged. "Do you notice that before you met (*name of the deceased*) you were a whole person and actively engaged?"

10. Another device using the same procedure is to have the client imagine the lost person as an inner guide (Sherman & Fredman, 1986). He can discuss any situation with or seek advice from the guide. Since this is a projective process, the person is basically empowered to solve his own problems.

3. CASE EXAMPLE

Rita is a 51-year-old woman whose husband was recently killed by a drunk driver in an automobile accident. Therapy incorporated work on confronting the reality of the loss and on integrating the loss. Rita began to share her identity issues. Among them she expressed her feelings of abandonment, incompleteness, and incompetence as a widowed woman.

The therapist asked Rita to recall and tell some favorite stories about her husband. She started slowly and soon stories began to flow one upon the other. As she did she relaxed more and more, smiled and laughed repeatedly. The stories brought her close to her husband.

The therapist asked Rita to identify where in her body she most felt her husband. She said in her chest. The therapist suggested she just experience that feeling for a while. The therapist then said, "Notice, you have the feeling and value of your husband with you anytime you want right there in your chest. He is a part of you. He will always be there. The value and memory of him is something that you have added to yourself. You can probably even talk with him whenever you want."

Next, the therapist asked Rita to relax more deeply and imagine herself as she is now at this stage of her life. She was able to imagine herself visually as a whole and complete physical being. She was asked to make sure that there were no strings, cords, or anything else tying her physically to anyone else. She recognized herself visually as individually independent and complete. She repeated this observation several times in order to help integrate it.

The therapist suggested that Rita visualize herself as an infant lying in the crib complete, cute and wonderful. She was told how wonderful she is and how much she is wanted and appreciated just the way she is. Rita was then asked to imagine her adult self in the same scene. Her adult self told the child how wonderful she is and how complete she is as a child and how much she was loved. The adult self was told to hold and hug the child if it was alright with both of them. They held and hugged for some time. They both felt warm and enjoyed the experience.

The therapist followed a similar imagery procedure through succeeding stages of life emphasizing in each her wholeness, competence and lovableness. She observed in imagery that as an adult prior to marriage she worked effectively in her job, dated men, and managed her life well, though not perfectly. Finally she imagined her positive, effective and valued behavior during her long marriage. She pursued a career successfully; raised three children as the primary care-giver; was the sensitive one who more closely related to her children; and often gave solace and advice to her husband, as well as support in his career. The therapist had her review several times her effective behavior in the marriage and all through life. She then suggested to Rita that she would use all of those skills and traits now, even as a widow, and she would cope successfully with the challenges of her life. The therapist told Rita that all she had imagined would stay with her, comfort her, and help her to succeed. She then ended the imagery.

Together, Rita and the therapist affirmed Rita's wholeness, individuality, competence, and ability to connect with others closely all through life. Rita felt much encouraged as a result of this exercise.

4. USES

The Making the Self Whole Again exercise can be used with anyone capable of engaging in imagery from preschool years on. It works simultaneously on building separate identity and ego functioning while maintaining the connection with and the value of the person who was the object of the dependency. It acts upon both the beliefs and the roles involved in the relationship. By invoking "left hemisphere" analogical thinking, it bypasses the existing myths and defenses. This exercise can be adapted for use as an ego-building device in most instances of low self-esteem.

III. TIPS AND TACTICS FOR GRIEF WORK

A. Confronting the Loss

1. *The funeral.* The first step is to help the family deal with the reality of the loss. If the loss is a death, then making funeral arrangements, attending the viewing, wake, and funeral, and talking about the death with friends and relatives are all designed to help absorb the fact of the loss. Various cultures may have other customs.

2. *Repetition and validation of the event and the grief.* The therapist will validate the grief experienced and help the family members talk about the loss with each other as a shared experience. They may first have to talk about the event over and over again in order to figure out how it happened and try to make some sense out of it, especially if sudden, accidental, or suicidal. There is a usually fruitless search for reasonable explanations. Such discussions often help the survivors to draw closer together and even to settle some past differences.

3. *Cooperation in attending to the deceased's business.* Death leaves temporal affairs to be attended to. Personal effects, wills, bills, bank accounts, and so on are left in the hands of the survivors. Taking care of the business of the deceased provides another confrontation with reality. The therapist can provide emotional support in this process. This is an opportunity for family cooperation in doing the jobs either through an agreed upon division of labor or all together. Cooperating in the tasks helps to bond the survivors.

B. Integrating the Loss

1. *Recalling fond memories and stories.* The family is asked to recall and describe memories of the lost person or object. They can be prompted with

additional requests such as: "What were some of the funny things he did? What were some of the special things he did? What were some of the peculiar things he did? What is the first event in your life with him that you can recall?" Each recollection further bonds the family and helps to introject the lost one within the self. The memories also provide some healing balm.

2. *Looking at family photo albums together.* Similar to stories, photos recall the connections among people, help to bond the survivors, provide healing salve for the wounds, and help internalize the value of the lost one. Other kinds of memorabilia can also be used, such as diplomas, awards, newspaper stories, letters, and collectibles.

3. *Validating relationships between the lost one and each other member of the family and reducing blame and guilt.* Have each person describe his relationship to the lost one and what made it special. It is acceptable also to look at some of the negatives, pointing out that people and relationships are complex and contain many elements both positive and negative. The deceased had imperfections like the rest of us. Since there may be a lot of blaming and guilt in connection with the loss, each person's behavior may have to be examined in order to affirm that each did the best he/she could under the circumstances. With hindsight, we can always examine all the ifs of history.

If, indeed, errors were made, we cannot just platitudinously gloss over them. The errors can be sympathetically affirmed and repeatedly described and explained by the perpetrator. Counselor encouragement comes in the form of eliciting what behavior might serve in some small way to compensate for the error. The error is also placed in a larger perspective to counteract the person's or family's probable exaggeration of its impact. For example, the adult daughter chastises herself for not supervising more closely the caregivers in the nursing home, or the parents of the suicide victim accuse each other of not paying enough attention to the child, or one is blamed for being too strict. These clients need reassurance that they were not responsible for the person's demise. The daughter examines closely the death to recognize that the parent was ill and aging and died of natural causes. Perhaps closer supervision might in small ways have made the parent more comfortable, but each person can do only so much. She also had a job and a family to care for and did as much as she could is the conclusion elicited through joint examination of the situation.

Situations in which a client is indeed directly responsible for the loss, such as a death resulting from drunk driving, require a different strategy that space does not permit us to describe in this book.

4. *Talking to the deceased.* Using the empty chair, a photograph of the

deceased, or imagery, the client(s) are asked to imagine the presence of the lost person and talk to that person. The conversation can be used to tell him anything that the client failed to say before, either in love or anger; to ask forgiveness for any errors or omissions; to request help with the tasks ahead; to obtain permission to behave differently or do something uncovered in therapy that might be disloyal to him in the family system. More dramatically, the clients can be sent to the cemetery to hold the conversation at the grave site.

5. *Write a letter to the deceased.* Similar to talking is writing a letter to the person. The letter can describe how the clients feel about the person, his death, and all the other kinds of things suggested above in talking with the person. The type of letter prescribed can also be a review of their lives together. Some people may prefer to draw pictures of what they would like to communicate.

6. *Establishing a memorial.* In addition to a grave marker, some people find it helpful to integrate the loss by creating some kind of continuing memorial. Some examples are: creating a scholarship fund; dedicating an article to the deceased in church, synagogue, or mosque; sponsoring an institution or event; becoming personally active in a movement (Mothers Against Drunk Driving); naming a new child after the deceased; planting trees dedicated to the lost one; or setting up a memorial altar at home.

7. *De-idealizing the relationship.* At some point in the therapy, certainly not near the beginning, it is important for the survivor(s) to recognize the humanness of the one who died. There is a tendency to emphasize the good and the best when someone dies and to forget the faults, foibles, and perhaps even the destructiveness of the person. Idealization creates a model that cannot be matched in the real world and against whom the survivors cannot stack up either, dooming them to failure and always being not good enough. It's also hard to express anger, frustration and disappointment against a saint. De-idealization makes it easier for the survivors to establish new connections. Questions such as the following help to establish a more complete and humane picture: "What were some of the things missing in the marriage?" "Were there some things you wished that the person who died may have done differently?" "What were some of his peculiarities?" Some of the imperfections may also be elicited in many of the techniques described above.

C. Building Support and Identifying Resources

It is important to involve family and friends as a support group. Often, this will occur naturally. Once family and friends have been identified and encouraged to rally around, the clients experience a sense of worth and belongingness in the world that is often very heartwarming. However, there is a tendency for most people to drift back into their familiar routine shortly after the funeral, leaving the survivors basically to shift for themselves. In today's highly mobile society, key relatives and friends may also be geographically widely dispersed. If these things occur, the therapist may choose to assist the clients in initiating contacts or in developing or joining more organized support groups.

1. *Outreach*. Clients may need to be encouraged and taught to initiate reaching out to people by talking rather than by complaining. "I need some company tonight. Would it be all right if I came over for a couple of hours?" "I don't know how to do this thing. Could you please either do it for me or, better still, show me how?" When clients are depressed, it may be very difficult for them to reach out or even to see themselves as worthy enough to expect anything from others. It may be helpful in such cases to rehearse the calls in session by role playing and then have the client make some telephone calls from the therapist's office with the therapist beside him/her for moral support.

2. *The network session*. Such models are described by Rueveni (1979) for use in family crises and by Speck and Attneave (1973) for general use in family therapy. The client is asked to identify all people who do or could play an important function in the life of the clients: relatives, neighbors, current and former friends, clergyman, and even service providers in contact with the family, such as mailman, local merchants, landlord, or janitor. Those who cannot be physically present are invited to join in on conference calls and are fully included through the use of the speaker phone. The family's behavior and needs are discussed and each participant is asked for both ideas and the pledge of concrete actions in carrying out plans devised by the group that will be useful to the family.

It is important to avoid putting the family in a dependent position vis-à-vis the members of the group. The family holds an equal place in the deliberations and the planning in its behalf. The object is to empower the family through an infusion of positive resources rather than to have others take over the functions of the family. It is further designed to make the family consciously an active and significant member of a larger community. A follow-up session is held a month later to evaluate and revise the plan. Another follow-up session may be planned if deemed useful.

3. *The surrogate family or fellowship group*. Recognizing that some families are very small while others are spread over wide geographic areas, efforts can be made to create extended multigenerational family-like groups

of people who live in proximity to one another. These can be therapeutic groups professionally led as described by Lifton, Tavantzis and Mooney (1979) and Rueveni (1979). They may also be self-directed in much the same fashion as any extended family once the therapist has organized the group (Crane, 1974; Woodward, 1978).

Examples of this are fellowship groups encouraged by many churches and synagogues in which individuals and families join together for worship or celebration of holidays, births, and weddings; meet as friends and confidants; and assist with illness and mourning. The members have to be recruited from among a list of potentially congenial people. They need to formulate the goals of forming such a group and develop the roles and places that are to be occupied by its members. Each member must be validated as an individual and valued as a person. Differences are taught to be expected and valued. Methods for negotiating differences and resolving conflicts based upon positive proposals and mutual respect are emphasized and taught. As time goes on, the members develop a sense of shared history and experiences, belonging, significance, caring, and commitment—an experience of extended family-like relationships. Cooperative leadership develops within the group and the therapist facilitator withdraws (Sherman & Fredman, 1986).

4. *The grief support group.* Sometimes people are able to draw special sustenance from sharing with a group of people who are living through similar life experiences. In such a group, they may feel more truly understood and accepted. Problems presented and confronted elicit a sympathetic hearing. Solutions tried out by others are offered for consideration. Members can call upon each other outside of group for support or just sympathetic company. Such groups are often sponsored by, or at least housed in, community centers, community mental health agencies, and religious institutions. Less frequently, private practitioners offer grief groups. The groups may either be professionally led or organized as a self-help group. The therapist can investigate such groups as a referral resource either as an adjunct to therapy or, at some point, in place of therapy. It is beyond the scope of this chapter to present a model for the conduct of a grief support group.

D. Reorganizing the Family

When the family or spouse is ready, the next step is to reorganize the family system. The division of labor may require revision. The surviving parent may need to reassert the parental role. Surviving siblings may wish for reassurance that they do not have to either live for or compensate for the deceased. The family may have to learn to live on a lower economic standard. The surviving spouse may need to acquire a new occupation or update a former one. Child care may have to be provided. Welfare assistance may be necessary. Family myths and traditions may be challenged or reinforced along with the family's sense of identity. For example: "We are okay." "God will look after us." "We are survivors." "Here is further proof that we are hopeless and constant victims." "Mother is dead. We can no longer have Christmas and Thanksgiving at our house." "Now we are poor." In this context, reorganizing the family involves shifts in both roles and beliefs.

1. *The family meeting.* (See pp. 175–179 in this volume, as well as Manaster & Corsini, 1982; Sherman & Fredman, 1986.) This is a good vehicle for the family to identify in a democratic way the jobs that need to be done and to have the members accept responsibility for each one's share of the tasks based upon ability and other accepted family commitments, such as employment. To make the tasks more palatable, see the Appreciation Party and related techniques on pp. 29–31.

2. *Protecting the family hierarchy.* The therapist may choose to ally with the surviving spouse in family sessions to empower the parent in properly performing the executive function of the family (Minuchin, 1974; Minuchin & Fishman, 1981). As a result of being "too busy," too depressed, too needy, or too overwhelmed, the parent may give up the executive function or exercise it only inconsistently. This leaves a vacuum and one or more of the children will enter, leading to a power struggle in the family (see Chapter 12, Defusing and Redirecting the Power Play). The therapist coaches the parent in session on how to manage the children and reinforces the parent's energy and ability to assert proper leadership. A child who moves into a parental role is congratulated on his willingness to sacrifice his childhood or youth for the family and then relieved of his duty as the parent is empowered. To handle the defiant child, see some of the techniques in Chapter 12. The parent is further instructed that the children have also suffered a severe loss and require the comfort and reassurance of the parent. The therapist rehearses how to do that in session, if necessary.

3. *Enhancing positive customs and traditions.* The family needs to maintain its central position in the lives of its members. Therefore, customs and traditions that build cohesion and identity and help the members cope with the challenges of life can be reinforced or new ones introduced. Celebration of holidays, regular visits with friends or relatives, regular attendance at religious services, family story time, a quiet time to share the doings of the day, the weekly food shopping trip, and a communal fitness period are examples of the kinds of things that can be encouraged. Members agree

to take on specific responsibilities with respect to each custom. In that way, each person's significant and valued place in the group is reinforced, while the family remains a central locus of activity and satisfaction for the members.

4. *Building positive identity and myths.* Chapter 2, The Art of Encouragement (pp. 26–44) contains many suggestions that could be helpful in this stage of grief work.

5. *Building toward the future.* As the person and family reorganize and restore their confidence and optimism, it is helpful to look toward the future. What new things do they want to add to their lives? It may include the widow beginning to date looking forward to new rewarding relationships; getting a new pet; a child being able to leave home for college or marriage; acquiring a new occupation; moving to a new geographic location; redoing the home; or pursuing a new hobby or interest. The first step is to help the family dare to want new things by eliciting such ideas from them. The second step is to encourage them to start planning for changes. If they now have the courage and skills to plan for the future the therapist may begin the termination process for the therapy.

REFERENCES

Araoz, D. L. (1982). *Hypnosis and sex therapy.* New York: Brunner/Mazel.

Crane, J. A., Jr. (1974). The extended family in Santa Barbara: A new direction. *Journal of Liberal Ministry* 14:2, 23–25.

Dunne, E. J., McIntosh, J. L., and Dunne-Maxim, K. (1987). *Suicide and its aftermath.* New York: Norton.

Frantz, T. T. Editor. (1984) *Death and grief in family therapy.* Rockville, MD: Aspen.

Kubler-Ross, E. (1969). *On death and dying.* New York: Macmillan.

Lifton, W. M., Tavantzis, T. N., and Mooney, W. (1979). The disappearing family: The role of the counselor in creating surrogate families. *Personnel and Guidance Journal*, November, 7–19.

Manaster, G. and Corsini, R. C. (1982). *Individual Psychology.* Itasca, IL: Peacock.

Minuchin, S. (1974). *Families and family therapy.* Cambridge, MA: Harvard University Press.

Minuchin, S. and Fishman, C. (1981). *Family therapy techniques.* Cambridge, MA: Harvard University Press.

Orbach, I. (1988). *Children who don't want to live.* San Francisco: Jossey-Bass.

Peck, M. L., Farberow, N. L., and Litman, R. E. Editors. (1985) *Youth suicide.* New York: Springer.

Rueveni, D. (1979). *Networking families in crisis.* NY: Garland.

Richman, J. (1986). *Family therapy for suicidal people.* New York: Springer.

Sanders, C. M. (1989). *Grief: The mourning after.* New York: Wiley.

Sherman, R. and Fredman, N. (1986). *Handbook of structured techniques in marriage and family therapy.* New York: Brunner/Mazel.

Speck, R. V. and Attneave, C. A. (1973). *Family networks.* New York: Pantheon.

Woodward, K. (1978). The emergence of a new theology. *Psychology Today.* January, 47.

Worden, J. W. (1989). *Grief counseling and grief therapy.* New York: Springer.

ADDITIONAL RESOURCES

Dersheimer, R. A. (1990). *Counseling the bereaved.* New York: Pergamon.

Fremouw, W. J., de Perczel, M., and Ellis, T. E. (1990). *Suicide risk: Assessment and response guidelines.* New York: Pergamon.

Goldberg, J. (1989). *Pastoral bereavement counseling.* New York: Human Sciences Press.

Hassl, B. and Marnocha, J. *Bereavement support group program for children.* Muncie, IN: Accelerated Development.

Heilig, R. J. (1983). *Adolescent suicidal behavior. A family systems model.* Ann Arbor, MI: UMI Research Press.

Jacobs, D. and Brown, H. N. (1989). *Suicide: Understanding and responding.* Harvard Medical School perspectives. New York: International Universities Press.

Masterman, S. H. and Reams, R. (1988). Support groups for bereaved preschool children. *American Journal of Orthopsychiatry.* 58:4, 562–570.

Schowalter, J. F., Buschman, P., Patterson, P. R., Kutscher, M. T., and Stevenson, R. G. (1987). *Children and death. Perspectives from birth through adolescence.* New York: Praeger.

Siegel, B. S. (1989). *Peace, love, and healing.* New York: Harper and Row.

Suicide and ethnicity in the United States. (1990) Group for the Advancement of Psychiatry Report #128. New York: Brunner/Mazel.

Walsh, F. and McGoldrick, M. (1991). *Living beyond loss. Death in the family.* New York: Norton.

Name Index

Subject Index